MINNEAPOLIS ✳ ST. PAUL
Linked to the Future

Towery Publishing, Inc.

▲ ED BOCK / FROZEN IMAGES

Minneapolis ✻ St. Paul

▲ JEFFERY C. DREWITZ / FROZEN IMAGES

M I N N E A P O L I S ✳ S T. P A U L
Linked to the Future

By Barbara Flanagan and Mary Ludington

Profiles in Excellence and Captions by Amy Hanson

Art Direction by Jil Foutch

URBAN
TAPESTRY
SERIES
TOWERY
PUBLISHING, INC.

Linked to the Future

▲ CHRIS FAUST

Mⁱ ORE THAN 150 YEARS AFTER settlers first created a clearing on the St. Paul side of the Mississippi River, Minneapolis (OPPOSITE) and St. Paul (ABOVE) have grown into a metropolitan center where more than 2.5 million people live and work.

LIBRARY OF CONGRESS CATALOGING-IN-PUBLICATION DATA

Flanagan, Barbara.
    Minneapolis-St. Paul : linked to the future / by Barbara Flanagan and Mary Ludington ; profiles in excellence and captions by Amy Hanson.
        p.   cm. — (Urban tapestry series)
    Includes index.
    ISBN 1-881096-39-4 (alk. paper)
        1. Minneapolis (Minn.)—Civilization. 2. Saint Paul (Minn.)--Civilization. 3. Minneapolis (Minn.)—Pictorial works. 4. Saint Paul (Minn.)—Pictorial works. 5. Business enterprises—Minnesota--Minneapolis. 6. Business enterprises–Minnesota–Saint Paul.
    I. Ludington, Mary, 1956-   . II. Hanson, Amy, 1969-   .
    III. Title. IV. Series.
    F614.M6F53 1997
    977.6'579—dc21
                                                                    96-29990
                                                                        CIP

TOWERY PUBLISHING, INC., 1835 UNION AVENUE, MEMPHIS, TN 38104

PUBLISHER: J. Robert Towery
EXECUTIVE PUBLISHER: Jenny McDowell
NATIONAL SALES MANAGER: Stephen Hung
REGIONAL SALES MANAGER: Michelle Sylvestro
MARKETING DIRECTOR: Carol Culpepper
PROJECT DIRECTORS: Henry Hintermeister, Paul Withington
CREATIVE DIRECTOR: Brian Groppe
EXECUTIVE EDITOR: David B. Dawson
SENIOR EDITOR: Michael C. James
PROFILES MANAGER/ASSOCIATE EDITOR: Lynn Conlee
ASSOCIATE EDITORS: Mary Jane Adams, Lori Bond, Jana Files, Carlisle Hacker
ASSISTANT EDITOR: Jennifer Cobb
PROFILE DESIGNERS: Jennifer Baugher, Laurie Lewis, Ann Ward
TECHNICAL DIRECTOR: William H. Towery
PRODUCTION MANAGER: Brenda Pattat
PRODUCTION ASSISTANTS: Sandra Carter, Jeff McDonald

Minneapolis ✶ St. Paul

▲ CHRIS FAUST

CONTENTS

THE FIRST MINNEAPOLIS CITY
Hall stood at the junction of
Hennepin and Nicollet avenues, as seen
in this circa 1885 view (PAGE 7 INSET).
At the time, the building's clock tower
was the tallest structure in the city.
Today, such architectural icons as the
IDS Center and the Foshay Tower, as
well as the Pillsbury Center, First Bank
Place, and Norwest building, define the
Minneapolis skyline (PAGES 6 AND 7).

PAGES 6 AND 7: TOM NELSON / FROZEN IMAGES
PAGE 7 INSET: MINNESOTA HISTORICAL SOCIETY

Linked to the Future

o get a good feel for the Twin Cities, it pays to do as the natives do, no matter how strange our local customs might seem at first. ✳ So grab a walleye taco—a flour tortilla stuffed with, no kidding, walleyed pike, Minnesota's official state fish—and get yourself to the river. The Mississippi, of course. Stand on the historic century-old Stone Arch Bridge that spans the river in downtown Minneapolis and look around you. A lovely hunk of breathing space, right? It's wide open and breezy—and what a view!

Then, listen a sec. Yes, that's St. Anthony Falls—the mighty source of waterpower that helped to build this city—as it continues to churn the flowing river. If you happen to be standing on the bridge in spring or early summer, the snowmelt makes the flowing water energetic enough to toss some spray onto your face.

Look around. From right here in the middle of the great river—buffeted by our ever-blowing, extra-fresh air—the vista includes a stunning new skyline and the aging remnants of the original Minneapolis. Much of what glistens on the cityscape was built in the last 40 years. Minneapolis is redoing itself.

What a thrill it would be (for me, at least) to see Minneapolis in its infancy around 1850, or during the 1870s and 1880s when lumber and flour milling dominated the economy and created a prairie boomtown.

As picturesque as those times were—and several important artists found them to be so, including Alexis Fournier, who painted the riverfront during those years of growth—I continue to wonder why Minneapolis doesn't project the same aura of grace and elegance and, yes, romance that other Mississippi River cities do.

For more than 100 years, St. Paul's wealthiest and most prestigious families have built their homes on beautiful Summit Avenue (above). One of the boulevard's more noteworthy tenants is the 3,000-seat Renaissance-style Cathedral of St. Paul (opposite), which stands high on St. Anthony Hill, a short distance from the state capitol.

Take St. Paul, for example. Although I always get a lift from Minneapolis' sleek and shiny cityscape, St. Paul has managed its historic properties better. The cities may be "twins," but it is undeniable that they are unique—each possessed of its own character, its own quirks, and a huge array of its own charms.

To get a good look at what I'm referring to, put the unfinished portion of that walleye taco in the proper trash receptacle and leave the Stone Arch Bridge. Then walk downstream from Minneapolis and cross the Mississippi to the downtown riverfront promenade along Kellogg Boulevard in St. Paul. From here, you can look across your right elbow up fabled Summit Avenue, anchored by the handsome Cathedral of St. Paul. Summit is a grand old boulevard as renowned and as romanticized as any other on the Mississippi River, and deservedly so. It reminds you that St. Paul is an enchanting river city, a place of irresistible vintage buildings and exuberant heritage festivals.

Summit Avenue is most famous because of one young man who lived here—novelist F. Scott Fitzgerald. The stories Fitzgerald wrote about his youth in St. Paul are only one chapter in the ongoing saga of the Twin Cities. His words still capture a fascinating St. Paul of the past. Several paintings of old Minneapolis achieve a similar effect—Fournier's *Lake Harriet by Moonlight* and Robert Koehler's *Rainy Evening on Hennepin Avenue* are two examples—but Fitzgerald's stories offer as good a description of a time and a place as any art form you'll find.

▲ CHRIS FAUST

As the northern terminus for steamboat travel on the Mississippi River, St. Paul was a bustling center of frontier enterprise as early as the 1840s. Taken in 1859, this photo shows steamers *Grey Eagle*, *Frank Steele*, *Jeannette Roberts*, and *Time and Tide* docked at St. Paul's lower levee (OPPOSITE). Today, paddleboats provide one of the best views of the downtown St. Paul skyline.

Although Minneapolis and St. Paul are definitely Mississippi River towns, outsiders are often surprised to learn that fact. New Orleans, sure. St. Louis, of course. Memphis, Vicksburg, Natchez, no doubt. But not the Twin Cities.

An obvious reason is because we are located so far north, and most folks tend to think of the Mississippi as a southern river. Maybe outsiders who think we live in a deep freeze need reassurance—after all, lutefisk doesn't smell as sweet as honeysuckle and magnolias. (What? You don't know lutefisk? Well, it's a dried codfish concoction that turns up only in the wintertime on local menus—and, yes, it's as Scandinavian as it sounds.

Minneapolis ✴ St. Paul

I think those who really care about the great river will eventually find Minneapolis and St. Paul because we're en route to the source. The Mississippi begins approximately 200 miles north of the Twins as a rivulet in Minnesota's Lake Itasca State Park. It's a special historic spot because only there can you walk, hop, skip, or jump across the greatest of U.S. rivers. How's that for a picturesque memory?

Linked to the Future

There's truth to the adage "You can't judge a book by its cover." Once a swamp, the clear blue waters of Lake Calhoun today provide a tranquil escape from life in the city (BELOW). Even critics who call the Frederick R. Weisman Art Museum an eyesore can appreciate the provocative exhibits inside its metal frame (OPPOSITE).

t is here, at the northernmost port on the Mississippi, that today's Twin Citians dream of a future metro area that is as productive and innovative as the one nurtured by those intrepid residents who settled the place back in the 1840s. ✳ In the more than 150 years since settlers first created a clearing on the St. Paul side of the river above the big bluffs, Minneapolis and St. Paul have grown into a metropolitan center where more than 2.5 million people live and work. Annually, thousands more come to enjoy the scenery, the friendly ambience, the fishing, and, yes, even the misunderstood weather. What surprises them most is the influential cultural scene and the fact that the Twin Cities abound in major-league and semiprofessional sports.

Our first tourists arrived early. French voyageurs, or fur traders, were the region's first "campers." As a result, many streets have French names, and Our Lady of Lourdes Church on the Minneapolis riverfront continues to be designated as "the French parish."

New Englanders also arrived early on in the city's history to seek their fortunes and to raise families that created and cared about Minneapolis, then and now. Some of those families are still here—among them such names as Pillsbury, Gale, Washburn, Crosby, Morrison, Eastman, Chute, Stevens, and Phelps. Walker, Winton, and Fullerton were among the lumbermen. Donaldson and Dayton opened the important retail stores, as did Elizabeth Quinlan, a young woman of Irish ancestry who, early in the 20th century, founded Young-Quinlan, a local women's specialty store that set the standard for upscale shops across the United States. (Stanley Marcus, of the Neiman Marcus family in Texas, was even sent by his father to learn retailing firsthand from Miss Quinlan.)

Minneapolis ✳ St. Paul

Among the 19th-century visitors were naturalist and writer Henry David Thoreau, who stayed in a boarding house on Lake Calhoun and was thrilled to discover that pocket gophers inhabited the lakeshore too. The old riverboater Mark Twain was also a fairly regular visitor during his lecturing years.

Famous Norwegian violinist Ole Bull made annual visits, occasionally accompanied by Jenny Lind, the singer known as the "Swedish Nightingale." By that time, many Scandinavian newcomers had arrived to provide Bull and Lind with adoring audiences. Today, a bronze statue of Bull in Minneapolis' Loring Park is a focal point for Norwegian-American events, while the American Swedish Institute,

For more than 12 years, St. Paul's West Side neighborhood has paid homage to its Hispanic roots with a Cinco de Mayo celebration that includes a colorful parade, festive music, and plenty of food and crafts.

also in Minneapolis, features a handsome portrait of Lind. Minneapolis continues to be a home to descendants of the Scandinavian settlers who came here more than a century ago—a heritage that is celebrated year-round. Svenskarnes Dag (Swedish Day) in June, for example, is the largest gathering of Swedes and Swedish-Americans outside of Sweden itself.

Although Johnson is the name that continues to dominate the local telephone book, new spice has been added to the mix with the addition of emigrants from Asia, Africa, and the Caribbean. The influence of these ethnic groups is most evident in local restaurants, which truly serve international food.

For its part, St. Paul was settled by German and Irish immigrants, who were mainly Catholic. (Not surprisingly, the Catholic Archdiocese has its headquarters in St. Paul.) In later years, a large Hispanic community grew in the city. And yes, St. Paul also has a sizable population of

Swedish immigrants who lived in a district known as (another surprise) Swede Hollow.

The original settlers of the Twin Cities were, of course, Native Americans who had roamed the northern prairies for centuries. These tribes greeted the newcomers when they arrived at the Mississippi landings—albeit not entirely enthusiastically—and the convergence between the Old World and the New was, as these meetings went, a friendly one. Things even remained cordial for a few years. The Dakota, called Sioux by white settlers, were the dominant tribe until they were challenged by the Ojibwa (Chippewa) for the Minnesota territory. After a Sioux uprising against American soldiers in 1862, both tribes were sent to reservations, where many continue to live in relative isolation and considerable poverty. In recent years, however, legalized gambling on the reservations has helped upgrade living conditions and offer new jobs, especially at the Las Vegas-style casino in Prior Lake, located 30 minutes from downtown Minneapolis.

THESE CHILDREN KNOW THERE'S much more to Minnesota winters than subzero temperatures and several feet of snow.

Although much of their land was taken, area tribes have managed to pass down their heritage over the years. For example, Native American art, music, and dance are regularly displayed in the Twin Cities. George Morrison, an Ojibwa artist whose work has been collected by major American museums, has two pieces in downtown Minneapolis—a sidewalk sculpture of granite on the Nicollet Mall and a totem in LaSalle Plaza. One of the most successful Native American novelists is Little Falls' Louise Erdrich, whose books, including the acclaimed *Love Medicine* and *The Bingo Palace*, reflect tribal life and spirituality.

Along with an abiding interest in Native American culture is a renewed effort to provide more opportunities for our original residents. Minneapolis has the Bear-Hawk American Indian Museum. The Minneapolis Institute of Arts boasts a permanent collection of superb Native American art. St. Paul is home to offices of the Minnesota American Indian Chamber of Commerce for business entrepreneurs. And there is an American Indian Opportunities Industrialization Center for job training, the American Indian Research and Policy Institute, and the Two Feathers Fund for philanthropic ventures. St. Paul also offers an authentic look at Native American history at Indian Mounds Park. The park, located on the river close to downtown, was an early Indian burial ground.

Although the Twin Cities have made great progress in honoring the real influence of Native Americans on the area, Henry Wadsworth Longfellow's romanticized Indian hero Hiawatha continues to be a presence in Minneapolis. Sometimes it's pervasive:

The land that eventually became the Twin Cities was originally purchased from the Sioux and Ojibwa Indians in the first half of the 19th century. Native Americans continue to maintain a strong political and cultural presence in the area.

Streets in one corner of the city, for example, are named for characters in the literary work. And in Minnehaha Park, there's a statue of Hiawatha carrying the Indian maiden Minnehaha across Minnehaha Creek. Ironically, the work was created by Scandinavian artist Jacob Fjelde. In recent years, a statue of Little Crow, a famous Sioux chief, was erected in the park. This one, however, is the work of an American Indian sculptor, Ed Noisecat.

There is no doubt that Twin Citians have to be hardy types, because winter here can make you frostbitten and frantic, especially in heavy snow or icy traffic jams. ✻ And yet, for more than 30 years, our nimble-thinking city fathers have made the "freezin' season" easier to live with by building more bridges. Not the kind that cross the Mississippi River—we have enough of those. These enclosed spans, which set a national trend for downtowns everywhere, are known as skyways. They link office blocks in both of the Twin Cities' downtown areas at the second-story level, offering locals a relief from heavy winter clothing and an easy way to get about town on foot without having to cope with the frigid blasts of January and February.

Minneapolis ✻ *St. Paul*

When visitors dare to come to the Twin Cities during the winter, they not only take comfort in the shelter of the skyways, but they also take refuge in the biggest enclosed shopping mall in the world. Located in Bloomington, the largest contiguous suburb in the metropolitan area, the dazzling Mall of America draws tourists and shoppers from around the globe to a retailing wonderland complete with Knott's Camp Snoopy, a seven-acre glass-domed amusement park, in its center. (Inspiration for Camp Snoopy, of course, comes from the comic strip characters in *Peanuts*, created by cartoonist Charles Schulz, a native of Minneapolis and a former resident of St. Paul whose best friend was named Charlie Brown.)

But really, why marvel at the cleverness of the bundled-up natives who have learned to

TWIN CITIANS FIND PLENTY OF ways to escape the elements. Miles of heated skyways link businesses, museums, residential space, retail establishments, and government buildings (OPPOSITE), while the Mall of America, the largest enclosed shopping complex in the country, boasts approximately 425 retail stores and dozens of entertainment options (ABOVE).

Linked to the Future

live—or rather, endure—a possible three months of below-zero days? Because long winters have given Twin Citians time to think. And thinking has brought results. Just look at the list of Fortune 500 companies that are headquartered in the Twin Cities area and you'll see.

We gave the world Scotch™ tape and Post-it® Notes from 3M, Wheaties ("The Breakfast of Champions") and Betty Crocker's recipes from General Mills, financial services from Norwest, and Honeywell's electronic devices.

The Minneapolis-St. Paul Metropolitan Airport is the number one hub for Northwest Airlines, which was founded here and continues to have its main offices in the suburb of Eagan. The airport, by the way, is the same one that Little Falls native Charles Lindbergh flew into and out of during his famous 1927 nonstop transatlantic flight. Lindbergh's homecoming to

Minneapolis ✳ St. Paul

Minnesota was staged on Minneapolis' Nicollet Avenue, which is now redesigned as the Nicollet Mall

for pedestrian shoppers.

One of the nation's largest retailers, Dayton Hudson Corporation, which operates Marshall Field's in

Chicago, Hudson's in Detroit, and Target Stores everywhere, was founded in Minneapolis. The company's

flagship department store, Dayton's, and its headquarters are both located on the Nicollet Mall.

Those winters also inspired Minnesotans to invent snowmobiles for outdoor activities and

Nordictrack machines for indoor exercise. The area's most recent retailing success, Rollerblade Inc.,

promoters of the in-line skating craze, began in a suburban Twin Cities basement. Scott Olson, the

young inventor who perfected the skates, also recently introduced the Rowbike, a rowing machine on

a bike that serves as an another unusual exercise vehicle.

TWIN CITIANS DON'T STAY INDOORS just because there's snow on the ground. Ice-fishing tents and snow caves are a few of the notable features of Minnesota's wintertime architectural landscape.

Linked to the Future

The IDS Tower, with its glass-roofed Crystal Court, is considered to be one of architect Philip Johnson's best designs. Located on Nicollet Mall, the building houses offices of IDS Financial Services, an investments subsidiary of American Express.

Other well-known companies with home offices here include Medtronic (medical devices); West Publishing (law books); Bemis Company (packaging materials); St. Paul Companies, Lutheran Brotherhood, and ReliaStar (insurance); and Ceridian (computers). Cargill, one of the largest privately owned firms in the world, was founded in the Twin Cities in 1865 and continues to maintain its executive offices in a Minneapolis suburb.

Currently, the wealthiest man in our midst is Curtis Carlson, a son of Swedish immigrants who created Carlson Companies, a multifaceted empire of hotels, travel agencies, and restaurants. Even more impressive is the fact that he started it all with trading stamps.

The Twin Cities have also been a center for medical research and treatment. It was here that Sister Elizabeth Kenny, the Australian nurse with a new treatment for polio, was allowed to first practice. And for decades, the University of Minnesota has been a leader in cancer research, organ transplants, and other medical innovations.

TWIN CITIES THEATERS HAVE hosted their share of audiences over the years, from this crowd waiting to see the premier of the film *Sister Kenny* (OPPOSITE) to the hundreds of people who lined up for the recent revival of the classic musical *Show Boat* (RIGHT).

Minneapolis ✴ St. Paul

uring the middle years of the 19th century, the Twin Cities became a summer-time vacation spot for wealthy southern families. They would travel up the Mississippi on spacious paddleboats and stay in hotels with wraparound porches that overlooked the river and caught those refreshing summer breezes. ✳ It wasn't long, though, before a young Canadian immigrant, who began working in St. Paul as a dock hand, built a mighty railroad. James J. Hill, one of the Twin Cities' first millionaires, founded the Great Northern Railroad (now known as the Burlington Northern) and located its headquarters in St. Paul. The firm's main offices have since moved to Washington State.

Known as an empire builder for extending his railroad from Minnesota to the Pacific Northwest, Hill put one of his plummier stops just west of Minneapolis on the shore of Lake Minnetonka. There, overlooking Lafayette Bay, he also built a fine hotel that was an easy railroad trip from the two nearby downtowns. By the late 1880s and early 1890s, tourists had abandoned the riverfront for the lake, and summer tourism thrived.

People continue to flock to Lake Minnetonka and White Bear Lake outside St. Paul in both summer and winter. However, the long-overlooked Minneapolis riverfront has been re-discovered not only by tourists, but by local residents as well. (Incidentally, the Stone Arch Bridge, a landmark that Hill built in 1883 to accommodate his railroad, is now one of the best in-line skating routes in town. It connects to a citywide—and soon countywide—route that will allow commuters to leave their cars at home and skate or bike to work.)

Nicollet Island dominates the downtown riverfront. It boasts a village of occupied historic houses—many of them reclaimed and restored by their original owners—as well as the Nicollet Island Inn, an old sash-and-door factory that was turned into a charming hotel. Another hotel, the Whitney, is housed in one of the historic mills on the riverbank.

ORIGINALLY CALLED "JIM HILL'S Folly" after chief railroad executive James J. Hill (OPPOSITE, THIRD MAN FROM LEFT), the Stone Arch Bridge provided a crossing for Hill's St. Paul, Minneapolis, and Manitoba railroads.

▼ CHRIS FAUST

Minneapolis ✳ *St. Paul*

In St. Paul, the downtown riverfront has been in more constant use over the years. Current plans will bring even more excitement to the riverbank, including the new and improved Science Museum of Minnesota, which will house a wraparound theater.

One particular surprise that St. Paul offers river-loving tourists in summer is the floating bed-and-breakfast moored near the popular No Wake Cafe, both of which are fast becoming local land, er, watermarks. Summer tourists can also ride the river in replicas of the old paddle wheelers. Several times a season, those queenly passenger boats travel upriver to St. Paul to pick up fares. Just as it was a century ago, it's still a big day when the *Delta Queen* or one of its sister paddle wheelers is docked in St. Paul.

For many years, the Padelford Packet Boat Co. has luxuriously carried sightseers along the St. Paul waterfront (ABOVE). For a true taste of life on the Mississippi, stop by for a meal at the renowned No Wake Cafe (OPPOSITE).

When I said that St. Paul was better at preserving its historic buildings than Minneapolis, I was perhaps stretching the point a bit. Actually, there is a great deal of long-standing enthusiasm for preservation and recycling of historic buildings for contemporary use in *both* cities. In St. Paul, such early residential areas as Summit Hill and Ramsey Hill attracted young residents who were eager and willing to do the hard work necessary to reclaim the neighborhoods.

Minneapolis was somewhat behind St. Paul in realizing the importance of historic preservation, but today, the city can boast a nationally recognized warehouse district—blocks of 19th- and 20th-century warehouse buildings that have been turned into housing, theaters, restaurants, offices, and art galleries. And when you move away from the Mississippi River and into the residential neighborhoods of both cities, you might be astonished, or perhaps overjoyed, at the blocks of parklands you see.

Minneapolis' park system, which has received national honors as the best among major cities,

Minneapolis ✳ St. Paul

includes more than 6,500 acres of parks and lakes. St. Paul has 3,000-plus acres of parkland inside the city, including the crown jewel, Como Park, with its 100-year-old glass-paned conservatory—a favorite wedding location—and its friendly old city zoo. (The newer 485-acre Minnesota Zoo, located in the suburb of Apple Valley, is the second largest in the United States.)

Surrounding the Twin Cities, the metropolitan area features county parks and recreation areas covering close to 50,000 acres. There is room for every kind of outdoor activity in the regional system—even in winter. No, the hills aren't mountains, but cross-country skiing, ski jumping, dogsledding, and snowmobiling are all part of the action.

My first glimpse of Lake Calhoun, the city lake that I now call my own, was a shock . . . a happy jolt really. You see, I grew up in Iowa, where lakes are few and far between. Minneapolis has 22 good-sized lakes inside the city limits. My lake—and I can call it that because I live so close and all taxpayers are owners—is about four miles around, making it almost perfect for a hike, a bike ride, or a turn on in-line skates.

EVEN AS EARLY AS 1927, HENNEPIN Avenue had established itself as the heart of the downtown Minneapolis business district. Today, thousands of people head daily to the boulevard's establishments to work as well as play.

Lake Calhoun also has its own yacht club of young, old, and very young sailors who make the summer views unusually pleasant. In winter, you'll see ice-fishing huts on the lake and those daring young things with their ice sleds "sailing" along with the wind.

The snow can arrive early in the fall, but usually Mother Nature waits until around Thanksgiving before socking it to us. Late December can bring on the big freeze with below-zero temperatures that often extend into January and February. Curiously, there is usually a warm-up in time for St. Paul's Winter Carnival, an annual romp that has been luring thousands to the great and icy outdoors since 1886.

Winter usually wraps up by April, when the ice breaks up on area waterways and spring's earlier blooms peek out. In fact, in 1996, when Arnold Schwarzenegger filmed *Jingle All the Way* in the

Minneapolis ✳ St. Paul

Twin Cities in late April, the crew had to substitute dried potato flakes for snow on the roofs of houses. (And that year, with April showers came . . . you guessed it, mashed potatoes.)

Incidentally, the moviemaking business is a new and profitable one for Minnesota and the Twin Cities. In recent years, the Minnesota Film Board, with help from two interested state governors, has brought many film crews to town. Among the more memorable movies to use the Twin Cities as a backdrop are *Fargo* by Joel and Ethan Coen, brothers who grew up in the Minneapolis suburb of St. Louis Park, and *Grumpy Old Men* and *Grumpier Old Men*, two popular comedies starring Jack Lemmon and Walter Matthau. It was the grumpy men's costar Sophia Loren, however, who *really* stopped traffic every time she relaxed by walking around downtown St. Paul.

Lake Harriet (opposite) and Lake Calhoun (above) are two of the largest lakes in Minneapolis. Along with Lake of the Isles, they make up the city's renowned Chain of Lakes. All three are connected by paved paths that are ideal for biking, walking, jogging, or in-line skating.

People often ask me what I like best about these two cities or where to go for a jolly good time. And I always ask them what *they* like, because the Twin Cities have everything . . . well, almost everything. We don't have mountains. ✳ Music lovers know that Minneapolis and St. Paul not only have inspired accomplished composer Antonín Dvořák to write his acclaimed symphony *From the New World*, but also boast two of the world's finest orchestras—the St. Paul Chamber Orchestra and the Minnesota Orchestra, formerly the Minneapolis Symphony Orchestra. The concert schedule is crowded with dozens of other performing arts organizations as well. Music lovers can attend top-notch performances by the Minnesota Opera and the innovative programs of the Plymouth Music Series, while dance connois-

FOUR NEW CONDUCTORS WHO are forever changing the way Minnesotans think about classical music include (FROM LEFT) Hugh Wolff, music director, St. Paul Chamber Orchestra; Bill Eddins, associate conductor, Minnesota Orchestra; Bobby McFerrin, creative chair, St. Paul Chamber Orchestra; and Eiji Oue, music director, Minnesota Orchestra.

seurs can enjoy a collection of excellent dance companies. All of these major professional performing arts organizations, which regularly tour across the country and overseas, make their headquarters in the Twin Cities.

True, we have nothing as anchored as W.C. Handy's *St. Louis Blues* or Chuck Berry's *Memphis, Tennessee* to put us on the pop culture map. No one

hums a tune about Minneapolis or St. Paul—not even troubadour Bob Dylan, a small-town boy from Iron Range whose singing career began in a coffeehouse near the University of Minnesota.

Although no hit song has been written about us yet, we have "reared" our fair share of superstar singers. Besides Dylan, the Artist Formerly Known as Prince, and the Andrews Sisters, Minnesota boasts the unforgettable Judy Garland, a Grand Rapids youngster who played vaudeville in the Twin Cities as a child and then returned as a star to sing a salute at the 1958 statehood centennial celebration in Minneapolis.

Theater is also rich and varied in the Twin Cities. Irishman Sir Tyrone Guthrie established one of the world's most famous regional theater companies in Minneapolis, the Guthrie Theater, which is now headed by another Irish native, Joe Dowling of Dublin's Abbey Theater. The Children's Theatre Company is equally world renowned, as is the Theatre de la Jeune Lune, a creative French-American company—both in Minneapolis. St. Paul offers the Penumbra Theatre Company, the principal African-American professional acting company in Minnesota, as well as the Great American History Theatre, which presents original plays based on regional history and folklore. And that's not all. At last count, the Twin Cities area was second only to New York City in presenting professional live theater on dozens of stages.

Writers have always thrived in the Twin Cities—thanks again to those long cold winters, I suppose—and writing workshops continue to be a part of the cultural picture. In addition to Fitzgerald, such novelists as Sinclair Lewis, Robert Penn Warren, and Saul Bellow have taught at the University of Minnesota. Meanwhile, news-

FEW MUSICIANS HAVE GAINED the degree of fame and notoriety enjoyed by Minneapolis' own Prince Rogers Nelson. Today, fans and critics alike reluctantly call him the Artist Formerly Known as Prince.

men Delos Lovelace, who wrote the original screenplay for the movie *King Kong*; Frederick Manfred of *Lord Grizzly* fame; and TV's Harry Reasoner and Eric Sevareid all began their writing careers with Twin Cities newspapers. Harrison Salisbury, a longtime *New York Times* correspondent and author, got a less glamorous "professional" start here; his first hometown job was pushing grain carts at the Pillsbury "A" Mill on the downtown riverbank. Two writers who saw their books become Broadway hits and major movies were Minneapolis' Thomas Heggen (*Mr. Roberts*) and St. Paul's Max Schulman (*Barefoot Boy with Cheek*).

Today's best-selling authors who live and work in or near the Twin Cities include Garrison Keillor, Louise Erdrich, Michael Dorris, and Robert Bly. August Wilson experimented with his work at the Playwrights Center in Minneapolis, while Brian Friel got a boost in his playwriting career as a Guthrie Theater intern.

Fans of Broadway musicals will find the best revivals on stage at the professional Chanhassen Dinner Theatre in suburban Chanhassen. And the oldest professional acting company in the area is the Old Log Theater overlooking Lake Minnetonka.

Labeled as the longest-running comedy playhouse in the United States, Dudley Riggs' Brave New Workshop and Instant Theatre is in Minneapolis. St. Paul counters with America's favorite humorist, Keillor, who performs many of his *A Prairie Home Companion* radio shows in the restored F. Scott Fitzgerald Theater in St. Paul.

Touring shows and concert artists play the Ordway Music Theatre, a new St. Paul gem, or the splendidly restored State and Orpheum theaters in Minneapolis. The acoustically superb Orchestra Hall in Minneapolis is a mecca for the world's greatest musicians. Target Center in Minneapolis, home of the National Basketball Association's Minnesota Timberwolves, also hosts rock concerts, ice shows, and circuses.

The Hubert H. Humphrey Metrodome, Minneapolis' downtown domed stadium, is where the Minnesota Vikings professional football team, the Minnesota Twins Major League Baseball team, and the University of Minnesota football team play. The Metrodome has also been the scene of one Super Bowl game, two World Series competitions, the NCAA Final Four basketball finals, a Billy Graham evangelistic rally, and an international Scandinavia Today celebration. The stadium was named for Hubert Humphrey, a former Minneapolis mayor who served in the U.S. Senate and as Vice President of the United States.

TWO LONGTIME ATTRACTIONS in the Twin Cities include Minneapolis' world-renowned Tyrone Guthrie Theater, currently under the artistic direction of native Irishman Joe Dowling (OPPOSITE), and the Cafesjian's Carousel in St. Paul's Town Square Park (BELOW). Each unique piece of the carousel, which has 68 horses and two chariots, was hand-carved in Philadelphia in 1914.

◄ STORMI GREENER / MINNEAPOLIS STAR TRIBUNE

In addition to a long list of attractions and things to do, both cities also have elaborate convention centers that are undergoing expansions. Visitors can choose from a variety of activities, including gambling casinos, speed skating tracks, a spectacular summertime amusement park, and a complete menu of museums. St. Paul offers the Minnesota Historical Society's History Center, the new Minnesota Children's Museum, the Science Museum of Minnesota, and the Minnesota Museum of American Art.

Minneapolis boasts three important art museums—the public Minneapolis Institute of Arts, our encyclopedic collection of art through the ages; the Walker Art Center, famous for its contemporary collection that includes pieces in the Minneapolis Sculpture Garden, the largest outdoor urban sculpture garden in the United States; and the Frederick R. Weisman Art Museum on the University of Minnesota campus, with a varied art collection that is housed in an architectural marvel of a building designed by Frank Gehry. It can even be said that the

Twin Cities' sphere of influence in the fine arts is far reaching: St. Paul native Paul Manship's

gilded *Prometheus* sculpture is prominently displayed in the main plaza of New York City's

Rockefeller Center.

St. Paul also has the Minnesota State Capitol, which overlooks downtown and boasts the

world's largest unsupported marble dome, and the five-story James J. Hill House, built in

1891. Additional Minneapolis attractions include the American Swedish Institute, a grand

mansion filled with art and fine furnishings, and Fort Snelling, the original government outpost

overlooking the Mississippi River that dates back to the 1820s. During the 1840s, the fort

commander was Captain Seth Eastman, today recognized as one of the important early artists

who painted images of the American West. And St. Paul has one of the country's most unique

wonders among its many attractions: the fanciful Cafesjian's Carousel, a historic marvel

featuring 68 hand-carved animals.

*P*OPULAR ENTERTAINMENT VENUES light up the evening landscape in Minneapolis. The Target Center arena, home of the Minnesota Timberwolves, offers state-of-the-art accommodations and holds just over 19,000 people (OPPOSITE). The recently renovated State Theater, located on Hennepin Avenue, hosts national as well as local performances (ABOVE).

Minnesota Children's Museum

PLAYHOUSE

ADMIT ONE

Minneapolis has its own share of out-of-the-ordinary attractions. The city's only planetarium is in the downtown branch of the public library. The First Avenue Club, a popular nightspot located in the old bus depot, is a contemporary landmark because Prince (you know, the Artist Formerly Known as . . .) got his big break in show business on its stage and set his movie *Purple Rain* there. And, then, there is the Foshay Tower, a 31-story office building that is a replica of the Washington Monument. It was built in 1929 by a Minneapolitan who just loved the Washington, D.C., landmark. Well, why not?

As you can see, we really do have a lovely hunk of breathing space right here in the Twin Cities. From the stunning views at the Stone Arch Bridge downtown to the residential neighborhoods that stretch out from the riverfront, from a thriving business community to an active and progressive performing arts scene, Minneapolis and St. Paul have a great deal to offer residents and visitors alike.

So don't be surprised if you find yourself, walleye taco in hand, falling in love with the Twin Cities. Simply listening to St. Anthony Falls, feeling the spray, and taking a deep breath of our cool, fresh air will draw you in. And you're sure to be hooked forever. ✳

ART COMES IN MANY FORMS AT the Minneapolis Sculpture Garden. Composed of a 52-foot-long spoon bearing a nine-and-a-half-foot-diameter cherry, *Spoonbridge and Cherry* by Claes Oldenburg and Coosje van Bruggen has become an icon of the Twin Cities' strong artistic culture (LEFT). Sporting its own variety of sculpture is the Minnesota Children's Museum, where exhibits are designed especially for children and encourage learning through hands-on experience (OPPOSITE).

*F*ireworks over the world's largest ice palace help Minnesotans celebrate the season at the St. Paul Winter Carnival, the oldest winter celebration in North America (PAGES 40 AND 41).

PAGES 40 AND 41: TOM NELSON / FROZEN IMAGES

Minneapolis ✳ *St. Paul*

With the approaching dusk, the vitality that is shared by St. Paul (opposite) and Minneapolis (above) begins to shine. In Minneapolis, such structures as First Bank Place, the Norwest building, and the IDS Center house some of the Twin Cities' most successful movers and shakers (pages 44 and 45).

Linked to the Future

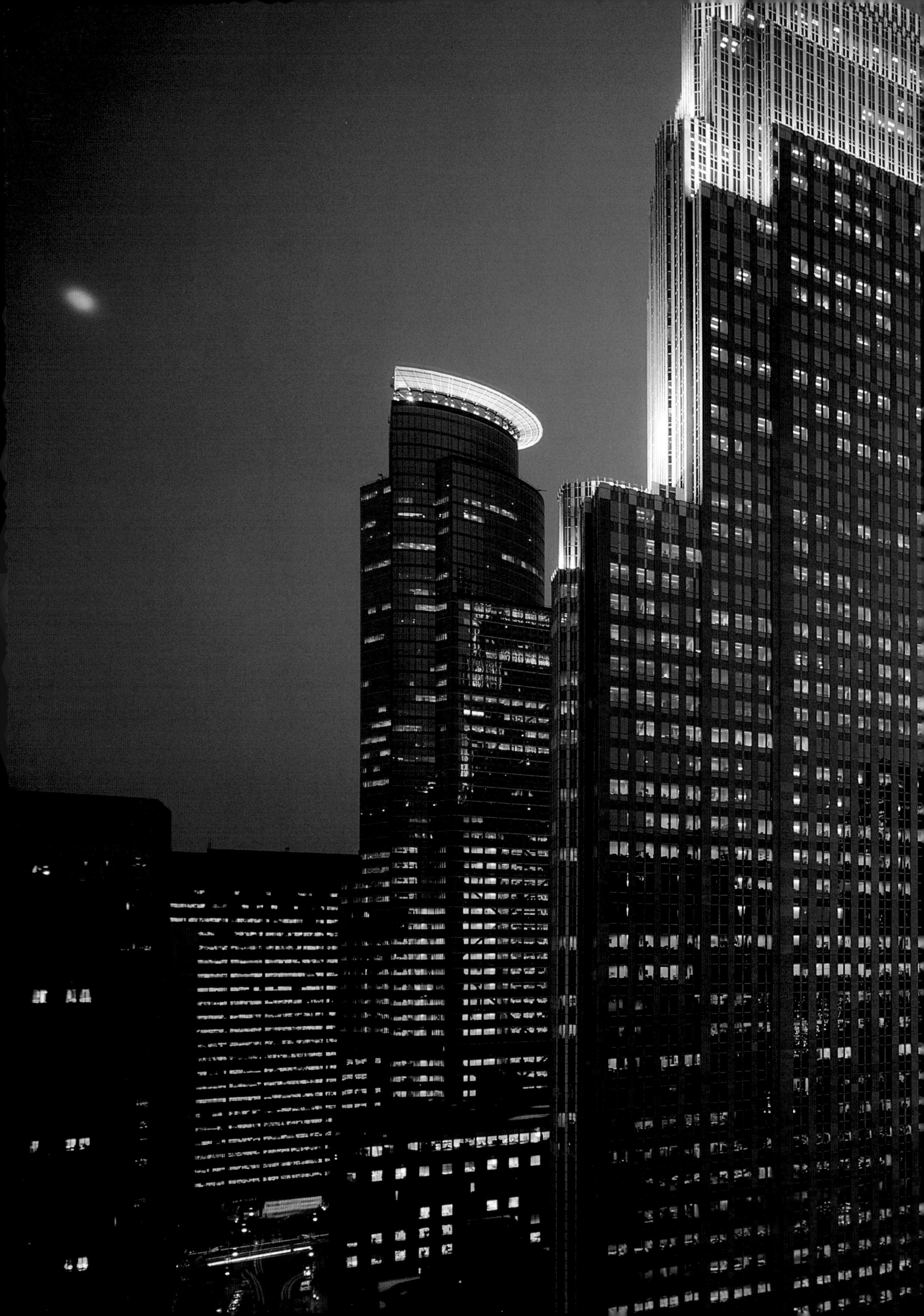

THE CAREFUL OBSERVER WILL discover reflections of power and beauty alike in downtown Minneapolis. Specifically, First Bank Place's distinctive crown (PAGE 46) and the 42-story Piper Jaffray Tower (PAGE 47) provide examples of the innovative and contemporary designs found in the city's differing architectural patterns.

PAGE 46: CHUCK PEFLEY / FROZEN IMAGES
PAGE 47: JEFFERY C. DREWITZ / FROZEN IMAGES

$\mathcal{T}$HE TARGET CENTER ARENA IN downtown Minneapolis hosts numerous sporting and special events, including all home games for the Min-nesota Timberwolves professional bas-ketball team. The arena's geometric elegance is mirrored in the natural landscape of downtown Minneapolis.

WHETHER YOUR TASTE LEANS toward the contemporary or the traditional, downtown Minneapolis offers something for everyone. The clean, sleek lines of the Pillsbury Center (PAGE 52) are no less beautiful than the intricate carvings found atop the historic State Theatre (PAGE 53). Once the city's tallest structure, the Foshay Tower, standing proudly between the IDS Center and Cesar Pelli's Norwest building, is a replica of the Washington Monument (ABOVE). Another dominating presence in downtown Minneapolis is the Metropolitan Centre office building (OPPOSITE).

PAGE 52: RICHARD HAMILTON SMITH / FROZEN IMAGES

PAGE 53: ED BOCK / FROZEN IMAGES

Minneapolis ✳ St. Paul

MINNESOTA HISTORICAL SOCIETY

Nicollet Avenue in Minneapolis had long been known as the retail center of the upper Midwest before it was transformed into a pedestrian mall in the late 1960s. Today, shoppers share the busy sidewalks with area businesspeople.

ED BOCK / FROZEN IMAGES

Minneapolis ✳ St. Paul

No matter your vantage point, the views around Minneapolis are spectacular. From the pedestrian bridge over Hennepin Avenue, spectators can see the downtown skyline and the Basilica of St. Mary (OPPOSITE BOTTOM). Meanwhile, the clock tower of Minneapolis' city hall and courthouse may look to be at eye level from this angle, but the structure actually rises 345 feet above the pedestrians walking along Fifth Street (LEFT).

Minneapolis ✳ *St. Paul*

THE MINNESOTA HISTORY CENTER in St. Paul houses an array of historical documents, artifacts, books, photographs, maps, manuscripts, and exhibits that bring the state's past to life. Recently completed, the three-story complex was clearly designed with beauty as well as function in mind.

M INNESOTA'S MAJESTIC CAPITOL
building in St. Paul has been
the center of the state government
since 1905. Within its interior is the
beautiful rotunda, where a symbolic
glass star set in brass adorns the
marbled floor.

Minneapolis ✴ *St. Paul*

High atop the capitol sits one of the largest unsupported marble domes in the world. Although commonly referred to as the "golden horses," the sculpture at the base of the dome is actually titled *The Progress of the State*.

A STROLL DOWN PICTURESQUE Summit Avenue in St. Paul will take you past the new library at Macalester College (CENTER), the governor's mansion (BOTTOM LEFT), and the historic James J. Hill House (BOTTOM RIGHT).

Minneapolis ✳ *St. Paul*

ONE OF ST. PAUL'S MOST FAMOUS residents was F. Scott Fitzgerald, who wrote *This Side of Paradise* while living on Summit Avenue. Here, Fitzgerald and his wife, Zelda, are pictured at Dellwood in September 1921, a month before their daughter, Scottie, was born.

THOUSANDS OF PEOPLE RECOGNIZE the resonating voice of Garrison Keillor, whose popular radio show, *A Prairie Home Companion*, can be heard nationwide on National Public Radio.

Minneapolis ✳ St. Paul

MINNESOTA POET AND AUTHOR Robert Bly is often credited with sparking the men's movement of the early 1990s.

*Minneapolis * St. Paul*

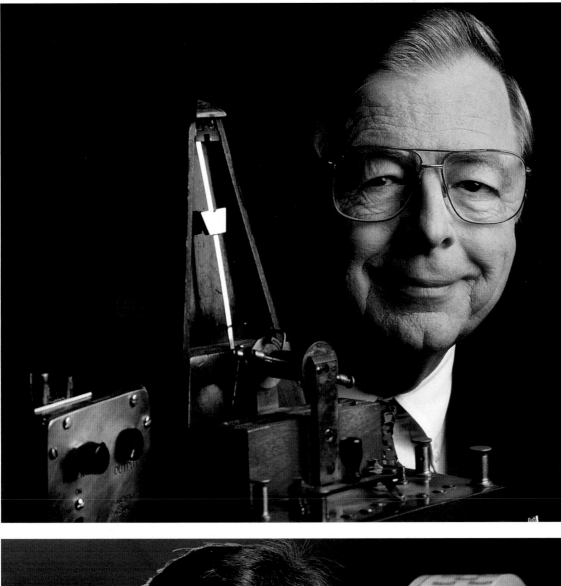

WHERE WOULD THE WORLD BE without barber poles, pacemakers, and Breathe Right strips? Thanks to Minnesota inventors William Marvy (OPPOSITE BOTTOM), Earl Bakken (TOP), and B.C. Johnson (BOTTOM), we won't have to find out.

THE BRIGHT LIGHTS OF MINNEapolis (TOP) and St. Paul (BOTTOM) showcase the splendor of the Twin Cities, currently under the leadership of Minneapolis Mayor Sharon Sayles Belton and St. Paul Mayor Norm Coleman (OPPOSITE), who occasionally work together on projects involving the two cities.

Though not exactly the stuff of fairy tales, these three "castles"—Minneapolis' city hall and courthouse (TOP), the American Swedish Institute (BOTTOM LEFT), and Our Lady of Lourdes Church (BOTTOM RIGHT)—evoke visions of times gone by. The Landmark Center in St. Paul (OPPOSITE) won an American Institute of Architects award for its restoration. This 1902 building originally housed the federal courts and post office.

▶ WALTER DEPTULA

Minneapolis ✳ *St. Paul*

T HESE SIGNS OF THE TIMES PRESENT a visual reminder of Minneapolis' commercial history.

CHUCK PEFLEY / FROZEN IMAGES

I̶N MINNEAPOLIS' EARLY YEARS, St. Anthony Falls provided water-power for lumber and flour mills. Its locks are also vital to the safe naviga- tion of the upper Mississippi by coal and grain barges as well as by private pleasure craft.

76

*Minneapolis * St. Paul*

LOCK & DAM NO. 1
NOV. 16, 1916.

MID THE SLEEK, CONTEMPORARY
lines that now dominate downtown Minneapolis, there are traces of
the architectural style that existed in
the city's earliest years. The Medical
Arts Building still houses many of the
city's most prominent physicians and
specialists (TOP). The Pillsbury "A"
Mill, built on the east riverbank in
1881, was once the world's largest mill
of its type (BOTTOM).

$\mathscr{D}$URING THE HEYDAY OF THE lumber industry in Minneapolis, many manufacturers and dealers had offices in the Romanesque-style Lumber Exchange Building, which was built in 1885 (LEFT). The Flour Exchange Building also illustrates the intricate detail found in architecture during that period (TOP RIGHT). The Stone Arch Bridge, which linked the city's milling district with the growing downtown area, is now listed as an engineering landmark on the National Register of Historic Places (BOTTOM RIGHT).

The STONE ARCH BRIDGE in Minneapolis originally carried trains across the Mississippi River. Today, bicycles and in-line skates provide the fastest means of transportation.

A NATIONALLY RECOGNIZED PARK system and a plethora of welcoming lakes make the Twin Cities the perfect setting for such outdoor activities as skateboarding and in-line skating.

EAR-ROUND, TWIN CITIES
residents make the most
of Minnesota's seasons.

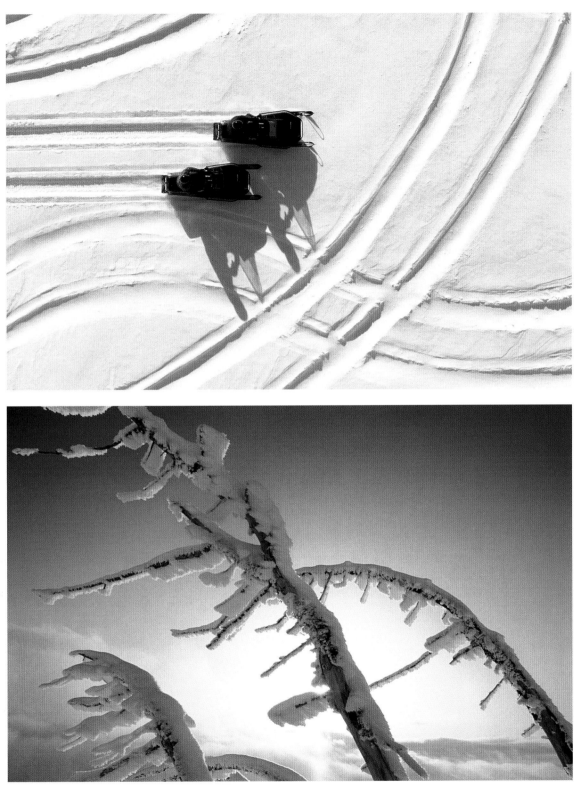

IX SOME WATER WITH FREEZING temperatures, and the result is a winter wonderland of beauty and fun.

RANSIT MAY NOT BE SO RAPID during the winter months, but getting from point A to point B is often much more fun. Twin Citians of all ages prove that ice skates are the best way to travel on Lake of the Isles. Even these peewee hockey players know enough to make sure the ice is frozen solid before venturing out too far.

*E*VEN THE MAJESTIC, CASCADING Minnehaha Falls in south Minneapolis' Minnehaha Park are no match for winter's silencing freeze.

Linked to the Future

FAIRY TALES DO COME TRUE AT the annual St. Paul Winter Carnival on Harriet Island (PAGES 92 AND 93). In 1992, thousands of local construction journeymen and registered apprentice workers volunteered time and talent to help construct one of the world's largest ice palaces.

PAGES 92 AND 93: CONRAD BLOOMQUIST / HILLSTROM STOCK PHOTO

Minneapolis ✳ St. Paul

Many Twin Cities residents figure that if they're going to live in a place that looks and feels like the North Pole, they may as well make the most of it. No doubt Santa feels right at home during the many cold December days.

At historic Fort Snelling, "officers" reenact everyday army life in the 1820s (top). Meanwhile, this army of headless figures keeps watch at the Minneapolis Sculpture Garden (bottom). The exhibit, titled *Black Flag*, was created by artist Alexander Calder.

$\mathcal{F}$ROM THE HUSTLE AND BUSTLE of the Minneapolis-St. Paul International Airport to the solitude and serenity of Fort Snelling National

Cemetery, everyday life in the Twin Cities is full of contrasts and idiosyncrasies.

THE LINES BETWEEN CITY AND country are often blurred in the more suburban regions of the Twin Cities. Here, the parking ramp at the world-famous Mall of America in Bloomington shares a stretch of land with a herd of sheep.

Minneapolis ✳ *St. Paul*

VISITORS TO THE MINNESOTA Zoo in Apple Valley can discover and enjoy more than 1,700 animals, and see thousands of plants in exhibits representing the natural habitats of the zoo's residents.

CHERYL WALSH BELLVILLE

JUDY OLAUSEN

Minneapolis ✳ St. Paul

ROM SUMMER RODEOS TO THE races at Canterbury Downs, Minnesotans love their horses, of course, for both entertainment and companionship.

W HETHER IT BE MAY DAY celebration participants (LEFT) or this towering craftsman, built entirely of scrap metal, at the Minneapolis Institute of Art (RIGHT), Twin Citians prove they are head and shoulders above the rest.

Minneapolis ✳ *St. Paul*

$\mathcal{T}$HE WINNERS, BY A FOOT OR two, are the lazy, hazy days of summer in the city. Hiding in a box is one way to find shade, but a cool dip in Lake Harriet will no doubt bring quicker relief from the heat.

▼ GERALD KOLLODGE

FROM MINNESOTAN PAUL Granlund's *Birth of Freedom* outside Westminster Presbyterian Church to the orangutans at Como Zoo in St. Paul, from the Minnesota gopher mascot at the State Fairgrounds to a larger-than-life snowman in north St. Paul, one can't help but appreciate the many faces of Minneapolis-St. Paul.

Minneapolis ✳ St. Paul

▶ HOWARD M. CHRISTOPHERSON

Minneapolis ✳ St. Paul

▲ JOEL SHEAGREN

THE REST OF THE COUNTRY MAY chuckle at Minnesota's notoriously long winters, but this scene proves that no one is laughing harder than Twin Cities residents themselves. Anyone up for a rematch?

On Monday nights during the summer, hundreds of people attend outdoor walk-in movies in Minneapolis' Loring Park. The movies and ensuing camaraderie are free, but viewers need to bring their own popcorn and candy.

THEY'RE NO SISKEL AND EBERT, but the cast of *Mystery Science Theater 3000* have gained quite a reputation—and quite a following—in the Twin Cities and nationwide. The show, which recently made its debut on the big screen as a feature-length movie, was created by a handful of Twin Cities natives and is still produced locally.

The arts in the Twin Cities grow out of a multitude of aesthetics—from contemporary to traditional, from tribal to experimental. Melissa Birch (TOP LEFT) is a well-known performance artist. Myron Johnson (TOP RIGHT) is artistic director of Ballet of the Dolls Dance Company in Minneapolis. And Patrick Scully (BOTTOM), artistic director of Patrick's Cabaret, has provided a place for hundreds of local artists and performers to make their dreams come true.

Minneapolis ✳ St. Paul

DANCE IS ALIVE AND WELL IN the Twin Cities, thanks to such performers as (CLOCKWISE FROM TOP LEFT) Joe Chvala and the Flying Foot Forum, in a scene from *Mjollnir—The Hammer of Thor*; the duo of Kari Margolis and Tony Brown, in *Vanishing Point*; and Shawn McConneloug and her orchestra, whose *Corporal Mortification*, played to rave reviews.

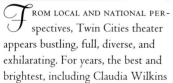

Ｆｒｏｍ ｌｏｃａｌ ａｎｄ ｎａｔｉｏｎａｌ ｐｅｒ-spectives, Twin Cities theater appears bustling, full, diverse, and exhilarating. For years, the best and brightest, including Claudia Wilkins (TOP LEFT) and Kim Hines (TOP RIGHT), have graced the stages of local theaters big and small. Playwright, actor, and storyteller Kevin Kling often collaborates with fellow actor Michael Sommers, the result of which is always outstanding (BOTTOM LEFT). Jungle Theater Artistic Director Bain Boehlke (BOTTOM RIGHT) felt the Lyndale/Lake Street neighborhood in south Minneapolis deserved a theater to call its own.

Minneapolis ✳ St. Paul

ALONG WITH SUCH MAINSTAYS as the Guthrie and the Children's Theatre Company, several mid-size companies have made a permanent home in the Twin Cities area. St. Paul's Penumbra Theatre, famous for its annual *Black Nativity*, is Minnesota's only African-American professional theater company (TOP). The Theatre de la Jeune Lune is best known for pushing the creative envelope through acting that is highly physical, visual, and witty. Dominique Serrand (BOTTOM), one of the company's original founders, still collaborates on and performs in nearly every production.

Minneapolis ✶ St. Paul

𝒟ESIGNED TO RESEMBLE A TRA-ditional European opera house, St. Paul's Ordway Music Theatre is home to the Minnesota Opera and the St. Paul Chamber Orchestra. Since its inception in 1985, the theater, which is currently under the leadership of President and CEO Kevin McCollum (RIGHT), has hosted local and national acts, as well as a number of touring Broadway shows. It also plans a series of concerts for young people each season.

THE STRENGTH OF THE TWIN Cities arts community lies in its depth and dimension. In addition to outstanding theater, dance, music, and visual arts, Minneapolis-St. Paul offers some of the best comedy venues and performers around. "Mr. Ron," the oldest-known female impersonator, has been performing here for more than 25 years (LEFT), while native comedienne Marilyn Belgum (RIGHT) has performed on *Late Night with David Letterman* and *The Tonight Show* with Jay Leno, as well as on stages throughout the metropolitan area.

Minneapolis ✳ St. Paul

MARC NORBERG

For nearly 40 years, Dudley Riggs (LEFT) and the company members of his Brave New Workshop have been performing satirical comedy shows that are sometimes politically incorrect, usually right on target, and always hilarious. Meanwhile, the Hey City Stage & Cafe, operated by Sandy Hey (RIGHT), is probably best known for its long-running show *Forever Plaid*, but the club is also considered to be one of the best places to see comedy in the Twin Cities.

𝒯HE PSYCHIC FAIR HELD IN 1996 at the Mall of America in Bloomington helped give new meaning to the slogan "Reach out and touch someone."

Minneapolis ✳ St. Paul

*I*T'S NO JOKE: THE MEN AND women in blue do an outstanding job of keeping Twin Citians safe and sound.

When the St. Paul Saints minor-league baseball team rolled into town in 1993, "Take me out to the ballgame" took on new meaning. Team President Mike Veeck (LEFT) believes it's not whether you win or lose, but how much fun you have in the process. This number one fan (RIGHT) seems to agree with that philosophy.

FORMER ST. PAUL SAINT DARRYL
Strawberry gained a lot of fans in
Minnesota before being called up to
join the world-champion New York
Yankees in July of 1996.

THE YEAR 1996 MARKED THE END of an era in Minnesota Twins baseball when Kirby Puckett was forced to retire due to a medical condition. The Twins' all-time leader in hits, runs, doubles, and total bases, Puckett will long be remembered for his contributions on and off the baseball diamond.

When the Twins won the World Series in 1987 and 1991, the entire community came out to celebrate. Ticker-tape parades in both cities left no doubt in anyone's mind as to how Twin Citians feel about the home team.

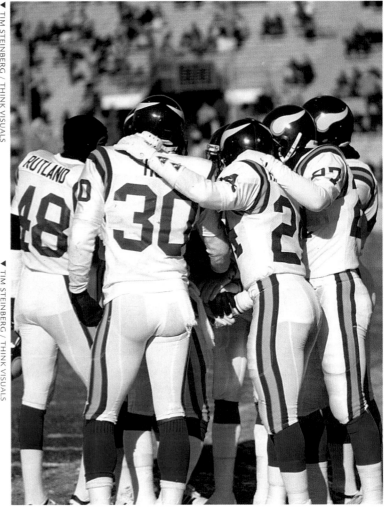

Lso known as the Purple People Eaters, the Minnesota Vikings are actually named for the fearless Nordics who possessed an aggressive will to win. That desire is shared by many Vikings supporters, who were especially fanatic in 1996 when quarterback Warren Moon (TOP LEFT) led the team to a 5-0 record, the best start in years.

Minneapolis ✳ *St. Paul*

ANDY HAYT / NBA PHOTOS

𝒮INCE 1989, WHEN THE NBA awarded the Twin Cities a professional basketball team, the Minnesota Timberwolves have gotten better and better. Two recent additions to the team—Kevin Garnett, who jumped to the NBA directly from high school (LEFT), and Tom Gugliotta, a record-setting forward (RIGHT)—have increased enthusiasm levels on the court as well as in the stands.

Minneapolis ✳ St. Paul

WHETHER THEY ARE SLAM-dunking a basketball at the corner playground, cheering a teammate's home run, or tossing the winning boccie ball, Minnesotans of all ages take to the great outdoors once the snow melts.

MINNESOTANS TAKE GREAT pride in encouraging young athletes to follow their dreams, and getting teenagers to participate is never a problem. Such high school athletic clubs as the Bloomington Jefferson boys track team receive tremendous financial and volunteer support, while young boxers hone their skills at the Circle of Discipline boxing club in south Minneapolis.

RUNNING FROM THE LAST WEEK of August until Labor Day, the Minnesota State Fair is affectionately known as the "Great Minnesota Get-Together." One of the largest state fairs in the nation, it features exciting rides, agricultural exhibits, livestock, farm equipment, local and national performers, an enormous midway, and food booths as far as the eye can see.

Minneapolis ✳ St. Paul

ICKEY'S ISN'T THE ONLY Twin Cities locale where time seems to have stood still. Minnehaha Liquors on East Lake Street and the Jiffy Car Wash in St. Louis Park remind us of an era when poodle skirts were in, rock and roll was born, and service always came with a smile.

After World War II, the renewed boom in automobile ownership—as well as the availability of air travel—significantly eroded railroad passenger traffic nationwide. The local railroad freight business, however, continued to prosper until the early 1980s, when Burlington Northern Inc. moved its corporate offices from St. Paul to Seattle. Many trains now rest quietly, reminding us of a time gone by.

▲ CHRIS FAUST

$\mathscr{P}$EOPLE RARELY THINK OF
industry resembling beauty, but
as these photos show, similarities can
be found in the most unusual places.

THE ESTABLISHMENT IN 1851 OF
the University of Minnesota was
a significant achievement in laying the
foundations for public education in the
state. Today, annual enrollment totals
approximately 50,000 undergraduate
and graduate students from around the
world. Northrop Auditorium (TOP and
LEFT), with its distinctive Romanesque-
style pillars, stands proudly at the
north end of the university's mall.
Named for former university president
Cyrus Northrop, the auditorium hosts
hundreds of special events and concerts
each year.

Minneapolis ✶ St. Paul

144

WHETHER AT THE LORING PARK pool in Minneapolis (OPPOSITE) or in a backyard bathtub (LEFT), area youngsters seem to know the cardinal rule of summertime: Wear as little as possible and head toward the water.

W<small>HAT'S THE USE OF BEING A KID</small> if you can't enjoy some of life's more pleasurable experiences?

$\mathcal{A}$ GROUP OF YOUNG "SHARP-
shooters" learn the tricks of the
trade with photographer Keri Pickett
and the Youth Photography Project.

Although Minnesotans celebrate year-round, many fairs and
festivals arrive just in time for summer
and keep going until the last falling
leaf signals winter's return. Face painting and pony rides are just a couple of
the activities everyone can enjoy.

Each summer, the Loring Block
Party celebrates Minneapolis' diverse
population (OPPOSITE). Thousands
of Twin Citians flock to Loring Park
to take in the parade, check out the
small midway, or spread a blanket
and enjoy the talents of local artists
and musicians.

TICKETS
$1

Minneapolis ✳ *St. Paul*

$\mathcal{S}$T. PAUL'S HARRIET ISLAND WAS one of the stops on the Lolla-palooza tour in 1994. An afternoon rain shower added to the fun as young adults enjoyed the music of some of the country's most prominent alterna-tive rock groups.

Minneapolis has produced its fair share of popular musicians over the years. During the 1960s and 1970s, Minnesota-born Bob Dylan (top) wrote, recorded, and performed as the voice of those who worked to end discrimination and war. More recently, Soul Asylum lead singer Dave Pirner (bottom right) has helped rocket his band to the top of the charts with the song *Runaway Train*, while singer/songwriter Paul Westerberg (bottom left) has gone on to a critically acclaimed solo career following the breakup of his group, The Replacements.

Minneapolis ✳ *St. Paul*

*T*HE 1,200-SEAT FIRST AVENUE Club has gained national prominence, thanks to the movie *Purple Rain*. Hundreds of local and national musicians perform on its stage every year, and audiences rarely leave disappointed.

$\mathcal{E}$VEN IF YOU DON'T KNOW their names, you should hear some of the popular bands that are revolutionizing the local music scene. The

Suburbs, for whom R.E.M. opened at a Navy Island concert in 1983, is an alternative rock band whose name is synonymous with Minneapolis music

(TOP). The group Suicide Commandos, pictured here before their 20th anniversary concert, is often given credit for initiating the Twin Cities' rock scene

(BOTTOM LEFT). Savage Aural Hotbed is an alternative percussion band with an impressive local following (BOTTOM RIGHT).

Minneapolis ✳ *St. Paul*

TONY NELSON

𝒯HE GROUP EIGHT HEAD BLENDS together the voices of three Twin Cities virtuosos into one harmony that will leave you wanting more (TOP). Meanwhile, Run Westy Run (BOTTOM LEFT) and singer/songwriter Barbara Cohen (BOTTOM RIGHT) have made names for themselves locally as well as nationally, and each has been awarded several Minnesota Music Awards.

Most visitors to the area don't think of blues music when they think of the Twin Cities, but when such musicians as Spider John Koerner (LEFT), or Tony "Little Sun" Glover and Dave Ray (RIGHT) hit the stage, newcomers will quickly forget they're not in Memphis, Tennessee.

*L*ocal sax legend Eddie Berger (LEFT) will take you places you've never been before, and you won't even have to leave your seat.

Meanwhile, Johnny Lang (RIGHT) may still be a teenager, but he's got the soul of an old bluesman.

𝒟ANCERS MAKE IT ALL LOOK SO easy, but behind every brilliant performance is a brilliant choreographer. Here, Diane Waller of the Minnesota Dance Alliance demonstrates the moves that made her an expert at her craft.

THE ART OF MAKING SNOW ANGELS is not unique to Minnesota, but there's little doubt that Minnesotans are among the best snow angel artists in the world. While no choreographer is needed for *this* endeavor, using precise, well-rehearsed moves will produce the best results.

Minneapolis ∗ St. Paul

No matter the medium, Minnesotans like to demonstrate their artistic prowess in sculpture. Local citizens carve designs in snow and ice during the St. Paul Winter Carnival, in sand as part of the Minneapolis Aquatennial, and in butter during the Minnesota State Fair.

164

MINNESOTA'S WILDLIFE PROVIDE ample opportunities for hunters and bird-watchers, as well as inspiration for decoy carver Karen Lesch (OPPOSITE) and for artist Roger Preuss (ABOVE).

Minneapolis ✳ St. Paul

William L. McKnight
3M
Omnitheater

MAYBE THE FACT THAT Minnesota is the land of 10,000 lakes helps explain our apparent fascination with water creatures. Or maybe we build, sculpt, and paint them because it's easier than dragging out a rod and reel and catching them the old-fashioned way.

Linked to the Future

Like many large urban areas, the Twin Cities can claim a mix of many ethnic groups, including Native American, African-American, Asian, Latino, and European. The Phillips Neighborhood Gateway Project, created by St. Paul artist Rafala Green, shouts "We will survive" to all who pass the corner of Franklin and Chicago avenues, making a powerful statement in one of Minneapolis' toughest neighborhoods.

Minneapolis ✳ St. Paul

CHILDREN OFTEN TEACH ADULTS about what's important and what's not. This little girl knows it doesn't matter what color your skin is: Cool bricks still feel nice on a warm summer day. Meanwhile, Cultural Toys Founder Jake Miles is doing his part to bridge the cultural gap by creating and producing toys that celebrate diversity (BOTTOM).

*Minneapolis * St. Paul*

$\mathcal{T}$WIN CITIANS START EARLY IN
their quest for athletic excellence.
Here, a young ballerina prepares to
dazzle her audience (OPPOSITE),
while 1996 Olympic gymnast John
Roethlisberger, who trains under his
father at the University of Minnesota,
shows off one of his moves in the un-
expected surrounds of a local brewery
(LEFT).

Minneapolis ✳ St. Paul

INGER TINY TIM, WHOSE SONG
Tiptoe through the Tulips gained him
international fame, married Minneapo-
lis-born Miss Sue in 1995, and lived
with her in the Twin Cities until his
death in 1996. This field of not-so-tiny
tulips is a sure sign of spring in the
Twin Cities, but look quickly because
they don't stay around for long.

Flowers bloom year-round at the Como Park Conservatory in St. Paul. Four main rooms—the Palm Room, the Sunken Garden, the Fern Room, and the North House—provide an escape that smells as beautiful as it looks. In addition, the conservatory's spectacular seasonal shows, such as this winter display (BOTTOM), help draw some 500,000 visitors annually.

Linked to the Future

In the spring of 1982, the new St. Paul Farmers' Market opened at East 5th and Wall streets in downtown St. Paul (above and opposite top). Every weekend from May to November, hundreds of people stop by to purchase fresh, locally grown vegetables, fruits, flowers, and honey.

LAYNE KENNEDY

I F YOU'RE HEADING OUT ON Saturday morning to the Minneapolis Farmers' Market, go early. Located just west of downtown Minneapolis on Lyndale Avenue, the market is packed by 8 a.m. and by noon the pickings get slim (BOTTOM LEFT AND RIGHT).

Minneapolis ✳ St. Paul

Although blond, blue-eyed Scandinavians with heavy Norwegian accents make up a fair share of the Twin Cities population, our community includes a wide variety of cultures and nationalities. And small specialty stores, such as Bill's Imported Foods (LEFT), make it easier for residents to maintain such customs as a traditional Polish Mardi Gras celebration (OPPOSITE BOTTOM).

LOCAL ARTISTS TAKE GRAFFITI to a whole new level. This scene of a street in Venice (TOP) is painted on the outside of Gluek's Restaurant in downtown Minneapolis, while a more abstract work adorns the side of the Valspar Paint building (BOTTOM).

Beginning the third week of July, the Minneapolis Aquatennial is a nine-day festival honoring the city's lakes and rivers. There are two parades, including the Grande Day Parade (BOTTOM) and a Torchlight Parade, as well as numerous other activities that are fun for all ages. The annual Milk Carton Boat Races (TOP) draw hundreds of spectators to the shores of Lake Nokomis in south Minneapolis.

INNEAPOLIS' LAKE HARRIET
provides a perfect setting for
sports and exercise enthusiasts, a band
shell for music lovers, and a quiet rest-
ing place for everyone in between.

AT ANY TIME OF THE YEAR, NEARLY 1,000 area lakes provide a perfect setting for an array of recreational activities. Many anglers agree that, regardless of whether they bring home dinner, the satisfaction lies in the process of trying. Others prefer the frozen waters that provide a stable surface for skating and sledding.

Minneapolis ✻ St. Paul

PROFILES IN

◆ Richard Hamilton Smith / Frozen Images

A look at the corporations, businesses, professional groups, and community service organizations that have made this book possible. Their stories—offering an informal chronicle of the local business community—are arranged according to the date they were established in the Minneapolis-St. Paul area.

Advance Circuits, Inc. ◆ Advance Machine Company ◆ AmClyde Engineered Products, Inc.
American Express Financial Advisors Inc. ◆ Andersen Consulting ◆ Augsburg Fortress, Publishers
Automatic Products international, Ltd. ◆ AVR, Inc. ◆ Best Buy Co., Inc. ◆ Building and Construction Trades Council
Cargill, Incorporated ◆ Carlson Companies, Inc. ◆ Centex Homes/CTX Mortgage ◆ Cummins Power Generation
Cuningham Group ◆ Dayton Hudson Corporation ◆ Dotronix Inc. ◆ Dynamark, Inc. ◆ Fairview
Faribault Foods, Inc. ◆ Federal Cartridge Company ◆ Fisher-Rosemount Systems, Inc. ◆ General Mills, Inc.
Robert Half International, Inc. ◆ Hamline University ◆ Hauenstein & Burmeister, Inc.

EXCELLENCE

Hennepin County Medical Center ✦ Hines ✦ IDS Center, a Heitman Property ✦ Innovex

Interactive Technologies, Inc. ✦ Jostens Inc. ✦ KARE 11 ✦ Katun Corporation ✦ Lagerquist Elevator

Land O'Lakes Inc. ✦ Landscape Structures Inc. ✦ Lawson Software ✦ M E International, Inc.

MEDTOX Laboratory Inc. ✦ Medtronic, Inc. ✦ Midwest Guest Suites ✦ Minnesota Mutual Life Insurance Co.

Minnesota Twins ✦ Norstan Inc. ✦ Northern States Power Company ✦ Northwestern College

Norwest Corporation ✦ Owens Services Corporation ✦ Jay Phillips Center for Jewish-Christian Learning

Piper Jaffray Companies Inc. ✦ Polka Dot Dairy/Tom Thumb Food Markets ✦ The Ramada Plaza Hotel

Regal Minneapolis Hotel ✦ ReliaStar Financial Corp. ✦ ROI Systems, Inc. ✦ The St. Paul Companies

The Saint Paul Hotel ✦ St. Paul Port Authority ✦ Slumberland, Inc. ✦ Smarte Carte, Inc.

Snyder's Drug Stores, Inc. ✦ TREND enterprises, Inc. ✦ University of St. Thomas

Upsher-Smith Laboratories, Inc. ✦ Villaume Industries, Inc. ✦ Waterous Company

1853 - 1924

1853
THE ST. PAUL COMPANIES
1854
HAMLINE UNIVERSITY
1866
GENERAL MILLS, INC.
1880
MINNESOTA MUTUAL LIFE INSURANCE CO.
1882
AMCLYDE ENGINEERED PRODUCTS, INC.
1882
LAGERQUIST ELEVATOR
1882
VILLAUME INDUSTRIES, INC.
1885
RELIASTAR FINANCIAL CORP.
1885
UNIVERSITY OF ST. THOMAS
1886
WATEROUS COMPANY
1887
HENNEPIN COUNTY MEDICAL CENTER
1889
BUILDING AND CONSTRUCTION TRADES COUNCIL
1894
AMERICAN EXPRESS FINANCIAL ADVISORS INC.

Minneapolis ✳ St. Paul

1895
Cargill, Incorporated
1895
Faribault Foods, Inc.
1895
Piper Jaffray Companies Inc.
1897
Jostens Inc.
1902
Dayton Hudson Corporation
1902
Northwestern College
1906
Fairview
1910
Advance Machine Company
1910
The Saint Paul Hotel
1916
Northern States Power Company
1917
M E International, Inc.
1919
Upsher-Smith Laboratories, Inc.
1921
Land O'Lakes Inc.
1922
Federal Cartridge Company
1923
Hauenstein & Burmeister, Inc.

IN 1995 THE ST. PAUL COMPANIES REPORTED RECORD EARNINGS FOR the third consecutive year, with net income up 18 percent. Operating earnings increased 12 percent. And the company also increased its dividend 10 percent, completing a string of 10 straight annual dividend increases. Clearly, many people are doing many things right at Minnesota's oldest, ninth-largest corporation. Headquartered in St. Paul, The St. Paul Companies provides

property-liability insurance, reinsurance, and insurance brokerage products and services worldwide. The company, originally named St. Paul Fire and Marine Insurance Company (which remains the name of its main insurance subsidiary), opened its doors in 1853. The first real test of its strength and viability came with the panic of 1857. Nationwide, 47 mutual insurance companies, all founded as recently as St. Paul Fire and Marine, were forced to close, taking more than $2 million of policyholders' money with them. To pay the bills and keep afloat, St. Paul Fire and Marine sold its office furniture. With the proceeds, debts were paid and promissory notes were returned to all policyholders. When all was said and done, St. Paul Fire and Marine had only $83 on the books, almost no furniture in its office—and its integrity intact.

Events from the well-worn pages of history books help trace the company's history: the Chicago fire of 1871, the San Francisco earthquake of 1906, World War I, the Great Depression, and World War II. In each case, St. Paul Fire

and Marine proved itself a dollar-for-dollar company—one that paid its claims based on the full policy value. And with each payment, the company helped solidify its reputation as a leader in the insurance industry.

Such commitment to its policyholders, shareholders, and employees is a primary reason "The St. Paul"

remains one of the world's most successful and fastest-growing insurance businesses in an industry that is fighting for growth. Says The St. Paul Companies' Chairman Douglas Leatherdale: "The industry in the United States is growing more slowly than the economy overall, in a dramatic contrast to the 1960s and 1970s, when it was a fast-grow-

ing field that was solidly outpacing the national economy. Competition is likely to lead to consolidation and restructuring of the industry, and it's very likely that the major players of the 1990s and beyond are going to be very different than the major players of the 1980s."

But with a capital base that has never been stronger and a focus on the future, Leatherdale is confident that The St. Paul will remain among the leaders. "Our long-term strategy is to achieve a distinct competitive advantage in this industry by providing customer-focused products and excellent service on a worldwide basis, resulting in superior long-term return for our shareholders," says Leatherdale. "The essence of that strategy is to continue to build on our outstanding track record in key U.S. and international markets that offer promising growth and profit opportunities."

A Plan for Continued Growth

With domestic growth slowing, The St. Paul sees major opportunities for growth in the international marketplace, particularly in Europe and emerging markets. The company, for example, already the leading medical liability insurer in the United States, has found new markets for products for health care providers in the United Kingdom, Spain, and the Netherlands. Latin America and South Africa are other growth markets worth watching, according to Leatherdale. "We have been in the international marketplace for over 100 years—long before the global economy was a fact of life," says Leatherdale. "Then and now, The St. Paul's ability to expand globally has been leveraged off the expertise developed in the United States. This strategy made sense when we wrote our first policy in Canada in 1866, and it continues to be the key to our success today."

In spite of The St. Paul's global outlook, the company has never lost sight of its core value: to remain profitable while conducting business

using the highest ethical standards. To ensure that this goal is consistently achieved, The St. Paul keeps close tabs on its customers and their needs. This focus on markets and customers is one of the reasons The St. Paul decided in the early 1980s to center its resources and capabilities on the business it knew best: property-liability insurance. The company's business units serve different customers and pursue different strategies, but they share a common core of skills, capabilities, and cultures.

The company's commitment to the people it serves also includes the communities in which it does business. Dating back more than 14 decades, the company has supported the communities from which it gains both employees and business. In 1994 The St. Paul Companies contributed more than 2 percent

of its operating earnings to ensure quality education for children, support the arts, reinvigorate families and communities through neighborhood-based housing developments, and identify resources for use by leaders in the nonprofit sector. "The measure of our success is how we grow the value of The St. Paul, whether that value comes in the form of dividends for our stockholders or a richer sense of community in the cities in which we are located," says Leatherdale.

THE ST. PAUL FIRE AND MARINE INSURANCE COMPANY IS STILL THE MAIN INSURANCE SUBSIDIARY OF THE ST. PAUL COMPANIES.

EACH YEAR, HAMLINE UNIVERSITY IN ST. PAUL CLOSES its commencement ceremony with the following words from John Wesley: "Do all the good you can, by all the means you can, in all the ways you can, in all the places you can, at all the times you can, to all the people you can, as long as ever you can." More than mere rhetoric, the words symbolize the values Hamline has brought to its students for nearly 150 years. "Our students

come from places as close as Apple Valley and as far away as Zimbabwe," says Larry Osnes, president of the university. "Some are quiet; some, outspoken. Some are from big cities; others, from small towns. They come to our professional and graduate schools from over 100 different colleges. They're different in many ways, yet they seem to have one thing in common: they value service to others."

A HISTORY OF FIRSTS

Hamline is the only college or university in Minnesota that can truly say, "We're number one!" A university from the start, Hamline was founded in 1854, when Minnesota was still a territory. The university's founders wanted to provide a values-centered liberal arts education in an atmosphere of equality and intellectual freedom. Today, that focus remains, as does the founders' strong belief in a forward vision and a pioneering spirit. Hamline was truly a "new American university" from its founding.

Always a leader in education, the university granted the state's first bachelor's degrees in 1859—to sisters Elizabeth and Emily Sorin; awarded its first master's degrees in 1863; and offered the state's first legal and medical programs. In 1895 Hamline hosted the nation's first intercollegiate basketball game. In 1924 Hamline created America's first academic exchange program with China's Peking (now Beijing) University. In the late 1970s, Hamline's College of Liberal Arts was the first college in the country to establish a computer literacy requirement. And in 1994, Hamline offered Minnesota's first advanced writing degree. Today Hamline University

BISHOP LEONIDAS HAMLINE, THE UNIVERSITY'S FIRST BENEFACTOR, WAS SCULPTED IN 1995 BY HAMLINE UNIVERSITY ART PROFESSOR AND NATIONALLY KNOWN SCULPTOR MICHAEL PRICE. BISHOP HAMLINE STANDS AT THE "CROSSROADS" OF THE CAMPUS, FACING OLD MAIN (ABOVE).

OLD MAIN, HAMLINE UNIVERSITY'S CAMPUS LANDMARK, WAS BUILT IN 1884 AND IS LISTED ON THE NATIONAL REGISTER OF HISTORIC PLACES (RIGHT).

is a high-quality, nationally ranked, liberal arts university with more than 3,000 degree-seeking students in the College of Liberal Arts, School of Law, and Graduate School.

A GROWING UNIVERSITY

Hamline University currently operates three schools, and is planning for more. But no matter how many schools lie in the future, they will always share one philosophy—make the world a better place.

Hamline's College of Liberal Arts attracts students from 40 states and 37 countries, and is ranked as "very selective" in *Cass and Birnbaum's Guide to American Colleges*. It is also listed as a top-caliber liberal arts college in two prestigious publications: *Barron's 300: Best Buys in Higher*

Education and *Peterson's Competitive Colleges*. Each year the college is listed among the top 120 in the category "national liberal arts colleges" in the annual *U.S. News & World Report* Best Colleges issue. The undergraduate curriculum—the Hamline Plan—is a set of flexible, goal-oriented graduation objectives designed to prepare students for success in today's constantly changing world. The Hamline Plan has attracted national attention and has been used as a case study in workshops on curriculum reform throughout the country. An innovative legal studies major is one of 37 major areas of study that Hamline undergraduates can choose.

Hamline University School of Law is a highly ranked, regional law school with nationally recognized

expertise in alternative dispute resolution; Native American policy study; and religion, law, and ethics studies. The school offers a three-year, full-time day program with flexible scheduling options for all-morning or all-afternoon classes. Because Hamline is the smallest law school in Minnesota, students receive a quality education in an atmosphere that is personal and supportive. In fact, Hamline University School of Law has one of the best faculty-student ratios in the country according to a new publication, *Judging the Law Schools*. Hamline has also been named one of the 35 best law schools in the country for women, based on a survey by *The National Jurist*.

The Hamline University Graduate School has expanded its service throughout the state and its programs have achieved a national reputation. The Graduate Education Program offers both master's and doctorate degrees; several cutting-edge specializations—including teaching English as a foreign language, English as a second language, teaching and technology, gifted education, and middle school licensure; a Center for Global Environmental Education; and innovative coursework in continuing education serving over 8,000 educators. Hamline Graduate Education is known for its superb teachers who model an approach enphasizing practical, real-world experience.

The Graduate Liberal Studies Program with a Master of Arts in Liberal Studies and a Master of Fine Arts in Writing sets the pace for challenging interdisciplinary coursework that is propelled by students' own lives and career explorations. In the writing program, students apprentice with master teachers to practice their craft.

The Graduate Public Administration Program is an all-inclusive educational approach for public policymakers. Hamline offers a Master of Arts in Public Administration, a Master of Arts in Nonprofit Management, and a Doctorate in Public Administration. A Master of Arts in Conflict Management will begin in the fall of 1997. Faculty bring broad-based, relevant expertise to the progam.

"Our goal is always to create extraordinary learning opportunities that promote transformations in personal, professional, and institutional lives," says Osnes. "Aiming to instill the skills, abilities, and vision needed for the future, every program challenges students through critical thinking and through examination of issues of societal and cultural import."

A Cut Above

According to Osnes, there is no doubt that the Hamline University envisioned by its founders is alive and active today, and is enjoying a growing national reputation. "The best way we know to judge how we're doing is to look at our 'product,' that is, our graduates," says Osnes. "Our graduates are valued by all who come to know them. They make a contribution wherever they go, in whatever career field they choose. But even more important is the fact that all of our graduates leave here with a philosophy that goes beyond the basics. They honor the open exchange of ideas; they respect others; they make ethical decisions; they're committed to service and leadership. In short, they help make the world a better place."

CONSUMERS MAY NOT BE AWARE, BUT CHEERIOS, WHEATIES, AND dozens of other products they probably grew up with come from General Mills. ✳ In fact, General Mills is the second-largest cereal company in the world. But its success doesn't stop there. Products like Bisquick® and Hamburger Helper® also dominate their respective categories. And Betty Crocker®—a true American icon—turned 75 years young in 1996.

GENERAL MILLS IS THE SECOND-LARGEST CEREAL COMPANY IN THE WORLD (FAR RIGHT).

GENERAL MILLS' EVOLUTION INTO A PREMIER CONSUMER FOOD COMPANY TRACES BACK TO 1866, WHEN CADWALLADER WASHBURN BUILT HIS FIRST FLOUR MILL ON THE BANKS OF THE MISSISSIPPI RIVER IN MINNEAPOLIS (NEAR RIGHT).

LINKED BY MILLS

The history of Minneapolis mirrors the history of General Mills: Both the city and the company trace their roots to flour milling.

General Mills' evolution into a premier consumer food company traces back to 1866, when Cadwallader Washburn built his first flour mill on the banks of the Mississippi River in Minneapolis. The huge mill was called "Washburn's Folly," but its steel roller technology was a major new innovation in milling.

Eleven years later, Washburn formed a partnership with John Crosby and the Washburn-Crosby Company became one of the country's most prominent flour millers. When Washburn-Crosby merged with several other regional milling companies in 1928, the new company took the name General Mills.

Since 1880, when the company's flour won the Gold Medal at the international milling competition, the company has been a baking products leader. Gold Medal® Flour— as the product was renamed shortly thereafter—became the nation's leading flour, a market position it still

holds today, more than 100 years later.

Created as a signature in response to a 1921 promotion for Gold Medal Flour, Betty Crocker® now ranks as the 16th-strongest brand in the United States, according to a national survey, with more than 200 products and 20 to 30 new product introductions each year.

But the Betty Crocker name goes beyond food products. Through licensing agreements, hundreds of houseware items—from flatware and dishes to kitchen gadgets and appliances—sport the Betty Crocker signature, many in the Betty Crocker catalog. All are thoroughly tested and approved by home economists in the Betty Crocker Kitchens.

Betty Crocker's Cookbook, first published in 1950, is the biggest selling cookbook of all time, with well over 27 million copies sold internationally. More than 30 Betty Crocker cookbooks are currently in print and Betty Crocker's recipe magazine sells

monthly at checkout counters nationwide.

And, although Betty was never a real person, more than 600,000 consumers still call or write Betty Crocker each year seeking advice on cooking or baking projects, or information about General Mills products. Many consumers still insist on talking with Betty herself.

INNOVATIVE LEADER

General Mills is recognized as an innovative leader in the food industry, having developed the technology behind Fruit Roll-ups®, Pop Secret® microwave popcorn, Nature Valley® granola bars, and Bugles® corn snacks, in its Snacks Division, for example.

Yoplait® and Colombo® have made General Mills a major player in refrigerated yogurts. Colombo, the nation's first yogurt, also originated soft-serve frozen yogurt in 1971.

With number one or number two market positions in every category in which it competes, General Mills is one of Minnesota's best-known manufacturers.

After all, if some "Silly Rabbit" wanted to taste your Trix® cereal, you'd know what to say, wouldn't you?

BETTY CROCKER®, SHOWN HERE IN HER 75TH ANNIVERSARY PORTRAIT, IS THE 16TH-STRONGEST BRAND IN THE UNITED STATES, ACCORDING TO A NATIONAL SURVEY, WITH MORE THAN 200 PRODUCTS AND 20 TO 30 NEW PRODUCT INTRODUCTIONS EACH YEAR (NEAR RIGHT).

MANY OF GENERAL MILLS' ADVERTISING LOGOS, SUCH AS THE TRIX RABBIT, HAVE ACHIEVED HOUSEHOLD RECOGNITION NATIONWIDE (FAR RIGHT).

Minneapolis ✳ St. Paul

NORTHWESTERN COLLEGE IN ST. PAUL WILL BE THE FIRST TO admit that it is unique, even in regard to other Christian colleges. But no one is apologizing, because the same elements that make it unique also make it one of the most popular and successful private Christian liberal arts colleges in the state. And few can dispute the college's proven track record: this year, Northwestern College will celebrate its 95th anniversary; enrollment has

NORTHWESTERN COLLEGE IS LOCATED ON A BEAUTIFUL 100-ACRE CAMPUS ON LAKE JOHANNA IN SUBURBAN ST. PAUL (LEFT).

THE LITTLE GOTHIC CHAPEL ON THE ISLAND PROVIDES A RELAXING ATMOSPHERE FOR SOCIALIZING (BOTTOM LEFT).

reached its highest level, with nearly 1,400 undergraduate students from 40 states and 18 countries; and three new majors—biology, Spanish, and English as a Second Language—were added, bringing the total number of available majors to 41. Being different has never been better.

THE ETHICAL ADVANTAGE

Northwestern was initially a Bible and missionary training school founded in 1902 by Dr. William Bell Riley. Classes took place in First Baptist Church of Minneapolis. The school started with two professors and seven students. Under evangelist Billy Graham, Northwestern's second president (1948-1952), the student body grew to nearly 1,200 students. The college moved in 1972 to its current location on a beautiful 100-acre campus on Lake Johanna in suburban St. Paul.

Northwestern College today has evolved from a Bible college to become Minnesota's only private nondenominational Christian liberal arts college, offering a three-tier academic program that integrates faith and learning through biblical studies, liberal arts education, and professional preparation for produc-

tive living. "Our goal is to educate the whole student—spiritually, physically, emotionally, and intellectually," says Naomi Bloom, director of public relations. "We've found students are most successful in college, careers, and life when they have solid foundations in each of those areas."

To help accomplish that goal, Northwestern College offers opportunities for students to participate in drama, performing arts, athletics, journalism, broadcasting, and a wide range of student-run clubs. The college also coordinates mission/service opportunities worldwide for students, and has one of the strongest business internship programs available in Minnesota. Northwestern students have traveled as far as Japan and India as part of the college's international internship program.

Northwestern College also offers two nontraditional programs: Focus 15, which allows adults 25 years or older with two years of transferable college credit as well as meaningful professional and personal experience to earn a bachelor of science degree in business administration, organizational administration, or psychology by attending class one night a week; and the Center for Distance Education, which offers students—particularly working adults—the opportunity to take college courses and earn credit in the convenience of their homes. The first distance education major is intercultural ministries.

Bloom points out that having the Bible as the underlying foundation of one's education does prove extremely beneficial. "Prospective employers often comment on the 'ethical advantage' they find in our students," she says. "Ethics are such an enormous issue in today's workplace, and employers recognize that Northwestern students possess a strong sense of commitment, responsibility, and values. That is a tangible benefit to hiring a Northwestern College graduate."

FOUNDED IN 1880, MINNESOTA MUTUAL TODAY RANKS AS ONE of the nation's largest and most financially secure life insurance companies. In 1996 the company's commitment to community involvement and a family-friendly workplace earned it national recognition for corporate citizenship from the White House; *Computerworld* magazine recently rated Minnesota Mutual as one of the 100 best places to work in the country. ✳ Minnesota Mutual was

originally an assessment company, the Banker's Life Association of Minnesota, offering life insurance protection to the business pioneers of Minnesota's capital city, St. Paul. Much like the Twin Cities itself, Banker's Life prospered and in 1899 became Minnesota Mutual, a mutual company owned by its policyowners and dedicated to providing superior financial services.

Minnesota Mutual has developed a reputation over the years as a company committed first and foremost to the safety and security of its policyowners' funds. In fact, one of the leading independent national rating agencies, A.M. Best, cites the company's conservative financial management, excellent balance sheet, good profitability, diverse product portfolio, and highly productive distribution system as reasons for giving Minnesota Mutual its highest rating.

Impeccable financial strength is just one by-product of Minnesota Mutual's commitment to its customers. The company puts people first in everything it does. As a mutual company, Minnesota Mutual shares its success with policyowners through

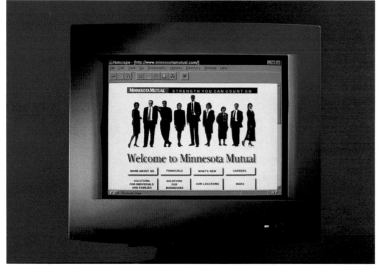

dividends. Focusing on customer needs, the company places policyowners' long-term interests ahead of short-term gains. "We are in the business of providing a promise to pay," says Robert L. Senkler, chairman and CEO. "Every decision we make reflects the fact that our promise has been good for more than 100 years and will be good 100 years from now."

Minnesota Mutual's focus on the customer is an essential ingredient to its long-term prosperity. Overall business retention is excellent, client surveys indicate historically high levels of satisfaction, and complaints are minimal. And the company continues to invest in current technologies to help give customers the service they expect and deserve. For example, in 1996 the company launched several Internet sites, offer-

ing product information instantaneously, including customized home owners' insurance quotes, and allowing pension plan participants to access their accounts.

TARGETING SPECIFIC MARKETS

Each of the company's five strategic business units has a defined purpose and specific target markets—yet all five share a common goal: to be the best at providing financial security and value for clients.

Minnesota Mutual's career agency system, the cornerstone of the Individual Insurance division, is another example of how the company puts people first. The company recruits the best agents and retains agents at twice the rate of the industry average. The personal service, professionalism, and ethical conduct

CUSTOMERS CAN LEARN ABOUT MINNESOTA MUTUAL'S PRODUCTS AND SERVICES THROUGH THE COMPANY'S WEB SITE AT HTTP://WWW.MINNESOTAMUTUAL.COM (BELOW).

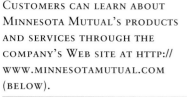

Minneapolis ✳ *St. Paul*

that a career agent offers make a real difference to the policyowner. Reflecting its strong consumer focus, Minnesota Mutual pioneered the development of adjustable life insurance in 1971.

The company's Financial Services division works with thousands of banks and credit unions to provide mortgage life, mortgage disability, and home owners' policies for their clients. Minnesota Mutual dominates the mortgage life market with more than a 60 percent share, while its nationwide career sales force, the only one exclusively serving the mortgage market, customizes programs to meet the needs of large financial institutions.

The Group Insurance division serves large, sophisticated employers who have complex employee benefit and tax-planning requirements. Minnesota Mutual is the only insurer endorsed by Farm Credit associations in all 50 states and maintains a solid 90 percent market share of the life insurance sold through the Farm Credit system. In addition to large employers and agriculture groups, the company provides extensive coverage to professional associations across the country.

Minnesota Mutual's Pension division provides full-service 401(k) plan management for small- and medium-sized companies. Minnesota Mutual customizes each plan to include asset management, government compliance, record keeping, tax reporting, and employee education. The company's pension plan participants benefit from its forward-looking approach to interactive communications, enabling participants to conduct more than 30 different transactions on-line.

The company's investment subsidiary, MIMLIC Asset Management Company, manages the company's assets. In addition, MIMLIC serves as an investment adviser primarily to smaller insurance companies with between $50 million and $5 billion of assets. Seeking performance advantage with minimum risk potential, investment professionals provide the

sophisticated asset management necessary to cope with today's complex and dynamic investment environment.

FINDING AND KEEPING THE BEST

Minnesota Mutual gives the highest priority to the needs of its associates. In each division, the company is committed to hiring and retaining the best and brightest. Opportunities for growth are part of the company's commitment to each associate. In an age of job hopping and precious little loyalty, Minnesota Mutual is particularly proud of its associate retention levels. "This is a good place to make a home," says Senkler. "It is a good place to grow in your career and do something worthwhile."

Senkler acknowledges it is simply good business to provide associates the tools necessary to become the very best at what they do. The company provides exceptional internal training and encourages associates to take advantage of tuition reimbursement for college courses. Minnesota Mutual's benefits package ranks in the upper tier for companies its size, and the company fosters a balanced approach to work and home life, recognizing that maintaining a sharp focus at work necessitates a commitment to life outside the office.

Over the years, the company's pioneering products, service commitment, and conservative investment philosophy, as well as the exceptionally high quality of its workforce, have combined to make Minnesota Mutual a national leader in financial services. Providing dignity in times of need, building dreams, and helping to secure a financial future full of promise: these are the many faces of Minnesota Mutual.

A MINNESOTA MUTUAL ASSOCIATE FOR 25 YEARS, CHAIRMAN AND CEO ROBERT L. SENKLER HELPS MAINTAIN THE COMPANY'S TRADITION OF TRUST, STRENGTH, AND INTEGRITY. "WE ARE GUIDED BY THE HIGHEST ETHICAL STANDARDS AND DEDICATED TO BEING THE BEST AT PROVIDING FINANCIAL SECURITY AND VALUE FOR OUR CUSTOMERS," SAYS SENKLER (ABOVE).

MINNESOTA MUTUAL HAS CALLED ST. PAUL HOME SINCE ITS FOUNDING IN 1880 (LEFT).

WHEN YOU THINK OF AmClyde Engineered Products, Inc., think big. Really big. St. Paul-based AmClyde, which designs and builds large specialty equipment for lifting, pulling, moving, and mooring the heaviest loads, dominates the tiny world of giant marine cranes lifting 1,000 tons or more. Of the 44 such cranes active today, 35 were designed and built by AmClyde. Among the company's claims to fame are twin

7,700-ton marine cranes with a combined lifting capacity of 15,400 tons (listed in the *Guinness Book of World Records*) and the world's largest mono-hulled crane ship, which has a lifting capacity of 5,500 tons. In 1996, AmClyde had sales of $90 million with a backlog of orders worth $40 million. And there's no sign of a slowdown anytime soon.

A Blending of Giants
Since the turn of the century, the companies of American Hoist & Derrick and Clyde Iron had offered their customers the very best in specialized industrial equipment, including cranes, winches, and other machinery. In 1987, Clyde and a unit

of American pooled their resources, employees, and 200 years of combined experience to better serve their customers. The result is AmClyde, the world leader in developing custom-engineered solutions for a wide range of specialized industrial requirements. From its headquarters in St. Paul, AmClyde employs a staff of nearly 250 professionals, which includes the largest group of crane and winch designers in the industry. The company also maintains eight regional offices around the world and has supplied equipment to more than 100 countries. Almost 60 percent of AmClyde's sales are international.

Although AmClyde products are not common in the Twin Cities

area, the company does have a local legacy: AmClyde designed and built the unique Movable Floor System for the Target Center, located in downtown Minneapolis. The Center needed to accommodate both professional hockey and basketball, so AmClyde designed a 2,300-ton floor that can move up or down five feet to optimize seating and viewing for each event.

Big Cranes and More
AmClyde's business straddles the private and public sectors, with many contracts coming from the navy, army, and the corps of engineers. AmClyde and its predecessors, for example, have delivered more than 75

TWO FLOATING MARINE CRANES ARE REQUIRED TO LOAD CREW QUARTERS—A SIX-STORY BUILDING WEIGHING 4,100 TONS— INTO POSITION ON AN OIL PLATFORM IN THE NORWEGIAN SECTOR OF THE NORTH SEA (RIGHT).

LOADS ARE ATTACHED TO GIGANTIC HOOKS WITH SLINGS THAT ARE 12 INCHES IN DIAMETER (LEFT).

percent of the U.S. Navy's shipyard cranes in the past 25 years. However, AmClyde's primary focus is on custom-engineered equipment for clients with special needs that cannot be met with existing products. The company has designed marine and land-based cranes that are the largest and most technically sophisticated of their kind.

Along with innovative new designs, AmClyde's aftermarket group manufactures replacement parts and employs service professionals to upgrade vintage equipment. Massive record rooms at the company's St. Paul facility store blueprints for thousands of machines manufactured by AmClyde and its predecessors since 1892. Since AmClyde owns the design rights to these custom-built machines, the company focuses nearly 20 percent of its current operations on refurbishing and retrofitting the thousands still in use around the world.

In addition to its preeminent standing in the crane business, AmClyde has created a significant niche supplying mooring systems to the offshore oil industry. AmClyde is unique among suppliers in that it has concurrently developed and refined conventional rotary winch, traction winch, and linear winch technology. The company also benefits from the move toward deeper waters, since it is one of the few suppliers equipped to handle the demands of deepwater offshore drilling. An alliance with the Japanese firm MODEC will further enhance AmClyde's growth in providing a patented floating oil platform.

AmClyde is tackling the sugarcane industry as well, in the form of a joint venture under the name AmCane International. The business has developed a revolutionary separator that divides the raw cane material components into high-value, revenue-producing by-products.

At the heart of AmClyde's success is its engineering design capability. The company provides pure engineering consulting, helping cus-

tomers develop innovative solutions to complex problems. Engineering excellence is a constant goal, and has resulted in a total of nine local and national Outstanding Engineering Achievement awards over the past eight years. But unlike most traditional consulting firms, AmClyde goes further, offering customers complete turnkey and warranty capabilities, including all necessary fabrication, field assembly, and quality assurance services. Even after a project is complete, AmClyde stands behind it, providing ongoing technical support and service.

"We have a strong desire to remain as the big crane professionals," says Senior Vice President Terrie Thompson, "but we're finding uses for our product in nontraditional markets." Thompson stresses that AmClyde's core business provides a solid foundation for the current transition the company is experiencing. "We have been a $50 million to $60 million company, are now a $90 million to $100 million

business, and are in a transition to even higher levels," says Thompson. "Our goal has always been to position ourselves for growth in areas that will complement our core businesses. Thanks to our careful attention to strategic planning and a number of key acquisitions, we are positioned to successfully take that next step as a company and expand our areas of expertise while still excelling at the things we do best."

THE 600-TON "GOLIATH" CRANE WAS DESIGNED AND BUILT FOR HALLA'S SAMHO SHIPYARD IN MOKPO, KOREA. HALLA ALSO BUILT SMALLER 40-TON CRANES THAT ARE UNDER LICENSE FROM AMCLYDE (TOP).

AMCANE'S REVOLUTIONARY SUGARCANE SEPARATION SYSTEM OPENS UP POTENTIALLY HUGE NEW MARKETS FOR AMCLYDE (BOTTOM).

Lagerquist Elevator

OR 115 YEARS, LAGERQUIST ELEVATOR, A WHOLLY OWNED subsidiary of Dover Elevator International, Inc., has been helping people in the Twin Cities and the upper Midwest reach greater heights than they ever before thought possible. Lagerquist is a full-service vertical transportation equipment company providing installation of passenger, freight, and residential elevator equipment, along with other means of vertical transportation, such as

wheelchair lifts, dumbwaiters, escalators, and stage and industrial lifts.

"Whatever type of elevator is needed, we can supply it," says Peter Nelson, marketing manager. "High-rise, mid-rise, low-rise, pre-engineered, and custom-built elevators are no problem for us. Our professionals will work closely with contractors, architects, and building owners to make sure their needs are completely met." Lagerquist also provides maintenance services to ensure that elevators are running at optimum performance, as well as complete modernization services to keep elevators updated and safe.

Dover, the leading manufacturer of elevators in the United States, manufactures a complete line of traction and hydraulic equipment, including car sling and platform, pit equipment, machines, controllers, power units, valve systems, and door equipment. Quality, dependability, and the latest in technology are what Dover Elevator products are all about. Exacting manufacturing processes ensure the Dover product's competitive edge.

MORE THAN A CENTURY OF SERVICE

Gust. Lagerquist and Sons, Inc. was founded in 1882 by a Swedish immigrant named Gustav Lagerquist, who started out doing repair work and selling hand-operated equipment. By 1900 Lagerquist and his group had produced a line of hand-operated elevators and drum machines, manufactured in Minneapolis out of their own Water Street foundry. The location was moved to 614 Bradford Avenue North in 1923 and remained there for about 60 years.

In 1981 the property on Bradford Avenue was purchased by the Metropolitan Transit Company, and consequently Lagerquist was forced to move. As a result of both Minneapolis' and Lagerquist's desire to keep the company in the city, an agreement was reached for Lagerquist to purchase property at 1801 West River Road North. This new building was completed in 1982. However, visitors to the company's headquarters can still see the original Bradford Avenue North street signs, which were given to the company by the City of Minneapolis, in the building's lobby.

In 1936 Lagerquist became a Rotary Lift distributor for Oildraulic elevators, a move that gave the company a greater degree of recognition in its territory. In 1962 company officers decided that Lagerquist would become a total distributor of Dover Elevator equipment. Ten years later, the company was sold to the employees; it continued to grow steadily during the 1970s. In 1985, the company was purchased by Dover.

To date, Lagerquist is the largest and leading elevator company in the Twin Cities area, employing approximately 150 people and possessing approximately $400,000 in replacement parts necessary for maintenance, repair, and construction. The company's marketing territory covers Minnesota, North Dakota, South Dakota, Montana, parts of Wisconsin, and Wyoming.

BUILDING A CITY
While Lagerquist has helped to build, literally, the Twin Cities area, it has also helped to develop a strong

LAGERQUIST'S NEW HEADQUARTERS IS LOCATED AT 1801 WEST RIVER ROAD NORTH IN MINNEAPOLIS.

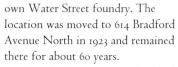

sense of community among its residents. Carl and Frank Lagerquist, sons of the company founder, were dedicated to the Masonic Lodge and its many community projects. Frank was a 32nd-degree Mason, and Carl served as Imperial Potentate of the Zuraha Shrine Temple. Carl was also very active in the Shrine Burn Hospital. For many years, Carl selected and organized the Shrine Circus acts that performed in Minneapolis. After Carl's death in 1977, the company established a memorial in his name and donated a defibrillator to the Shriner's Hospital for Crippled Children, where Carl had been a lifetime board member.

Many Lagerquist employees contribute time and money to local charitable organizations. Lagerquist executives and employees have also been instrumental in the formation of numerous elevator industry organizations, including the National Association of Elevator Safety Authorities and the Elevator Escalator Safety Foundation.

GROWING BIG BY STAYING SMALL

After more than a century of service, Lagerquist has become synonymous

ELEVATOR HOISTING ENGINE
TRACTION TYPE   DESIGN "OT-2"
MANUFACTURED BY
GUST. LAGERQUIST & SONS
MINNEAPOLIS, MINN.

with quality; that's why the biggest names in construction rely on Lagerquist for their highest-profile projects: the Dain Tower, Target Center, City Center, Convention Center, Lutheran Brotherhood Building, and new Federal Courthouse in downtown Minneapolis; West Publishing's new facility and City Hall in St. Paul; Carlson Towers, Normandale Lake 8500 Tower, and Veteran's Administration Hospital in the surrounding Twin Cities area, just to name a few.

"We're proud of our record dating back to 1882 and prouder still of keeping pace with today's

fast-moving elevator technology," says Nelson. "Being a part of the Dover Corporation allows us to benefit from their marketing strategies and sales efforts. We also have the financial backing of a Fortune 500 company, which allows our customers to know we'll be part of this industry for years to come. We've built our reputation by providing the highest-quality products and services, and by being responsive to the needs of our local customers. That's the strategy that has made us who we are, and that strategy will never change."

CLOCKWISE FROM TOP LEFT: GUST. LAGERQUIST AND SONS, INC. WAS FOUNDED IN 1882 BY A SWEDISH IMMIGRANT NAMED GUSTAV LAGERQUIST, WHO STARTED OUT DOING REPAIR WORK AND SELLING HAND-OPERATED EQUIPMENT.

GUST. LAGERQUIST AND SONS, INC. EXPANDED INTO ELEVATOR HOISTING ENGINES IN THE EARLY 1900S.

IN 1985 LAGERQUIST WAS PURCHASED BY DOVER CORPORATION. LAGERQUIST NOW SUPPLIES SUCH ELEVATOR PARTS AS GEARED TRACTION MACHINES, WHICH BEAR AN ELEVATOR CAPACITY OF 6,000 POUNDS.

WHEN TALK TURNS TO WAR HEROES, ONE USUALLY THINKS OF those men and women who gave their lives on the front lines. It's sometimes easy to forget the quiet heroes, the ones who never set foot in enemy territory, but who played a crucial role in our country's victory. The employees of St. Paul-based Villaume Industries, a 115-year-old wood-products firm, fall into that category. ✳ When World

War II began, Villaume was making boxes, doing millwork, and selling lumber in St. Paul. By war's end, Villaume had shipped 2 million boxes to ammunition plants and made boxes for K rations. The company also won a contract to produce wing, tail, and fuselage parts for gliders like those used in the invasion of Normandy. Villaume went from 130 to 1,500 employees in less than six months. "It was pretty crazy," says Louis Villaume, grandson of the founder and the one who handled that massive payroll with one assistant. By 1944, when he left for the navy, Villaume had seven or eight helpers to keep track of three shifts a day, six days a week. Government contracts totaled more than $15 million.

"We were a viable subcontractor because of our experience in woodworking, even though we didn't have experience with airplanes," says President Nick Linsmayer, a great-grandson of Villaume's founder. All told, Villaume made about 1,500 gliders, which cost some $25,000 apiece to make because they required so many parts. For some employees, the work was just a job, but for many, Linsmayer says, "There was a genuine feeling that we were actually doing something to help win and end the war."

BUILDING FOR THE FUTURE

Villaume was a pioneer St. Paul company. Eugene Villaume had come to St. Paul from France in 1873 as a woodworker. In 1881 he and his brothers established the Villaume Box and Lumber Company at the base of bluffs on the Mississippi River's west side.

The company grew, acquiring other small companies and eventually

becoming well known for the quality of its woodworking, cabinetry, and store fixtures. Villaume produced church interiors for local and out-of-state churches, and the mahogany doors and trim on the top 25 floors of St. Paul's First National Bank Building, as well as the interior of the nearby Northern States Power Building, the Ramsey County Courthouse, and the St. Paul City Hall.

Villaume's reputation for quality crates was given special credence in 1898 when the company received an order from a farmer in Colorado for a season's supply of melon crates.

Depending on the harvest, the order called for anywhere from 10 to 20 railroad boxcars filled with crates. Villaume made sure the company was protected against disasters such as crop failure, plant shutdown, and material destruction "by fire or otherwise." He was precise in his contract letter about the quality and workmanship. Ends were to be nailed together with three cement-coated nails, cleats would be beveled, and the lumber would be "good, merchantable basswood free from knots and other defects affecting strength."

CLOCKWISE FROM TOP: WHEN WORLD WAR II BEGAN, VILLAUME INDUSTRIES WAS MAKING BOXES, DOING MILLWORK, AND SELLING LUMBER IN ST. PAUL.

VILLAUME PRESIDENT NICK LINSMAYER

VILLAUME FOUNDER EUGENE VILLAUME

VILLAUME INDUSTRIES LED THE
WAY IN RECOGNIZING THE COST
AND DESIGN ADVANTAGES OF
PREENGINEERED AND CUSTOM
BUILT TRUSSES.

AN INDUSTRY PIONEER

In the mid-1950s, Villaume pioneered the use of the wood truss in the Minnesota construction market. At that time, wooden trusses were being held together with plywood gussets. When Paul West created his "Gizmo Gusset"—the original metal connector, or "gusset" plate—Villaume was one of the first companies to use it.

In the mid-1980s, Villaume Industries was the first component manufacturer to test a prototype of the Auto-Omni computer-controlled saw from Engineering Services Co., in Rochester, Minnesota. Unlike previous saws, the Auto-Omni has a fifth blade that speeds up cuts for scissor trusses. "More than 100 years of experience has given us the insight and courage for deciding what new technology to adopt, how to identify market changes early, and the best ways to address them," says Linsmayer.

Today Villaume Industries' truss business is strong, accounting for nearly two-thirds of the company's total business, and Linsmayer continues to keep close tabs on industry trends. "Within the last

few years, the percentage of houses using manufactured trusses has risen from 65 percent to 95 percent," he says. "Every home owner wants a house that looks different from all the others. We can do that, with trusses as small as 10 inches or as long as 120 feet—in 30,000 different designs."

While no longer in the ornamental or architectural woodworking industry, Villaume continues to produce wood pallets, crates, specialty wood products, and—after 115 years—boxes. With 120 employees, the company is the largest manufacturer of industrial wood products and components (trusses) in the Twin Cities area, and certainly one of the best known for quality, craftsmanship, and dependability in the entire north central United States.

"We're a survivor company that was founded on what has been and continues to be the Villaume commitment: to put the customers' needs foremost," says Linsmayer. "Some of our customers have been with us for nearly 80 years. I think that says a lot about our ability to provide top-quality service while at the same time adapting to the needs of the industry." Linsmayer says that in terms of the future, the company will continue to do what it does best—produce cost-effective, quality wood products—but he will keep his eyes open. "Our strategy has always been to grow from our strengths."

VILLAUME RELIES ON THE PALLET
DESIGN SYSTEM (PDS) TO CAL-
CULATE THE SAFEST AND MOST
EFFICIENT PALLETS FOR ITS
CUSTOMERS.

I N 1885, ARCHBISHOP JOHN IRELAND SAW A NEED FOR A Catholic, liberal arts institution offering a values-centered career-oriented education. ✷ Responding to that need, he founded what has become the University of St. Thomas, the largest private university in Minnesota. Home to 5,000 undergraduate students and more than 5,200 graduate students, St. Thomas offers 28 master's and three doctoral programs in addition to its 67 undergraduate majors.

BETTER PROGRAMS, MORE LOCATIONS

Over the years, St. Thomas has continued to look to the community for direction in terms of development and growth. That outward vision was one of the primary reasons the university developed its graduate program in business in 1974. "We recognized that not everybody could afford to quit his or her job and go back to school full-time," says the Rev. Dennis Dease, president. "We saw that more options were needed for those people who wanted to keep working while getting their MBA." The Graduate School of Business, with an enrollment of about 3,000, is now the fifth largest in the United States.

That same reasoning was behind St. Thomas' decision to offer classes in downtown Minneapolis. "We took a look at our numbers and realized that a majority of our graduate business students were coming from Hennepin County, and that many of them worked in downtown Minneapolis," says Dease. Classes first were held at a remodeled department store. The university opened a permanent $25 million campus in fall 1992. The campus enrolls 2,200 students.

READY FOR THE FUTURE

The university's new $30 million science and engineering center is still another example of St. Thomas' commitment to the larger community. "Science is booming among undergraduates at St. Thomas, as it is across the nation," says Dease. "With more than 30 percent of our prospective pool of students looking very seriously at careers in science and health-related fields, we saw significant value in having the latest resources and technologies available to enhance their learning experience." The new center will be home to the undergraduate departments of biology, chemistry, geology, manufacturing engineering, mathematics, physics, and quantitative methods-computer science, as well as graduate programs in software and manufacturing systems engineering.

The university's more than 1,500 employees include 650 full- and part-time faculty, and a support staff of 900. The student-faculty ratio is about 17-to-1. An increasing emphasis is being placed, as an urban university, on service learning programs and community service. "We must be more than just *in* the city," Dease says. "We must be *of* the city."

THE O'SHAUGHNESSY-FREY LIBRARY CENTER IS LOCATED ON THE UNIVERSITY'S ST. PAUL CAMPUS (RIGHT).

THE UNIVERSITY OF ST. THOMAS SERVES THE TWIN CITIES AREA WITH SEVERAL LOCATIONS, INCLUDING THE MINNEAPOLIS CAMPUS (BELOW).

RELIASTAR FINANCIAL CORP.

OUNDED IN 1885, RELIASTAR FINANCIAL CORP., FORMERLY The NWNL Companies, is a Minneapolis-based holding company that provides financial security through individual life insurance and annuities, employee benefits, retirement plans, life and health reinsurance, mutual funds, and personal finance education programs. The company's goal is to be a lifetime partner delivering integrated financial solutions to its customers. ✳ The company

began in 1885 as the Northwestern Aid Association, a mutual assessment organization. It became known as Northwestern National Life Insurance in 1901. In 1927 it adopted a dual stock and mutual ownership structure that remained in effect until 1989, when it converted to a completely shareholder-owned company and The NWNL Companies succeeded Northwestern National Life as the parent organization. The NWNL Companies changed its name to ReliaStar Financial Corp. in 1995. Currently, ReliaStar is the 12th-largest publicly held life insurance holding company in the United States.

"ReliaStar has been growing rapidly in recent years. We're adding new businesses, expanding our portfolio of financial products and services, and finding new ways of making these products and services available to consumers. As a result, we can better meet our customers' changing financial security needs over their entire lifetime by serving them what, when, and how they want to be served," says John G. Turner, chairman and chief executive officer. "We changed our name to ReliaStar to create a brand identity that would link all of these products and services under one name. We believe that having a single name makes it easier for our customers to work with us again and again as they go from one point in their financial life to the next."

REACHING CUSTOMERS MANY WAYS

Buying preferences of today's consumers are changing. Many people still prefer to work with a traditional insurance agent or financial adviser,

THOMAS SCHNETZ

but a growing number of consumers are meeting their financial security needs by purchasing products and services at their work sites or through their banks. ReliaStar is therefore expanding to include these outlets. As a result, customers not only have more ReliaStar products to choose from, they also have more ways to buy them.

Consumers—particularly Baby Boomers—also are becoming increasingly aware of the need to take responsibility for their own financial security, as the role of employers and government diminishes. In order to make sound decisions, they are seeking information and education about financial matters. ReliaStar has added Successful

Money Management Seminars, Inc. (SMMS) to its family of companies in order to meet this need. A leading provider of personal finance education, SMMS presents seminars on a variety of topics through a network of licensed instructors. ReliaStar will leverage SMMS across its entire family of companies. "SMMS enables our businesses to provide their customers with high-quality financial education services, thus building an advisory relationship that grows over time," says John H. Flittie, ReliaStar president and chief operating officer. "These relationships are a great way to help us achieve our vision of developing lifetime partnerships with our customers."

FOR MORE THAN 30 YEARS, THE CORPORATE HEADQUARTERS OF RELIASTAR FINANCIAL CORP. HAS BEEN ACCLAIMED AS AN ARCHITECTURAL HIGHLIGHT OF MINNEAPOLIS. THE COMPANY HAS GROWN DRAMATICALLY SINCE THE BUILDING WAS BUILT IN 1964, PROMPTING THE CONSTRUCTION OF TWO ADDITIONAL BUILDINGS, ONE OF WHICH APPEARS IN THE BACKGROUND.

Linked to the Future

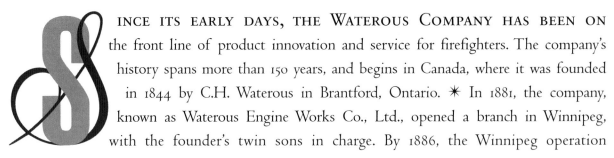

SINCE ITS EARLY DAYS, THE WATEROUS COMPANY HAS BEEN ON the front line of product innovation and service for firefighters. The company's history spans more than 150 years, and begins in Canada, where it was founded in 1844 by C.H. Waterous in Brantford, Ontario. ✳ In 1881, the company, known as Waterous Engine Works Co., Ltd., opened a branch in Winnipeg, with the founder's twin sons in charge. By 1886, the Winnipeg operation

had grown beyond the capabilities of local distribution facilities, so the company decided to move to St. Paul, a growing transportation and wholesaling center. A private development company interested in the growth of the southern St. Paul area offered the Waterous brothers free land on which to build a new factory. The new building, located less than a mile from the present-day facility, was already in operation by the time South St. Paul was incorporated in 1887.

In St. Paul, The Waterous Company originally manufactured steam fire engines, hook and ladder trucks, and chemical engines. In 1898, Waterous revolutionized fire fighting by introducing the first gasoline-powered pumper, and in 1906 the company produced the first gasoline-powered self-propelled pumper. It had two engines—one to propel the truck and one to drive the pump. The first single gasoline engine self-propelled fire truck, introduced in 1907, was another Waterous first.

In an ironic turn of events, the Waterous plant itself was destroyed by fire—not once, but twice. After the first fire in 1894, the factory was rebuilt in St. Paul on the west side levee, next to the Robert Street bridge, but then burned again in 1904. It was rebuilt on the same site, then moved to Fillmore Street in St. Paul in 1917. The grandson of C.H. Waterous, Fred Waterous, joined the company in 1920 and directed its operations from 1935 until it was sold to American Hoist and Derrick in 1965. In 1973, a new 140,000-square-foot plant was erected at the current South St. Paul location.

A POWERHOUSE OF PRODUCTS

Waterous built its last complete piece of fire apparatus in 1929 and has since concentrated on fire pumps, hydrants, valves, and accessories. Today, Waterous manufactures a variety of centrifugal pumps for fire protection and industrial applications, including mobile fire apparatus, por-

table pumps, skid mount pumps, trailer mounted pumps, aircraft rescue pumps, fireboat pumps, high-pressure pumps, deicing pumps, relief valves, discharge valves, and split shaft power take-off transmissions.

The company's fire hydrants—including the pacer hydrant and the trend hydrant—incorporate features that make them the hydrant of choice in many municipalities. These features include an attractive modern design, interchangeability of service parts, a traffic "break off" flange option, and a valve that can be completely replaced without digging up the hydrant.

Waterous entered the gate valve business in 1978 with the acquisition of the Traverse City Iron Works in Traverse City, Michigan. The Traverse City manufacturing and product line was moved to South St. Paul and included traditional metal seated gate valves that, together with hydrants, enabled the company to offer a complete line of water-

WATEROUS WAS THE FIRST MANUFACTURER TO OFFER A FIRE TRUCK WITH ONE ENGINE CAPABLE OF DRIVING THE VEHICLE AND PUMPING THE WATER (LEFT).

IN 1906, THE FIRST GASOLINE-POWERED SELF-PROPELLED PUMPER WAS INTRODUCED. IT HAD TWO ENGINES—ONE TO PROPEL THE TRUCK AND ONE TO DRIVE THE PUMP (RIGHT).

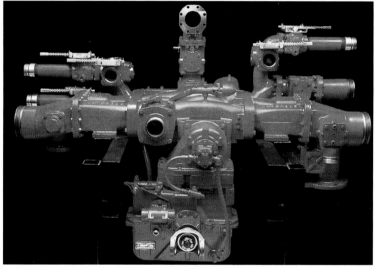

works and fire protection products. In 1981, the company introduced the Series 500 resilient wedge gate valve featuring a rubber-coated wedge that seals against an epoxy-coated body. This type of valve is quickly replacing traditional metal seated valves because it provides drop tight shut-off and superior corrosion resistance. Waterous is recognized as a leading manufacturer of resilient seated gate valves.

Product training has also been a key element of Waterous' business. Since 1958, the company's Mobile Training Unit has traveled the country, teaching firefighters how to maintain one of the most critical components of the fire truck, the fire pump. Training will continue to be a large part of Waterous' commitment to total customer service as new, more complex products are developed and introduced.

A Leader and Innovator

Consistent, high-quality performance through the years has made Waterous the most requested name in pumps, power takeoffs, valves, and hydrants for industry and fire service. But the company's products are only part of the reason Waterous continues to experience success, says Waterous President and Chief Executive Officer Donald Haugen. "The widespread acceptance and quality of our product line is certainly one of our strengths," he says. "But the company's commitment to serving its customers as well as its employees is what allows us to strengthen our relationships and grow in positive directions."

Haugen says those directions include actively promoting international sales, expanding the domestic sales base, further opening up the channels of distribution, and con-

tinuing to develop new products. "We've just released a new foam delivery system for use in firefighting, and we're optimistic that it could sell as well as our current pump line," says Haugen. "We feel we have the opportunity to position Waterous as the leader and innovator in the fire pump and waterworks industries, and we're doing everything we can to achieve that goal."

Already the largest manufacturing employer in South St. Paul, Waterous has added nearly 70 employees during the past four years, bringing the total number close to 350. And Haugen says he expects the company to be in double-digit growth rates for the next five years. But, he adds, the true measure of success involves more than numbers. "It gives all of us a good feeling to know we are producing a product that someday may help save a life."

CLOCKWISE FROM LEFT: THE COMPANY'S FIRE HYDRANTS— INCLUDING THE PACER HYDRANT AND THE TREND HYDRANT— INCORPORATE FEATURES THAT MAKE THEM THE HYDRANT OF CHOICE IN MANY MUNICIPALITIES.

TODAY, WATEROUS MANUFACTURES A VARIETY OF CENTRIFUGAL PUMPS FOR FIRE PROTECTION AND INDUSTRIAL APPLICATIONS, INCLUDING MOBILE FIRE APPARATUS, PORTABLE PUMPS, SKID MOUNT PUMPS, TRAILER MOUNTED PUMPS, AIRCRAFT RESCUE PUMPS, FIREBOAT PUMPS, HIGH-PRESSURE PUMPS, DEICING PUMPS, RELIEF VALVES, DISCHARGE VALVES, AND SPLIT SHAFT POWER TAKEOFF TRANSMISSIONS.

AMONG THE NATION'S HOSPITALS, HENNEPIN COUNTY MEDICAL CENTER (HCMC) ranks with the elite. In 1996, it was named by *Self* magazine as one of the 10 best hospitals in the country in which to have a baby, due in part to its low C-section rate and strong nurse-midwife program. In 1995 it was one of just a handful of public hospitals that made the top 100 list (with more than 1,000 evaluated) in *America's Best Hospitals*, a book compiled through surveys of

LOCATED IN DOWNTOWN MINNE-APOLIS NEAR THE METRODOME, HENNEPIN COUNTY MEDICAL CENTER HAS EXISTED SINCE 1887. THE CURRENT FACILITY WAS COMPLETED IN 1976, BUT RENOVATION AND REMODELING TO ACCOMMODATE NEW SERVICES AND PROGRAMS ARE ONGOING.

the nation's physicians and published by *U.S. News & World Report* magazine.

HCMC ranked among the top 100 in several specialties including cardiology, endocrinology, geriatrics, gynecology, orthopedics, gastroenterology, rheumatology, urology, and treatment of AIDS.

HCMC's teaching programs in these and other specialties are nationally recognized, and residency slots are highly prized. Estimates are that 25 percent of all physicians practicing in the Twin Cities metropolitan area received all or part of their advanced training at HCMC.

The training is provided by HCMC's staff physicians, the 250-plus members of Hennepin Faculty Associates (HFA)—who are also faculty in the University of Minnesota

Medical School. HFA physicians supervise nearly all patient care at HCMC, and between 20 to 30 are routinely listed among the Best Doctors in America.

FINANCIALLY HEALTHY

While marketplace pressures and reimbursement cutbacks from federal and state payers have forced the closure of many public hospitals across the country during the past few years, HCMC has operated in the black. It is one of a very few county hospitals nationwide to derive less than 10 percent of its operating revenues from county tax support.

HCMC is perhaps best known locally for its outstanding emergency services. HCMC physicians were leaders in the development of the emergency medical services system

in the metro area and established one of the first emergency medicine residency training programs in the nation. The Emergency Department's stabilization room, designed by former Chief of Emergency Medicine Ernest Ruiz in the mid-1970s, is still considered a model for emergency room critical care facilities.

In 1989 HCMC's commitment to emergency care and trauma services culminated in receiving verification from the American College of Surgeons as a Level 1 trauma center, the first hospital in the state to achieve this level of excellence in trauma services.

Not so well known but equally important to tens of thousands of patients is the large clinic system operated by HCMC. Between 280,000 and 300,000 visits annually are recorded by HCMC's network of primary care and specialty clinics. While the majority occur at HCMC's downtown location, patient visits continue to increase at off-site clinics located in the suburbs of Richfield and Brooklyn Center and at the Family Medical Center on Lake Street in Minneapolis. HCMC is also a partner in the Glenwood-Lyndale Community Clinic on North Bryant in Minneapolis. Development of these clinics is part of HCMC's ongoing commitment to provide easily accessible, quality health care services in neighborhoods convenient to patients.

A COMMUNITY RESOURCE

HCMC has been a valuable community resource since its founding in 1887 as City Hospital. For many years it met the needs of the community from inadequate, often temporary facilities. Infectious disease outbreaks, for example, would often

Minneapolis ✶ St. Paul

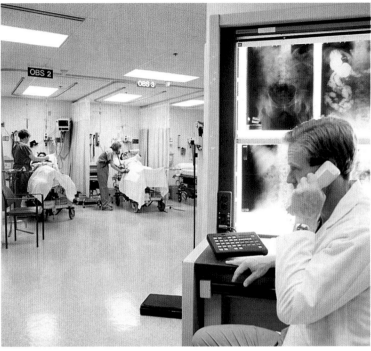

necessitate setting up quarters in schools or even tents on the hospital lawn.

Until 1976 when the present modern structure was completed, the hospital occupied a hodgepodge collection of buildings all constructed before 1912. Adverse conditions, however, gave rise to a remarkable esprit de corps among hospital staff, and the eventual demolition of "The General," as it had then become known, was a poignant occasion.

The new HCMC continued the pattern of outgrowing its space, and when the neighboring private hospital closed its doors, HCMC purchased the buildings, thus doubling its size, and began relocating and expanding services. The additional space has enabled HCMC to develop centers where patients with complex needs can be seen by multiple providers within a single location on the sprawling four-city-block campus.

The Center for Senior Care, the Hennepin Diabetes Center, the Orthopaedic Specialty Center, the Cardiac Care Center, the Hennepin Comprehensive Cancer Center, and the Occupational Medicine Clinic are all newly remodeled services housed in the additional space.

This space is also home to the hospital's extensive psychiatry services, including acute hospitalization and a Day Treatment Program; and the Knapp Rehabilitation Center, which includes a therapeutic pool and an Easy Street environment where patients with traumatic injuries or stroke can learn to readjust to the real world while still in the hospital.

A Wealth of Programs and Services

HCMC's long history includes a series of firsts in the metro area—services or programs started to meet community needs that others were unable or unwilling to provide. These include the Hennepin Regional Poison Center, established in 1972 and now handling more than 100,000 calls a year; Regional Kidney Disease Program, the founder of which, Dr. Claude Hitchcock, performed the first transplantation surgery and first hemodialysis in the region during the early 1960s; Nurse-Midwife Service, which celebrated 25 years in 1996; Burn Center, which has pioneered skin culturing; Sleep Disorders Center, the physicians of which have identified two new disorders; Bloodless Medicine and Surgery Program, for

patients who wish to avoid transfusions; and Women's Advocate Program, for victims of domestic abuse.

Yet another service to meet an urgent community need that began in the late 1970s has now developed into a full-scale Interpreter Services Program. What began in 1978 with three part-time, temporary Southeast Asian interpreters now comprises 18 full-time interpreters of languages including Russian, Somali, Spanish, Hmong, Vietnamese, Lao, and Cambodian. Interpreters for an additional 60-plus languages are available on a freelance basis.

Responding to the needs of the community is a tradition that began at HCMC with caring for the victims of typhoid epidemics before the turn of the century. It is a tradition of which the current staff members are very proud and one they hope to uphold far into the future.

CLOCKWISE FROM TOP LEFT: PATIENTS WITH SERIOUS TRAUMATIC INJURY ARE HELPED TO REGAIN AS MUCH FUNCTION AS POSSIBLE IN THE KNAPP REHABILITATION CENTER.

AN URGENT CARE CENTER IN HCMC'S MEDICAL SPECIALTY CENTER ON 7TH STREET TAKES SOME OF THE PRESSURE OFF THE HOSPITAL'S EMERGENCY DEPARTMENT ON 8TH AND PARK; THE ED IS THE BUSIEST IN THE STATE WITH UPWARDS OF 90,000 VISITS ANNUALLY.

TO SERVE THE NEEDS OF GREATER MINNESOTA, HCMC OWNS AND OPERATES A HELICOPTER SERVICE IN PARTNERSHIP WITH A PRIVATE HOSPITAL.

Bloomington's Mall of America—completed three months ahead of schedule and $25 million under budget—is a striking example of an innovative labor/management partnership that is winning Minnesota an international reputation for projects that routinely come in on time, under budget—or better. ✳ Communications, teamwork, and respect have long been part of the labor/management culture between

the state's unionized building and construction trades and their signatory contractors. But this spirit of cooperation took on new meaning in 1980, following a long summer of strikes and lockouts. To ensure that labor strife need never again delay a project's completion, the Minnesota Building and Construction Trades Council developed an agreement that would help serve as a guarantee to developers, contractors, and owners that their projects would be completed on schedule and on budget.

Since the first agreement was forged, project agreements have reshaped Minnesota's skyline— schools, banks, hospitals, shopping centers, sewage treatment plants, apartment complexes, and local, state, and federal government facilities. Whether the project has been a soaring skyscraper or a single-family home, the Council has kept its word. No project constructed in Minnesota under a project agreement has come in behind schedule or over budget. "Project agreements set a level of wages and benefits that are fair and equitable to workers and employers and are good for the community and, ultimately, the customer," says Dick Anfang, executive secretary of the St. Paul Building and Construction Trades Council. "Once in place, a project agreement creates an opportunity for a first-rate project. And that's what the Council is all about."

Organized for the Future

The history of the Minnesota Building and Construction Trades Council dates back to the turn of the 19th century. Construction trades were flourishing in Minneapolis after 1880 as a result of massive construction in the city, as well as in the residential, commercial, and industrial sectors. Construction workers wanted to be certain that they could count on satisfactory working conditions, along with fair wages for a full day's work. The success of the early trade unions soon led to the growth of other unions throughout the city. John Lamb, the state's first commissioner of labor, reported that in 1888, more than 80 unions were active in Minnesota, with 20 located in Minneapolis.

In 1889 the Minnesota Building and Construction Trades Council was formed to act as the "union of unions," a single entity that would help unite and lobby for the individual trade unions currently organized throughout the state. Today the Minnesota Building and Construction Trades Council is a vibrant organization comprised of 30 AFL-CIO Building Trades Craft Unions representing more than 30,000 journeymen and registered apprentice workers.

Over the years, the focus of the Council has shifted from securing decent work conditions and wages to training the workforce of the future. "In Minnesota we have come to expect a certain level of expertise," says Ray Waldron, business manager of the Minneapolis Building and Construction Trades Council, "and we accomplish that by investing in our people through a joint labor/management training program that not only prepares workers for today's construction challenges, but ensures they will master the future's new and changing technologies."

All qualified candidates are interviewed by employers and union

ONE OF THE MORE VISIBLE COMMUNITY PROJECTS THE COUNCIL HAS BEEN INVOLVED WITH IS THE CONSTRUCTION OF THE 1986 AND 1992 ST. PAUL WINTER CARNIVAL ICE PALACES.

Minneapolis ✳ St. Paul

representatives. The best are selected to enter a state-registered apprenticeship system that combines classroom-related instruction at the top technical colleges in the state with structured on-the-job training. Even after the apprentices graduate, comprehensive journeyman retraining programs keep workers up to date on the industry's needs and technologies. "Our overall training goal is simple," says Waldron. "We want to produce an individual with unmatched job skill, knowledge of the trade, and a positive attitude toward his or her union, employer, the public, and, most certainly, the paying customer."

GIVING BACK TO THE COMMUNITY

In addition to creating a better life for its members, the Minnesota Building and Construction Trades Council also helps to create a better life for those communities in which its members work and live. Council members have participated in many community service projects such as the United Way; Dollars Against Diabetes (D.A.D.'s); the Pipefitters' project "Heat's On;" the Plumbers' project "Water's Off;" the Electricians' Smoke Detector Program and

volunteer efforts for NET DAY; and the Carpenters, Cement Finishers, and Bricklayers building of many handicap ramps and the construction of an open-air urban market for community artisans and growers. Many local unions volunteered a summer's worth of work in 1993 to restore a condemned historical building into a functional neighborhood community center, saving thousands of dollars.

One of the more visible projects the Council has been involved with is the construction of the St. Paul Winter Carnival Ice Palace. After successfully constructing the Palace in 1986, the Council was again asked by the City of St. Paul to construct the Ice Palace in 1992. Building Trades members agreed to work on the Palace at one-half the present wage rates, donating approximately $100,000 for the project. In addition, Winter Carnival officials estimated that the total cost of the Ice Palace was reduced by $500,000 because of the skill and experience the union workers brought to the project.

Building Trades members toiled in double shifts from December 12 to January 20 to complete the "World's Tallest Ice Palace" on schedule. "Morale stayed high because workers

on the project knew they were doing something special to build pride in themselves, their unions, and their community." says Anfang. Few projects could better embody the spirit or the goal of the Minnesota Building and Construction Trades Council.

Local Unions that make up the St. Paul and Minneapolis Building Trades Councils include Asbestos Workers Local #34; Boilermakers Local #647; Bricklayers Local #1; Cabinet Makers Local #1865; Carpenters Locals #87, #851, and #1644; Carpet Layers Local #596; Cement Masons Local #633; Construction Drivers Local #221; Elevator Constructors Local #9; Glaziers Local #1324; International Brotherhood of Electric Workers Locals #110 and #292; Ironworkers Local #512; Laborers Locals #132 and #563; Lathers Locals #190; Millwrights Locals #548; Operating Engineers Local #49; Painters Locals #61 and #386; Pile Drivers Local #1847; Pipefitters Locals #455 and #539; Plasterers Local #265; Plaster Tenders Local #111; Plumbers Locals #15 and #34; Roofers Local #96; Sheet Metal Local #10; Sign, Display, Screen Local #880; Sprinkler-fitters Local #417; and Tile Layers Local #1.

FINANCIAL SERVICES IS ONE OF MINNESOTA'S LARGEST industries, and managing other people's money is one of its fastest-growing components. No company does that with more success than American Express Financial Advisors. Now into its second century of service, the company—known until recently as IDS Financial Services—is the undisputed leader in financial planning. ✳ Headquartered in Minneapolis in the renowned

tower that bears the IDS name, American Express Financial Advisors offers a wide range of financial services and products, including personal financial planning, mutual funds, insurance and annuities, certificates, and lending and brokerage services. With 2 million clients, 8,000 financial advisors in 176 cities nationwide, 5,100 employees in downtown Minneapolis, and more than $149 billion in owned and managed assets, the company has been the most consistently profitable American Express company over the past decade.

THE MAKINGS OF A GIANT

Investors Syndicate was launched in 1894 in a one-room office in the Lumber Exchange Building by John E. Tappan, a 26-year-old law student whose only previous business experience was working in collections in order to finance his night school studies. Tappan learned that the only way to settle overdue accounts was to help people organize a regular payment plan. Why, he reasoned, couldn't the same system be used to help people who weren't in financial trouble save for the future? With $2,600 and abundant confidence, he went into business.

Tappan began by offering a fixed-return investment known as a face amount certificate. Investors made small regular payments until the certificate matured, usually in 10 years, in order to collect the face amount of the certificate. Within a year, Tappan had investment contracts with 150 people in the Twin Cities. Within 20 years, his reserves had grown from the initial stake to $88,000. The company passed the million-dollar mark in 1918; by 1925,

when Tappan sold his interests at the age of 57, Investors Syndicate had assets of more than $12 million.

The company spread from coast to coast during the 1920s and 1930s. Its growth was based on individual salespeople who offered investment programs directly to the little guy— farmers, merchants, workers, home owners—usually in small towns. During the worst days of the depres-

sion, Investors Syndicate paid out $101 million on time to holders of matured certificates, establishing a reputation for reliability that would be basic to its future success.

Renamed Investors Diversified Services in 1949, the company invested money in industrial and construction loans in the postwar growth years, and guided the early years of Investors Mutual, the mutual

HEADQUARTERED IN MINNEAPOLIS IN THE RENOWNED IDS BUILDING, AMERICAN EXPRESS FINANCIAL ADVISORS OFFERS A WIDE RANGE OF FINANCIAL SERVICES AND PRODUCTS, INCLUDING PERSONAL FINANCIAL PLANNING, MUTUAL FUNDS, INSURANCE AND ANNUITIES, CERTIFICATES, AND LENDING AND BROKERAGE SERVICES.

fund begun in 1940 that today ranks among the world's largest. American Express acquired the company, then named IDS Financial Services Inc., in 1984, but it wasn't until January 1, 1995, that the company took on the corporation's name.

"As we enter our second century with a new name—American Express Financial Advisors Inc.—we are ready to continue our history of success," says Peter Lefferts, senior vice president, corporate strategy development. "We have built our business around the single, simple premise of helping people achieve their financial objectives through a long-term financial planning relationship with trusted and knowledgeable advisors. For more than 100 years that has been our philosophy, and that will continue to be our philosophy in the years to come."

Lefferts points out, however, that although the company's primary focus is helping clients manage their money safely and profitably, it's not all about figures on a ledger sheet. "We've had a long-term commitment to the Twin Cities community and to other communities in which we live and work," says Lefferts. "By supporting programs such as Women Venture, Junior Achievement, and Dakota, Inc., we give further credence to our mission to help people achieve financial independence. We've also long been recognized for our ability to train and grow leaders," he continues. "Our goal is to be the kind of company with which people want to build long-term relationships. That means doing more than just making the numbers."

INVESTING IN THE FUTURE

American Express Financial Advisors has long been recognized for its ability to nurture long-term, multi-product relationships with its customers. But the company realizes that to remain a leader it will need to attract new customers as well. For that reason, the company's future growth strategy is two-pronged: to

improve the performance of its traditional agent-based channels while also exploring potential new channels, including financial direct services. Financial direct services would allow American Express Financial Advisors to contact consumers and offer products and services they could obtain by calling an 800 number or by return mail.

Changes in traditional distribution methods include eliminating the cold-calling approach advisors have used in the past and experimenting with advertising, which the company has traditionally eschewed. The company has also introduced a number

of initiatives aimed at helping its financial planners work more efficiently, such as equipping them with personal computers on which to devise financial strategies. Lefferts says that the decision to pursue new distribution options was a response to marketplace realities. "We must be adept at serving customers who want to work with advisors and those who don't. You need a presence and capability in a variety of channels," he says. "Clients increasingly will have a choice of how to access you, and you have to accommodate the client need."

AMERICAN EXPRESS FINANCIAL ADVISORS TAKES PRIDE IN THE LEVEL OF SERVICE IT DELIVERS TO ITS CLIENTS AND HOLDS ADVISOR SUCCESS WORKSHOPS TO ENSURE TOTAL CLIENT SATISFACTION (ABOVE).

AMERICAN EXPRESS FINANCIAL ADVISORS HAS LONG BEEN RECOGNIZED FOR ITS ABILITY TO NURTURE LONG-TERM, MULTI-PRODUCT RELATIONSHIPS WITH ITS CUSTOMERS (LEFT).

CHANCES ARE GOOD THAT NO MATTER WHO YOU ARE, WHERE YOU live, or what you do, your life has somehow been touched by Minneapolis-based Cargill, Incorporated. Although it is America's largest privately held corporation, Cargill is hardly a household name. But the company supplies flour for bread, oil for salad dressing, concentrate for orange juice, beans for coffee, sweetener for soft drinks, malt for beer, peanuts

for peanut butter, cocoa for candy bars, salt and steak for barbecuing, and much, much more.

From its beginnings in 1865 as a country grain warehouse in Conover, Iowa, Cargill has grown into a global marketer, processor, and distributor of agricultural, financial, and industrial products. It provides farmers with services and inputs, including seed, feed, and fertilizer. It buys their crops and finds new markets and uses for them—processing wheat, corn, oilseeds, and fruits, as well as beef, pork, and poultry. Cargill manufactures steel, salt, and fertilizer. Its financial businesses are involved in capital markets, emerging economies, and various financial assets and futures brokerages. And it employs more than 76,000 people in approximately 1,000 locations in 66 countries around the world.

But numbers alone don't tell the whole story. "We touch the lives of millions of people in hundreds of communities in countless ways," says retired Chairman and Chief Executive Officer Whitney MacMillan,

great-grandson of the corporation's original founder.

"What ties Cargill employees together is more than what we do. It is how we do it," says Ernest Micek, Cargill's current chairman and CEO. "Our success as a business grew from our commitment to integrity and to adding value to the lives of the people and communities we are privileged to serve." According to Micek, that commitment has made Cargill the corporation it is today and will

continue to guide its growth in the future.

COMMUNITY COMMITMENT

Cargill knows that it takes many partners to build strong communities. No one agency or company can reach all of those in need today. But their combined efforts can make a real difference. For example, Cargill and Farm Safety 4 Just Kids, a non-profit organization dedicated to protecting children from becoming

CARGILL PRESENTS A FAMILIAR FACE THROUGHOUT RURAL AMERICA—WHETHER IT'S ELEVATORS, FEED MILLS, FERTILIZER OR SEED DISTRIBUTORS, FLOUR MILLS, OILSEED CRUSHING PLANTS, CORN MILLS, OR BEEF PROCESSING PLANTS (FAR RIGHT).

CARGILL'S FIRST GRAIN ELEVATOR IN MINNESOTA OPENED AT ALBERT LEA IN 1871 (RIGHT).

injured or killed while playing or working on a farm, have been partners since 1992. In the past several years, more than 200 Cargill businesses have created or are in the process of initiating chapters with Farm Safety 4 Just Kids, and have sponsored safety camps or hosted a variety of displays and events—including tours of working farms—to make children and their parents aware of the hidden dangers on farms. Other activities include discussions about fire safety, poisons and pesticides, cardiopulmonary resuscitation, and the danger of playing near farm equipment.

Dan Huber, a Cargill sector president and cochair of its farm safety campaign, explains that the corporation has been dedicated to serving farmers for more than 130 years, and that it's only fitting to serve their families as well. "Every year, about 300 kids are killed in farm accidents, and thousands are seriously injured," says Huber. "The partnership between Cargill and Farm Safety 4 Just Kids enables us to share our safety experience with farm communities and farm families. In our business and in our partnership, our goal is to prevent tragedies."

Farm safety for children is one of several Cargill Cares projects that attempt to involve employees throughout the company. Although it may seem a strange concern for a company with headquarters in the land of 10,000 lakes, another such project is Water Matters—At Home, at Work, and in Our Community, an international effort to improve water quality and promote water education. In this case, Cargill partnered with the National Geographic Society and The Conservation Fund to launch the project in 1995. As with its farm safety project, Cargill provides an annual donation of $100,000 in additional support for its locations to search out local partners on water quality projects.

In Nebraska, for example, five different Cargill businesses have worked together to promote children's education on groundwater issues, including activities at a statewide Children's Groundwater Festival. The businesses bolstered their efforts with the aid of the Cargill Partnership Fund—corporate matching funds to help locations respond to local community needs.

"Our Cargill Cares projects are designed to connect employees with local organizations, so they can work together to improve communities," says Jim Hield, manager of Cargill Community Relations. "Employees have really enjoyed those experiences. They not only contribute something to make their community a better place to live, they also learn new skills and have a lot of fun."

In addition to working on farm safety and water quality, Cargill has joined with organizations around the world to help alleviate hunger, promote literacy and education, sustain the arts, and improve health and human services. In 1996 alone, Cargill

MOLTEN STEEL FROM RECYCLED AUTOS AND OTHER STEEL GOODS POURS INTO A LADLE TAP AT NORTH STAR STEEL'S ST. PAUL, MINNESOTA, MINIMILL. THE INDUSTRIAL SIDE OF CARGILL INCLUDES NORTH STAR'S NINE MINIMILLS (FAR LEFT).

MANAGING THE RISKS OF TRADING BUSINESSES, NOW RANGING FROM FARM COMMODITIES TO FINANCIAL PRODUCTS, HAS BEEN A CORE SKILL AT CARGILL FOR MORE THAN 130 YEARS (LEFT).

contributed nearly $9 million to nonprofit organizations nationwide.

THE YEARS AHEAD

Cargill's growth and diversification from an Iowa grain warehouse to a successful global corporation puts it into a class shared by few. For more than 13 decades, the company's mission has remained constant: to provide essential goods and services required for the well-being of customers around the world—and, in the process, raise living standards.

As a privately held company, Cargill has been able to reinvest more of its earnings and take a longer term view of business success than companies beholden to stockholders. That commitment to growth has helped the company double in size approximately every six years for the past 60 years. Growing into new businesses and into new locations around the world provides dynamic careers for employees. Cargill has a tradition of attracting long-term employees, in large part because of the opportunities they have to seek new challenges and advance their careers. "We reinvest our earnings in businesses that grow and excel over the long haul," says Micek. "This builds opportunities for our employees, better service for our customers and suppliers, and stronger communities where we live."

As the developing countries around the world make progress, there will be more demand for the basic goods and services that are Cargill's stock-in-trade. As diets improve around the world, core Cargill businesses such as fertilizer, hybrid seed, animal feed, corn and oilseed processing, flour milling, and meat processing should continue their robust growth well into Cargill's second century of operations.

HAUENSTEIN & BURMEISTER, INC.

USTOMER EXPECTATIONS HAVE CHANGED SIGNIFICANTLY OVER THE past 10 years so that people now expect to conduct their banking at the touch of a button, their pizza to arrive at their door in 30 minutes, and their packages to be delivered overnight. In short, customers want to get the best products and services available in the shortest amount of time for the least amount of money—and success will come to the companies that can meet that demand.

Minneapolis-based Hauenstein & Burmeister, Inc. (H&B) plans to be one of those companies and is implementing several companywide changes to ensure that it will remain customer-focused. "We're hearing the call of our customers, and we recognize the need to continually change and improve to create the level of responsiveness and service they demand," says H&B President Robert Johnston. "Change is never easy, but we have a solid foundation and a forward-looking vision to guide us."

CHANGES AND GROWTH

The history of H&B dates back more than 70 years to 1923 when George Hauenstein of New Ulm began selling weather-stripping for wooden storm windows throughout cold-weather states in the upper Midwest. In 1927 he joined forces with Otto Burmeister, who held the patent for double-hung aluminum storm windows. Together, they formed Hauenstein & Burmeister, which provided residential home owners both options for improving the energy efficiency of windows.

During the late 1940s, the company branched into elevator entrance manufacturing, hollow metal and metal specialties, subcontracting, and architectural services. In order to remain competitive in the manufacturing of elevator entrances and related custom steel fabrication, a new and modern manufacturing facility and offices were built at the company's current site in Minneapolis.

The next 50 years brought many changes for H&B—franchises were acquired, new growth opportunities were pursued, core businesses were refined, and businesses were sold.

Then, in 1989, the company refocused its efforts on four core businesses: H&B Hollow Metal, which provides a complete package of hollow metal doors and frames, wooden doors, and finished hardware; H&B Interiors, a general contracting company providing complete interior construction services for commercial, industrial, office, and retail businesses; H&B Specialized Products, a key distributor and installer of indoor and outdoor seating, casework, gymnasium equipment, folding partitions, and lockers; and H&B Elevators, which supplies custom cabs and entrances to the major elevator companies and to independent elevator companies throughout the United States and internationally.

Employee training and increased employee involvement have ignited a renewed sense of energy and enthusiasm among H&B's 150 employees. The company recently developed an aggressive five-year plan to help it become more market- and customer-driven, cost competitive, flexible,

and responsive. The long-term goal: to double total company revenues by 1999. "H&B has enormous potential and a bright future," says Johnston. "Through improved processes, improved technology, improved personnel, and improved skill levels from employees, we will continue to grow more productive and profitable. The entrepreneurial spirit that created this company in the beginning is still alive and well, and will continue to propel us forward."

H&B ELEVATORS SUPPLIES CUSTOM CABS AND ENTRANCES TO THE MAJOR ELEVATOR COMPANIES AND TO INDEPENDENT ELEVATOR COMPANIES THROUGHOUT THE UNITED STATES AND INTERNATIONALLY.

H&B CONTINUES TO GROW MORE PRODUCTIVE AND PROFITABLE, UTILIZING THE LATEST DESIGN TECHNOLOGY AVAILABLE.

FARIBAULT FOODS

S INCE 1895, FARIBAULT FOODS HAS BEEN SERVING ITS CUSTOMERS and the grocery industry with food products of the highest quality. The company's name and its brands—including Butter Kernel, Kuner's, Pride, Pasta Select, and Mrs. Grimes—have always stood for dependability, an unswerving commitment to customer service, and the highest ethical standards. "These remain our central values," says Chief Executive Officer

Reid MacDonald, whose great-grandfather, Charles A. Vandever, was one of the company's first presidents. "They have helped us achieve success for more than 100 years, and they will help us remain successful as we move into the 21st century."

A CENTURY OF PRODUCTS

The mission of Faribault Foods is to market a full line of canned vegetables, dry beans, pasta, and prepared food through strong regional brands and top private labels. Currently, the company is also developing and manufacturing a wide variety of great-tasting recipe-type products that match exact customer

CLOCKWISE FROM TOP: FARIBAULT FOODS BOASTS 100 YEARS OF INNOVATION, SERVICE, AND QUALITY.

EMPLOYEES IN THE FARIBAULT PLANT OVERSEE AIR CLEANING, WASHING, AND OPTICAL COLOR SORTING TO ENSURE A DEFECT-FREE AND ALWAYS DELICIOUS FINAL PRODUCT.

FARIBAULT SPICES ITS BEANS WITH JUST THE RIGHT BLEND OF INGREDIENTS.

specifications. "Our customers have every right to expect the best, starting with product quality," says MacDonald. "We encourage specific lot approval and do our utmost to match products with buyers' specifications."

Faribault Foods was originally founded in 1888 in the town of Faribault, Minnesota, as Faribault

Canning & Preserving Company by a group of local entrepreneurs and incorporated in 1895 as Faribault Canning Company. The company was sold to the Vandever family in 1917. Vegetables were the company's mainstay in the early years, and they remain the company's best-selling product. "We are blessed to be located in one of the world's finest

growing areas for specialty vegetables," says MacDonald.

Processing facilities in Faribault and Cokato, Minnesota, as well as in Mondovi, Wisconsin, ensure that vegetables can be harvested at the peak of perfection and canned under quality assurance standards that exceed federal and state regulatory requirements. "Our equipment, systems, and training programs are designed to build quality into our products—from the ground up," says MacDonald.

Faribault entered the dry bean business with the 1983 acquisition of Kuner's and the 1988 acquisition of Mrs. Grimes—market leaders in Colorado and Iowa, respectively. Using their existing products as a base, Faribault has developed one of the most diverse lines of plain and sauced beans available in the market today. "We source most of our raw stock in the upper Midwest through cooperative agreements with individual farmers that allow us to control both quality and price," says MacDonald. "We inspect the produce in the field, scan the beans optically in the plant, and then add spices from approved suppliers. The result is bean products of the highest quality, ideal for the full range of health, ethnic, spiced, and prepared food adaptations."

As pasta products became more

The company also can formulate other prepared food, such as soups, chilis, and stews. "We offer shrink-wrapped packaging and combined shipments with other Faribault products," says MacDonald. "And we will assist customers in developing packaging to meet their specifications." To produce these value-added products, the company recently built a stand-alone addition to its plant in Cokato. The new facility is USDA-approved for meat processing and operates under stringent, HACCP-driven quality standards.

In order to bring new products to market rapidly, Faribault has drawn from internal and external resources to form a team of recipe creators, food scientists, and plant engineers. This group offers proven expertise in prototyping, reiteration, thermal processes, scale-up, and commercialization. Because product matching is so critical in the private label business, the team's expertise in ingredient technology is invaluable.

center stocks its full assortment of products. A high-speed packaging equipment and pre-labeling system also speed up the process. All of Faribault's information systems are fully EDI-capable. And, as part of the company's normal follow-up on orders, Faribault keeps its customers informed on order status, labels, freight rates, carrier selection, and pickup/delivery appointments.

When Faribault doesn't produce a product, the company sources quality-approved, competitively priced products from its network of suppliers. "Our goal is to earn 'preferred supplier' status from all our customers," says MacDonald. "We know that competing on product and price alone isn't enough; superior customer service is what it takes to hone our edge over the competition."

And superior customer service starts and ends with people. "While our technical strengths are primary,

MEAT-FILLED RAVIOLI IS PRODUCED IN FARIBAULT'S COKATO PLANT (FAR LEFT).

THE FARIBAULT TEST KITCHEN PROVIDES ONGOING QUALITY ASSURANCE AND NEW PRODUCT DEVELOPMENT (NEAR RIGHT).

GREGORY EDWARDS

popular, Faribault moved to take advantage of the market trend. The company's research-and-development team created a line of canned pasta products that precisely matches the national brand leaders in ingredients, taste, color, and nutritional value. Now, customers can buy "children's" and "family-style" products from a single source.

A CENTURY OF SERVICE
MacDonald acknowledges that customer satisfaction is the cornerstone of Faribault's success, so he emphasizes that the company works hard to deliver the best service in the industry.

Once a customer places an order, Faribault moves fast. The company's centralized distribution

we also focus a good deal of our energies on cultivating an atmosphere of team spirit, respect, and enthusiasm among our people," says MacDonald. "We hope it shows—in our service as well as in our products. We are proud of Faribault and of the history behind this company. We look to the future with excitement and energy."

PIPER JAFFRAY COMPANIES INC., A MINNEAPOLIS-BASED INVESTMENT and financial services firm, has been serving clients, employees, shareholders, and communities in Minnesota and throughout the United States for more than 100 years. Addison "Tad" Piper, chief executive officer and chairman of the board, attributes the company's success to a strong belief in the company's mission statement: "By placing the interests of our clients first, we serve the best

interests of our employees, our shareholders, and our communities."

This mission expresses a vision shared by the more than 3,000 employees of Piper Jaffray Companies and its four subsidiaries: Piper Jaffray Inc., a full-service securities broker/dealer and investment banking firm with retail sales offices in 17 states and capital markets offices in 16 cities; Piper Capital Management Incorporated, a money management company; Piper Trust Company, a provider of trust services to individuals and institutions; and Piper Jaffray Ventures, a private equity venture capital firm focusing its investments in growth industry sectors. Piper Jaffray Inc. is a member of SIPC, the New York Stock Exchange, and other major stock exchanges.

SERVING CLIENT NEEDS

Piper Jaffray Companies started as a small commercial paper business serving a handful of companies at the turn of the century. The company expanded into investment banking in the 1930s and investment management and trust services in the 1980s. Today Piper Jaffray Companies and its four subsidiaries provide a wide range of products and services.

Piper Jaffray Inc.'s Individual Investor Services business unit works with individuals and small businesses to analyze their investment needs. Then, from the company's diverse array of products and services, investment executives help develop the appropriate investment plan to serve those needs.

Expanding its operations into the arena of investment banking, the company participated in major public offerings for such future corporate giants as 3M, Archer Daniels Midland, Greyhound, Honeywell, and Pillsbury. Today Piper Jaffray Inc.'s Equity Capital Markets group provides superior equity capital services to both issuers and investors. Teams of professionals in research, corporate finance, institutional sales, and trading focus on five key industry groups: Consumer, Financial Services, Health Care, Technology, and Industrial Growth. Within each industry area, the company covers emerging industry niches with high investment and growth potential.

Since 1991 the Securities Data Company, Inc. has ranked Piper Jaffray as the number one underwriter of Midwest long-term municipal new issues in terms of volume. This ranking is a reflection of the high-quality client-focused underwriting, trading, and sales services Piper Jaffray's Fixed Income Capital Markets group provides to public finance clients and investors. Products include both taxable and taxexempt financing using traditional and nontraditional approaches. The company's expertise includes specialized financing knowledge in state and local governments, health care, housing and real estate, school districts and higher education, municipal and private utilities, and corporate debt.

A wholly owned subsidiary of Piper Jaffray Companies, Piper Capital Management provides global money management services for individuals, corporations, and institutions.

CLOCKWISE FROM TOP RIGHT: PIPER JAFFRAY'S FIXED INCOME CAPITAL MARKETS GROUP PROVIDES HIGH-QUALITY CLIENT-FOCUSED UNDERWRITING, TRADING, AND SALES SERVICES TO PUBLIC FINANCE CLIENTS AND INVESTORS.

PIPER JAFFRAY INC.'S EQUITY CAPITAL MARKETS GROUP PROVIDES SUPERIOR EQUITY CAPITAL SERVICES TO BOTH ISSUERS AND INVESTORS.

PIPER JAFFRAY INC.'S INDIVIDUAL INVESTOR SERVICES BUSINESS UNIT WORKS WITH INDIVIDUALS AND SMALL BUSINESSES TO ANALYZE THEIR INVESTMENT NEEDS.

The company offers standard and custom portfolios, and domestic and international products. Piper Trust, also a wholly owned subsidiary of Piper Jaffray Companies, offers trustee, investment-management, and administrative services tailored to the goals of each individual, business, and institutional client. Piper Jaffray Ventures, also a wholly owned subsidiary of Piper Jaffray Companies, offers equity growth capital to emerging companies that are still in private stages of financing. Its investment focus is primarily in the health care and technology industries.

CELEBRATING A CENTURY OF SERVICE

It's not every day that a company turns 100, so when Piper Jaffray Companies achieved this milestone in 1995, employees decided to celebrate in style with a four-part Centennial Community Initiative. In offices throughout the country, employees assessed the needs in their communities; identified projects that would help build strong, healthy families; and selected nonprofit partners to help address these needs. Overall,

the company contributed nearly $1.4 million to 85 projects, and employee volunteers maximized the positive impact of the grants by adding their time, talents, and energies to each project. As a result of its volunteer efforts, Piper Jaffray Companies was among 10 companies across the nation recognized in 1995 by the Points of Light Foundation. The company also developed a Family Lecture Series to stimulate community debate on social issues that affect families.

The spirit of giving is part of a long-standing tradition at Piper Jaffray Companies. Each year, the

company dedicates 5 percent of its pretax profits to civic and charitable causes. Piper Jaffray Companies gives matching funds to the charities in which company employees or their family members are active participants. In 1996 the Greater Minneapolis Chamber of Commerce awarded Piper Jaffray Companies a Quality of Life Award for its efforts to enhance the quality of life of its employees, its customers, and the communities in which it serves.

During its second century of service, the focus of Piper Jaffray Companies will remain on the principles that have made the company a success: placing the interests of its clients first; maintaining a balanced approach that allows for growth opportunities in all market cycles; and hiring professional, knowledgeable, and experienced employees who help foster an environment in which everyone is given a stake in the future. "We believe our industry expertise and our commitment to the highest level of client service will continue to strengthen our national presence," says Piper, "as well as benefit the people right here in Minneapolis and the Midwest."

F

OR 100 YEARS, JOSTENS INC. HAS BEEN PROVIDING PRODUCTS and services that help people celebrate achievement, reward performance, recognize service, and commemorate experiences. When the Minnesota Twins won the World Series in 1987 and 1991, Jostens made the championship rings. The company also made the 1986 Super Bowl rings for the Chicago Bears, including William "The Refrigerator" Perry's size 23 diamond-encrusted hunk of gold that fit around a Kennedy half-dollar. In fact, Jostens has produced 19 of 30 Super Bowl rings and 23 National Football League conference championship rings, more than any other company.

When the *Cheers* television show ended in 1993 after 11 years on the air, Jostens created a photo memory book for those who had worked on the show. Jostens also created the medals for the 1984 Summer Olympic Games and the 1988 Winter Olympic Games. And the company crafted the NBA championship rings for the Chicago Bulls.

But the company's bread and butter is not the high-profile, celebrity work. Jostens is more about the memories of the kid next door.

MAKING MEMORIES

Jostens makes more than half of all high school yearbooks sold in the United States, sells class rings in about 40 percent of the country's high schools, and prints more than half of the nation's high school diplomas. The company, with headquarters in Minneapolis, also prints graduation announcements and makes caps and gowns. "People turn to Jostens because we're the best at helping them celebrate important moments and achievements throughout their lives," says Robert C. Buhrmaster, president and chief executive officer. "In short, we help create memories."

Jostens has come a long way since Otto Josten founded his watch repair business in 1897 in Owatonna, Minnesota, and began making emblems, awards, and class rings for schools. The company expanded its school products line in the 1940s and 1950s to include graduation announcements, diplomas, and yearbooks. In the 1960s and 1970s, Jostens moved into school photography, graduation caps and gowns, and business recognition awards. A decade later, it began making customized products for colleges, universities, and other groups.

Jostens became publicly owned in 1959 and has been listed on the New York Stock Exchange since 1965. The company now has more than 6,500 employees, some 1,000 independent sales agents, and more than 20 plant and office facilities throughout North America. Sales agents also serve 50 foreign countries, including a new joint venture in Chile.

CELEBRATING THE PAST, ANTICIPATING THE FUTURE

The year 1997 marks Jostens' 100-year anniversary—but even as the company celebrates its history, its vision is firmly focused on the future. "The future entails building on our current business strengths and viewing our

IN 1897, OTTO JOSTEN OPENED A SMALL JEWELRY AND WATCH REPAIR SHOP ABOVE AN OPERA HOUSE IN OWATONNA, MINNESOTA. TODAY, JOSTENS SERVES CUSTOMERS WORLDWIDE, WITH 1996 SALES OF ABOUT $700 MILLION.

customers differently—not just as students or company employees, but as customers for life," says Buhrmaster. "That's a big change, requiring us to develop new ways to identify and reach customers. People participate in many organizations, activities, and associations—and all are opportunities for Jostens to help celebrate important moments and achievements."

With spending on employee awards by U.S. companies increasing, Jostens' Recognition business segment is developing programs and services in this growing market. Jostens helps companies create programs to provide incentives and recognition for employees who meet specific objectives important to the company's success, in addition to traditional service awards.

The company is also utilizing digital technology in its photography and publishing businesses, enabling Jostens to produce smaller, customized memory books for such special occasions as cheerleader camps and reunions.

Jostens recently introduced a "new millennium" line of 12 class rings aimed at students graduating around the turn of the century. "Research indicates that, as the new millennium approaches, year-dated

materials will become more important to consumers," says Buhrmaster. "And since most of our school-related business involves preserving memories with year-dated products, the millennium offers us a natural and unique opportunity to reach customers."

As part of its forward-looking vision, Jostens has spent the last several years modernizing its systems and refocusing on its strengths. The strategy seems to be working. In 1996 Jostens experienced record sales in its largest businesses: Printing &

Publishing, Jewelry, and Graduation Products. The Recognition business doubled its operating profits, and the company ended the year with record fourth-quarter sales and earnings.

All of this suggests a good start to Jostens' second hundred years. "As we move ahead, we will continue to take steps to simplify and focus on the things that truly add value for our customers throughout their lives," says Buhrmaster. "We've been helping to create memories for 100 years. And we plan to continue doing so for the next 100 as well."

JOSTENS HAS PROVIDED PRODUCTS FOR OLYMPIC CHAMPIONS, SUPER BOWL WINNERS, AND MORE THAN HALF OF ALL U.S. HIGH SCHOOL STUDENTS WHO COMMEMORATE THEIR SCHOOL YEARS WITH CLASS RINGS, DIPLOMAS, AWARDS, AND YEARBOOKS (TOP).

CAPTURING THE MEMORIES OF A LIFETIME IS WHAT JOSTENS DOES BEST. MEMORY BOOKS CELEBRATE SPECIAL OCCASIONS AND EVENTS, FROM SPORTS CAMPS AND REUNIONS TO CORPORATE GATHERINGS (BOTTOM).

MAKING THE WORLD 5 PERCENT BETTER, EVERY DAY" IS THE credo of the Dayton Hudson Corporation. For 50 years, the company—which operates Target, Mervyn's California, Dayton's, Hudson's, and Marshall Field's stores—has enriched the lives of people everywhere through its dedication to quality, fashion, and value, and an extraordinary commitment to the communities in which it does business. ✳ In 1902 a

Worthington, Minnesota, banker named George Draper Dayton began selling dry goods from a six-story building on the corner of Nicollet and Seventh Street in downtown Minneapolis. He built his business on the principles of customer satisfaction, liberal credit and return policies, and service, and over the years he developed a reputation in the retail industry that few other retailers have been able to match.

As well as a commitment to quality products and service, Dayton focused on giving back to the communities in which he did business. Dayton once wrote: "The thrills of relieving distress, of encouraging the young, of easing the footsteps of the weary—are these rewards not greater than the knowledge you have added thousands of dollars to your hoard? Success by contribution is open to every one. Success by acquisition is possible only to a comparatively few."

As far back as 1909, Dayton and his wife set aside $500,000 for charitable purposes. In 1917 Dayton established the Dayton Foundation, which supported such organizations as the YMCA, YWCA, and Salvation Army, as well as arts organizations and movements designed to improve interracial relations.

By 1946 six of Dayton's grandsons had joined the firm. Charitable giving had been substantial but irregular up to this point, so the decision was made to standardize the amount donated each year. The family set the annual giving amount at 5 percent of pretax profits—the maximum permitted by federal law. This generous policy is still adhered to today.

CLOCKWISE FROM TOP RIGHT: DAYTON HUDSON CORPORATION'S LONG-STANDING TRADITION OF GIVING BACK TO ITS COMMUNITIES HELPS STRENGTHEN FAMILIES, CREATING A BRIGHTER FUTURE FOR LOTS OF CHILDREN WITH DREAMS.

MORE THAN 200 DAYTON HUDSON TEAM MEMBERS AND THEIR FAMILIES PARTICIPATED IN THE GREAT TWIN CITIES CLEANUP, HELPING TO TURN THIS LITTERED CORRIDOR INTO PUBLIC WALKING AND BIKING PATHS.

EACH YEAR TARGET TEAM MEMBERS, IN PARTNERSHIP WITH HABITAT FOR HUMANITY, GIVE MUSCLE AND HEART TO BUILD DOZENS OF HOMES FOR FAMILIES IN NEED.

Some years ago, a survey identified the Dayton family as the "greatest positive influence on the evolution of the Twin Cities area as a vital, civilized, and attractive place to live." Few could argue with that distinction.

New Name, Old Values

In 1969 the Dayton Corporation merged with J.L. Hudson to form the Dayton Hudson Corporation, and the foundation was renamed the Dayton Hudson Foundation. Maintaining an emphasis on service to customers and communities, the Dayton Hudson Corporation today is the nation's fourth-largest general merchandise retailer, operating more than 1,100 stores in 35 states.

Dayton Hudson's generosity extends throughout its three operating companies—Target, an upscale discount store that provides quality merchandise at attractive prices in clean, spacious, and guest-friendly stores in 39 states nationwide; Mervyn's California, a 295-chain middle-market promotional department store that offers name-brand and private-label casual apparel and home soft goods in 16 states; and the Department Store Division, which offers trend leadership, quality merchandise, and superior service through 64 Dayton's, Hudson's, and Marshall Field's stores in nine states.

The company remains committed to its formula of making the world 5 percent better every day, and each operating company focuses its efforts in areas where it can make a difference in each community. "At Dayton Hudson, we've seen what 5 percent of our dollars can do," says Bob Ulrich, chairman and chief executive officer of Dayton Hudson Corporation. "We've watched communities prosper when businesses, nonprofit organizations, and neighbors work together. Through the past five decades, the causes have changed and the communities have evolved. We've worked hard to remain responsive to the ever changing needs of our customers, and will continue to do so as long as we're doing business."

Celebrating 50 Years of Giving

The Dayton Hudson Foundation philosophy states, in part, "[we] believe that philanthropy must help devise better solutions to improve the environments of those people living in the areas where we do busi-

ness." The Foundation accomplishes this goal by focusing on the arts and on social action programs—two significant areas that substantially contribute to the well-being of citizens and the economic development of their communities.

In 1996 Dayton Hudson announced its 50th anniversary of giving 5 percent of its federally taxable income to support nonprofit organizations. Since 1946, the retailer has contributed more than $350 million—or the equivalent of $19,000 a day—which is a record unmatched by any other retailer. To help celebrate the anniversary, teams of employee volunteers at more than 1,000 Dayton Hudson locations across the country planned and completed community service projects in their own neighborhoods on June 22. Called the Day of Giving, it was a special opportunity for team members and their families to join together to help their communities where help was most needed.

"We believe that it is our responsibility to help improve and build on the strengths of the communities in which we live and work," says Ulrich. "We hope that our efforts have encouraged and will continue to encourage other companies to support their communities with financial contributions and volunteer support, because as more companies contribute, it will really make a difference for all of us."

To that end, Ulrich sees the anniversary as a commitment to the future, as well as a celebration of the past. "There's no way to put a dollar value on what giving means to Dayton Hudson's business," says Ulrich. "Unquestionably, it creates goodwill, encourages customer support, and appeals to potential employees seeking socially responsible employers. It also improves the environment in which companies operate, and it strengthens the future of free enterprise. We believe that the business of business is much more than just making money," he continues. "And we will continue to operate with that philosophy in mind."

CLOCKWISE FROM TOP LEFT: HAVE BRUSH, WILL PAINT. TEAM MEMBERS PITCH IN TO SPRUCE UP HOMES OF ELDERLY RESIDENTS AS PART OF THE YEARLY PAINT-A-THON PROJECT.

IN 1996 DAYTON HUDSON CELEBRATED WHAT 50 YEARS OF GIVING 5 PERCENT OF COMPANY INCOME CAN DO.

IN METRO DETROIT MORE THAN 400 TEAM MEMBERS SPENT A SATURDAY PAINTING, PLANTING, AND PRUNING AT THE WATERFORD SENIOR CENTER.

DAYTON HUDSON'S COMMITMENT TO KIDS MEANS P.J. HUGGABEE WILL HELP COMFORT A CHILD ENTERING THE FOSTER CARE SYSTEM, AND THE ALL-AROUND SCHOLARSHIP WILL HELP A COMMUNITY-SERVICE-MINDED HIGH SCHOOLER REALIZE DREAMS OF HIGHER EDUCATION.

IN 1905 NORWEGIAN LUTHERAN IMMIGRANTS AND THEIR PASTORS formed the United Church Association with hopes of building a hospital near Fairview Park in north Minneapolis. Although the facility that eventually resulted from their fund-raising efforts opened in Riverside Park in 1916, it was given the Fairview name in honor of the association's original dreams. Today, Fairview is comprised of urban, suburban, and rural health care facilities across Minnesota.

A SYSTEM OF HEALTH CARE

Through its network of hospitals, clinics, ambulatory care programs, and affiliated physicians, Fairview offers high-quality preventive, primary, specialty, acute, and long-term care, as well as home care services in a coordinated, cost-effective manner. In the process, Fairview's 14,000-plus employees embrace core values and the principles of continuous quality improvement as a way of life. Fairview is also a partner with Fairview Physician Associates, a 750-member physician-driven care system.

The Fairview system includes Fairview Southdale Hospital in Edina; Fairview Ridges Hospital in Burnsville; Fairview Northland Regional Hospital in Princeton; the newly merged Fairview-University Medical Center in Minneapolis; University Medical Center-Mesabi in Hibbing; and Fairview Lakes Regional Medical Center, a combining of facilities in Chisago City, Forest Lake, and Rush City that will create a new regional medical center opening in Wyoming, Minnesota, in early 1998.

Fairview also owns and operates 30 clinics. Ambulatory care services at those sites are supplemented by 20 sports medicine, 22 behavioral, 12 retail pharmacy, and six orthopedic laboratory locations in the Twin Cities and surrounding areas. In 1995 Fairview affiliated with the Ebenezer Society, which operates four skilled-nursing and 13 senior housing facilities, and is a leader in long-term care.

INNOVATIONS AND GROWTH

Over the years, the Fairview name has been linked with many innovations in the management of health care, including the first full-service satellite hospital, Fairview Southdale in suburban Edina. President Emeritus Carl Platou pioneered the concept of a hospital holding company in 1971 as a response to the need for medical cost containment. And Fairview has been a leader in the sharing of hospital services: pediatrics and open-heart surgery between downtown Fairview and adjacent St. Mary's hospitals (before the two institutions merged to become Fairview Riverside); dialysis equipment between Fairview Southdale and Methodist Hospital in neighboring St. Louis Park; and pediatrics between Fairview Ridges Hospital and Children's Health Care.

In an environment characterized by shifting legislative priorities, the changing complexion of human services delivery, and an almost constant reshuffling of provider relationships, Fairview has responded with swift-

FAIRVIEW-UNIVERSITY MEDICAL CENTER PROVIDES A FULL RANGE OF HIGH-TECH SERVICES, AS WELL AS A STRONG EDUCATION AND RESEARCH FOCUS.

ness and innovation. Its Community Health Plan, for example, in partnership with Group Health, provided a system of care for uninsured people in transition, serving as a model that was replicated by the state of Minnesota.

So it came as no surprise when it was announced that the University of Minnesota Academic Health Centers would affiliate with the Fairview health system and that the University of Minnesota Hospital and Clinic (UMHC) would merge with the Fairview health system, adding a premier research and teaching hospital to Fairview's already outstanding system of health care facilities. Fairview-University Medical Center functions on two campuses as a single, Fairview-run entity, much like Fairview Southdale or Fairview Lakes Regional Medical Center.

MERGER PROVIDES COMPREHENSIVE PROGRAM

As a result of the merger, Fairview now offers patients a comprehensive range of coordinated services—from illness and injury prevention to treatment of the most unusual and complex medical cases. The center supports and expands the university's

education and research mission in a market-driven environment in which the university found it hard to compete as a stand-alone organization.

"Our goal has always been to create a high-quality, cost-effective, and accessible health care system," says Richard Norling, Fairview president and CEO. "We've never been afraid to take the steps necessary to help us achieve that goal. This is an exciting time for Fairview. This affiliation and merger is good for Fairview, it's good for the university, and it's good for the community as a whole."

Norling notes that Fairview has been working for some time toward a fully integrated system that allows patients to easily arrange for service and receive the care they need at any point in their lives, anywhere in the system. "Now we have a partner, the university, to fill out the range of services we provide," Norling says. "Our tradition of commitment to the communities we serve continues to inspire creative improvements in the quality of medical care and service to create value for patients and physicians alike."

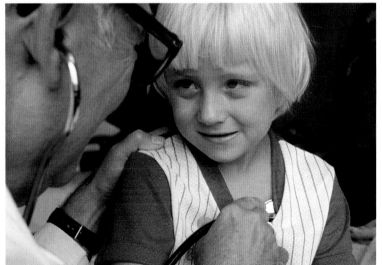

FAIRVIEW'S HEALTH CARE NETWORK INCLUDES FAIRVIEW PHYSICIAN ASSOCIATES, A GROUP OF NEARLY 750 PRIMARY AND SPECIALTY CARE DOCTORS WORKING IN NEIGHBORHOOD CLINICS THROUGHOUT THE AREA.

FAIRVIEW HAS ESTABLISHED PARTNERSHIPS WITH A VARIETY OF COMMUNITY-BASED ORGANIZATIONS TO WORK ON HEALTH CARE ISSUES THAT AFFECT THE PEOPLE THE SYSTEM SERVES.

W HEN MERRITT POND STARTED THE ADVANCE MACHINE Shop in 1910, the business repaired equipment for the grain milling industry in Minneapolis. The company's employees worked out of a small wooden building with a dirt floor located at 2613 Southeast Fourth Street, not far from the mills. ✳ To grow the business in the 1920s, Advance started machining repair parts for terrazzo floor grinders.

CLOCKWISE FROM TOP RIGHT: THE LOCATION OF ALL ADVANCE DEPARTMENTS AND FACILITIES IN ONE PLYMOUTH-BASED COMPLEX HAS ALLOWED THE DEVELOPMENT OF A TEAM MANAGEMENT APPROACH, ENSURING COOPERATION BETWEEN THE SALES AND MARKETING FUNCTIONS, AND THE MANUFACTURING AND ENGINEERING FUNCTIONS.

TODAY, ADVANCE EMPLOYS MORE THAN 600 PEOPLE AND MARKETS OVER 100 DIFFERENT MODELS OF FLOOR CLEANING AND MAINTENANCE EQUIPMENT THROUGH A NETWORK OF SOME 500 ADVANCE DISTRIBUTORS.

ADVANCE STARTED MANUFACTURING AUTOMATIC FLOOR SCRUBBING MACHINES SIMILAR TO THIS ONE IN THE EARLY 1950S.

Soon it started building its own terrazzo grinder, which became an industry standard by 1930. This early involvement in the floor industry set the course for the company's future, as Advance soon started making floor cleaning and polishing machines on a private label basis. Next, Advance manufactured and sold its own brand of floor machine, called Lowboy for its ability to "reach under" desks and furniture. With this solid start in the floor cleaning industry, Advance was able to survive the Great Depression of the 1930s.

From 1941 to 1945, Advance put its efforts into helping the American cause in World War II by making parts for B-17 bombsights. After the war, Advance decided to diversify its product line, expanding the floor machine models and adding wet-dry vacuums, automatic scrubbers, and eventually carpet cleaning equipment. As a result, the company firmly established its reputation as an industry leader in the innovation and development of floor care equipment.

GROWTH

The company's diversification led to a broad line of carpet and hard-floor cleaning products, which still make up the foundation of its Commercial Division. In 1974, Advance established its Industrial Division with the manufacture and sale of large heavy-duty rider sweepers and scrubbers. This presented a significant growth opportunity for the company that continues today.

Ground was broken and construction was begun in 1985 on the main building at Advance's Plymouth location. The new construction consolidated Advance corporate headquarters, manufacturing, and distribution, bringing all U.S. facilities together in the 500,000-square-foot complex. The location of all Advance departments and facilities in one complex has allowed the development of a team management approach, ensuring cooperation between the sales and marketing functions, and the manufacturing and engineering functions. The team concept is also used in conjunction with the dealer organization to form trust, cooperation, and long-term partnerships.

New Ownership

From the beginning, Advance was a family-owned corporation started by Merritt Pond, who passed ownership on to his son Harold Pond, who passed it on to his son Robert J. Pond. In 1989 Robert Pond sold the company to a group of financial investors. Five years later, Advance merged with Nilfisk A/S, a well-known Danish company manufacturing a broad line of industrial and commercial vacuum cleaners marketed worldwide.

Today, Advance employs more than 600 people and markets over 100 different models of floor cleaning and maintenance equipment through a network of approximately 500 Advance distributors in North and South America, the Far East, Australia, and New Zealand. European, Middle Eastern, and South African sales and marketing activities are managed through a network of Nilfisk subsidiaries.

Keeping Ahead of the Competition

Any company that can thrive for nearly 90 years is undoubtedly doing something right. Advance President Jack Cooney can think of several things his company is doing that set it apart from the competition. For starters, "Advance is especially proud of its manufacturing technology, which is unparalleled in the floor maintenance industry. As a vertically integrated manufacturer, Advance fabricates most product components and assembles products internally. This permits close monitoring of product quality throughout the manufacturing process."

Cooney goes on to say that this manufacturing process involves state-of-the-art technology and machinery, operated by skilled Advance technicians who turn raw stock into thousands of different product components, often with microscopic precision. The computerized powder-coat painting system automatically and efficiently moves parts through the proper paint booths and ovens with consistent quality.

The manufacturing process was converted from assembly line to a cellular system of manufacturing over a one-year period in 1993, allowing greater flexibility and tremendous improvements in quality. Final products are team assembled in cells before packaging and shipping to national and international destinations. According to Cooney, the use of this team concept "ensures the highest-quality productivity and value to Advance customers."

Advance also focuses a good deal of resources and energy on dealer training programs. The company invented the concept of Mechanized Maintenance Seminars, and provides both in-plant training and home-study courses to ensure that dealers are knowledgeable about the Advance products they sell.

Changing for the Future

Looking ahead, Cooney says, "We are on the brink of a technology transformation within the floor cleaning equipment industry that's going to affect every aspect of our business from marketing and manufacturing to delivery, sales, and service. The key is going to be tying this technology to customer needs. That's what feeds innovation in equipment and value-added services."

Advance is intensely focused on the customer, and continually collects a mix of input from market segments, dealers, and field sales representatives. Information gathered is studied and analyzed to recognize needs and trends, which in turn drive innovation in equipment and value-added services.

Sophisticated CAD/CAM engineering systems convert this information to manufacturing technology such as artificial intelligence, laser cutters, and robot welders. This technology, according to Cooney, results in consistent reliability while compressing production time. "We expect quick-paced change from decision maker desktops to the factory floor," states Cooney, "so our dealers can respond to their customers' equipment needs."

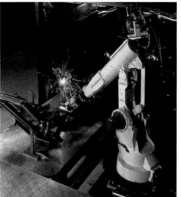

Other marketing services include education and training of both dealer sales and service personnel, as well as those who use the products.

The ability to communicate sales and marketing information with a strong dealer network is crucial, and Advance uses electronic data exchange technology to streamline that process. Computerized communication through internet and intranet will help both Advance and its dealers respond to changes and decisions as they are made.

Cooney believes developing technology continues to make the manufacturing and business outlook for the next century exciting with new challenges. "We don't approach the future with the idea of adapting to change," says Cooney, "but rather with the idea of creating it. Proactive choices in using the right tools and resources to manufacture the right products will make Advance a viable force in this marketplace well into the future."

Clockwise from top: Advance is a very vertically integrated manufacturer making 80 percent of product parts in-house, such as this rotationally molded tank.

Advance's manufacturing process involves state-of-the-art technology and machinery, operated by skilled technicians who turn raw stock into thousands of different product components.

Advance Machine Company operates one of the most technologically modern manufacturing facilities in the industry.

THE SAINT PAUL HOTEL

CHARLES LINDBERGH WAS A FREQUENT GUEST. SO WERE F. SCOTT and Zelda Fitzgerald. Even President William Taft rented a room during his visit. The fact is, everyone who was anyone stayed at The Saint Paul Hotel when they came to the city. It's nice to know that some things never change. ✳ As far back as 1908, St. Paul's leading businessmen realized the importance of a luxury hotel to the city's development. In a grand gesture, successful

entrepreneur Lucius P. Ordway challenged the business community with a pledge of $1 million if the St. Paul Business League would donate a site on Rice Park in the heart of St. Paul for construction of a new hotel. The challenge was accepted.

Determined that the new hotel would be of exceptional quality and design, the business leaders commissioned the New York firm of Reed and Stem, architects for Grand Central Station, to create the showcase hotel. The firm did not disappoint. When it opened its doors on April 8, 1910, The Saint Paul Hotel featured the latest in hotel comforts for its guests: a view from every room, a roof garden, a grand ballroom, and a fine dining room. It boasted 284 solid porcelain bathtubs and 300 washstands. Not unlike today, the hotel became the city's center of activity, popular not only with travelers for its fine guest accommodations, but also with local citizens for dining, entertaining, and celebrating.

The hotel fell on hard times in the 1970s, experiencing several management changeovers and, eventually,

complete shutdown in the summer of 1979. Fortunately, fate intervened in 1982, much as it had 70 years earlier, when the business community again realized the importance of a premier downtown hotel, and a $20 million refurbishing effort was soon under way.

DESTINATION: LUXURY

Today, The Saint Paul Hotel is again the crown jewel in the heart of downtown St. Paul. Restored to its original splendor, the hotel welcomes

business travelers with a unique combination of turn-of-the-century charm and modern-day convenience for the traveler.

Overlooking Rice Park, an oasis of beauty in a bustling metropolis, The Saint Paul Hotel is within walking distance of the renowned Ordway Music Theatre, historic Landmark Center, Roy Wilkins Auditorium, and St. Paul Convention Center. The city's indoor skyway system links the hotel to business, retail, and entertainment venues. The

CLOCKWISE FROM TOP RIGHT: THE SAINT PAUL HOTEL IS THE CROWN JEWEL IN THE HEART OF DOWNTOWN ST. PAUL.

DINERS LOOKING FOR DELICIOUS FOOD IN A CREATIVE SETTING FAVOR THE AMBIENCE OF THE CAFE.

THE ST. PAUL GRILL HAS BEEN CALLED ST. PAUL'S PREMIER DINING SPOT FOR ITS HIGH-QUALITY, UNPRETENTIOUS MENU ITEMS OFFERED AT A GOOD VALUE.

Minneapolis/St. Paul Airport, Mall of America, Metrodome, Target Center, and all that the Twin Cities have to offer are within a short drive with easy access via interstate highways I-94 and I-35. Complimentary shuttles to nearby business and entertainment centers are also provided.

Seven function rooms can accommodate up to 260 people for meetings and 350 for banquets. In addition, seven suites are available for smaller, private meetings. Each meeting room features independent lighting and temperature controls, multiple electrical and sound hookups, and private phone lines, and is wired and networked for audiovisual equipment.

Each guest room radiates the warmth, comfort, intimacy, and attention to detail that's expected of a grand hotel. There is fine art in every room, luxurious furnishings, and panoramic views. Other hotel amenities include daily turndown service, complimentary newspaper delivered to the room, complimentary coffee in the lobby, 24-hour security, full-time concierge services, indoor parking and valet service, a gift shop, and an exercise equipment in-room delivery program.

Unique to guests of The Saint Paul Hotel is the opportunity to indulge in afternoon tea. Held year round in the hotel lobby on select

days, the afternoon tea features live piano music; traditional tea scones, finger sandwiches, and sweets; and a chance for guests to step back to a more civilized time, if only for a moment.

Pastries aren't the only delicacies served at The Saint Paul Hotel. In fact, the hotel's two award-winning restaurants are known throughout the Twin Cities for upscale dining. The St. Paul Grill is a classic urban American grill restaurant and bar overlooking Rice Park. The Grill has one of the most extensive wine lists in the Twin Cities as well as one of the largest and most unique single malt scotch selections.

The Cafe is a cozy full-service restaurant featuring American regional cuisine. The menu combines time-honored American classics with the best of current trends in the U.S. culinary scene. It is comprised of selections that come from the South, Southwest, Heartland, Gulf Coast, East Coast, Pacific Northwest, and California regions. The Cafe is also considered a favorite place for breakfast by hotel guests and the local business community. Its consistent high standards for food and beverage quality and for service in its extensive catering business are carried out both in the hotel and at other sites around town.

The Saint Paul Hotel is the only Twin Cities hotel to be a member of the Historic Hotels of America, an exclusive association of 123 hotels throughout the country recognized for their historic character, their architectural quality, and the outstanding preservation efforts of their owners and managers.

Another of the hotel's distinguishing features is the beautifully designed English Cottage Garden that greets guests and visitors to the hotel in a most welcoming way. "Our goal is always to add value for our guests and to enhance the experience of staying at The Saint Paul Hotel," says Pam Schlemmer, director of marketing. "We want to create the quality standard and continue to earn our reputation as the luxury hotel in the Twin Cities."

THE SAINT PAUL HOTEL OFFERS 254 SPLENDIDLY APPOINTED GUEST ROOMS OR SPACIOUS SUITES REFLECTING THE CHARM AND GRACE OF AN ERA GONE BY (TOP LEFT AND TOP RIGHT).

THE SAINT PAUL HOTEL, WHICH OPENED IN 1910, WAS DESIGNED BY THE PREMIER ARCHITECTURAL FIRM OF REED AND STEM (LEFT).

ELECTRICITY IS ONE ASPECT OF LIFE OFTEN TAKEN FOR GRANTED. People flip on switches, plug in appliances, and adjust thermostats without much thought. But it hasn't always been that way. ✳ Waterwheels had been creating power for flour mills along the Mississippi since the middle of the century, but it wasn't until 1882 that electricity was first available for Twin Cities' homes and businesses. That year, the Minnesota Brush Electric Company

built a small hydroelectric station on St. Anthony Falls—one of the first hydro plants in the Western Hemisphere. Its inception marked the beginning of a new—and brighter—era.

In the Midwest, early electric generating plants were small and usually privately owned by men from the gas light business. But after the turn of the century, an easterner named Henry Byllesby began buying small power plants all over the Midwest. In Minnesota, Byllesby organized the Washington County Light and Power Company, bought the Stillwater Gas and Electric Company, and united the two as the Consumers Power Company in 1909.

In 1912, Byllesby added the Minneapolis Electric Company, formerly the Minnesota Brush Electric Company, which a year earlier had begun supplying its first coal-generated power from its new Riverside power plant. The new company was renamed Northern States Power Company (NSP) in 1916.

Today, with a net income of some $276 million and nearly 7,000

JERRY MILLER

employees, NSP is a major influence in the Twin Cities area.

A Far-Reaching Vision

NSP has long been known for its sound decisions and forward-looking vision. "So many of the decisions we make have the potential to have far-reaching, long-term consequences," says NSP Chairman, President, and Chief Executive Officer James J. Howard. "We need to be constantly looking forward, to be anticipating how things will be in five, 10, 20 years down the line."

One of the most significant of those visionary actions was NSP's

decision to merge with Wisconsin Energy Corporation (WEC) to form Primergy Corporation, a registered public utility holding company. Primergy will operate generation, transmission, and distribution facilities, providing electricity to nearly 2.3 million customers in Minnesota, Wisconsin, North Dakota, South Dakota, and Michigan. The company will also distribute natural gas to more than 750,000 customers in Minnesota, Wisconsin, North Dakota, and Michigan, and provide a variety of energy-related services throughout these regions.

NSP understands that low-cost electricity drives the region's economy. The merger will help keep rates competitive, which is the primary reason NSP and WEC decided to merge.

The merger will also help NSP grow and thrive in today's competitive environment, says Howard. "Because customers want more choices, and utilities will no longer enjoy monopolistic service territories, a merger of equals such as NSP and WEC makes sense," he continues. "Our expectation with Primergy is to achieve greater efficiencies and savings of about $2 billion over 10 years. These savings will help ensure competitive rates over the long term, which will strengthen the area economy and retain businesses and jobs."

In environmental protection, NSP has also been ahead of the times. More than 20 years ago the company began installing air pollution control equipment at coal-burning power plants to reduce sulfur dioxide emissions. The company reduced its sulfur dioxide emissions by 75 percent even as it

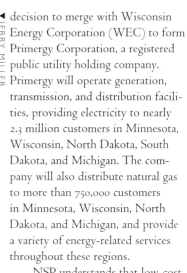

BETH THEISEN, PHOTOGRAPHER

JAMES J. HOWARD, CHAIRMAN, PRESIDENT, AND CHIEF EXECUTIVE OFFICER OF NSP

NSP IS A MAJOR SPONSOR OF THE ANNUAL TWIN CITIES UNITED NEGRO COLLEGE FUND WALK-A-THON AND HAS WON THE JUDSON BEMIS VISIONARY AWARD SEVERAL YEARS IN A ROW FOR RAISING THE MOST PLEDGE DOLLARS.

produced 60 percent more power with fossil fuels. Through this proactive approach, NSP also minimized the cost of meeting federal Clean Air Act requirements, passed by Congress in 1990, for 2000 and beyond.

NSP is proud of its commitment to economic development and its history of community involvement. The company recognizes that its success as an energy provider is directly linked to the success of the communities and businesses it serves. NSP offers a comprehensive set of programs to support economic development, improve education, and strengthen communities in the service territory. Its corporate contributions program targets grants toward empowering disadvantaged people to improve their lives, as well as the life of the larger community.

Poised for the Future

Howard points out that NSP's proactive business philosophy will be integral to the company's success, as industry restructuring at the state and federal levels continues to increase competition. "More open electric markets will enable commercial, industrial, and even residential customers to choose their energy suppliers," says Howard. "We want them to choose NSP." To make

this choice even more attractive to customers, NSP is investing in new technologies to improve productivity and customer service.

"We are well positioned for an intensely competitive future," says Howard. "We are committed to providing high-quality service

to our customers at low rates. We also will maintain our long-standing commitment to the environment and to the health and well-being of the communities we serve. We look forward to meeting the needs and expectations of our customers well into the next century."

CLOCKWISE FROM TOP LEFT: EMPLOYEES WORK HARD TO DELIVER SAFE, RELIABLE, COMPETITIVELY PRICED ELECTRICITY.

NSP'S GAS UTILITY SUPPLIES ST. PAUL AND ITS SURROUNDING AREA WITH NATURAL GAS AND RELATED ENERGY SERVICES.

THE RIVERSIDE COAL-FIRED ELECTRIC GENERATING PLANT NEAR DOWNTOWN MINNEAPOLIS IS PART OF THE NSP SYSTEM.

WHEN SHELDON WOOD FOUNDED MINNEAPOLIS ELECTRIC Steel Castings Co., predecessor to M E International, Inc., he began a philosophy of producing quality products that continues today. Such quality has helped make M E International a leading supplier of consumable wear parts for the mineral processing industry worldwide. ✳ The Wood family owned and operated the business in Minneapolis until 1971 when it was sold to Evans Products Company. The business grew rapidly during the 1970s, including an expansion of the Minneapolis facility in 1975. In 1976, with no room for expansion at the Minneapolis site and a projected doubling of market demand, the Evans Products Company approved the construction of an additional state-of-the-art manufacturing facility in Duluth.

In July 1980 the first casting was poured at the Duluth plant, which is the largest steel foundry built in North America since the 1940s. The Duluth facility produces alloy steel and white iron wear parts ranging in size from 200 to 16,000 pounds. Its unique vacuum molding process (V-Process) capability, experience, and proprietary technology combine to yield the world's largest tonnage of abrasion-resistant castings for mineral processing applications. The V-Process uses vacuum to hold the sand in place, eliminating the need for binders used in traditional foundries. This process improves product quality by producing a casting with a clean, well-defined surface finish and improved, accurate dimensions; it also provides improved control of the process. In addition, the process eliminates smoke and fumes from the pouring bay of the plant, creating a better work environment.

AN EMPLOYEE TAPS 25,000-POUND HEAT AT M E INTERNATIONAL'S DULUTH, MINNESOTA, FACILITY (RIGHT).

M E INTERNATIONAL'S WORLDWIDE BUSINESS ACTIVITY IS MANAGED FROM ITS CORPORATE OFFICE IN MINNEAPOLIS (BELOW).

The company's future brightened even more in 1987 when two steel companies, Armco Inc. and Stelco, announced a joint venture buyout. The joint venture consolidated the equipment and inventory from the Minneapolis operation into the Duluth plant and renamed the joint venture M E International. M E International acquired an additional facility in Tempe, Arizona, in April 1994. Like the Duluth facility, the Tempe facility produces alloy steel and white iron wear parts. Its No-Bake molding system provides wear parts with extremely tight tolerances coupled with excellent surface finish.

In 1994 GS Technologies (formerly Armco Grinding Systems) acquired the balance of M E International and subsequently merged with Georgetown Industries in 1995 to form GS Industries—now the parent company of M E International.

Raising the Standards

Throughout the company's history, key decisions have shaped its future as the largest producer of grinding mill liners in the world. In the 1960s there was a change in the company's business strategy that placed emphasis on servicing the mining industry. M E International offers metallurgical and design engineering services along with top-quality cast wear parts. The company works closely with its customers to improve grinding mill production, developing designs and choosing alloys that will extend liner life and reduce downtime. Sales engineers begin the process by analyzing a mill's requirements and offering suggestions for improved casting applications. M E International can then create a new design resulting in more consistent, reliable wear parts.

M E International focuses on a very narrow market segment within the foundry industry, but the company is known worldwide for producing mill liners that are very cost effective. M E International is committed to producing high-quality castings, rather than large quantities of castings.

Such commitment to quality is evident throughout every manufacturing step and sets the company apart from its competition. Second only to energy costs, liners are often the highest consumable cost for a grinding mill. Liners must fit, they

must be durable, they must wear consistently, and they must be easy to change out. For the past 75 years, M E International customers have known that they can count on these requirements being met.

The numbers tell the story: 1995 was a record year in gross sales in terms of both dollars and tons. And customers aren't the only ones who are noticing M E International's commitment to quality. In January 1996 M E International's Minnesota locations obtained ISO 9000 certification. The Minneapolis location was awarded ISO 9001 certification, which, in addition to a quality system for quality assurance in production and installation of a product, includes the requirements for design. M E International currently is the

only North American foundry producing mill liners with ISO 9001 certification.

What are M E International's plans as it heads into the next century? The company confidently strides towards fulfilling its goal of being the leading supplier of grinding mill liners and other consumable wear parts for the mining industry worldwide. Historically, the company has raised the industry standard for quality and innovation and will continue to do so. The company's responsiveness to customer needs and the reliability of its products have given it a solid foundation for success, and M E International plans to continue to build on that foundation both domestically and in the international marketplace.

Clockwise from top left: The Duluth foundry was dedicated in 1980.

M E International produces such alloy steel and white iron wear parts as this new mill liner, shown here with a worn mill liner.

A customer and an M E International employee inspect mill liner profiles.

M

INNEAPOLIS-BASED UPSHER-SMITH LABORATORIES, INC. MAY not be the largest pharmaceutical manufacturer around or the most well known. But the company's reputation—along with its annual sales—has continued to grow steadily over the past 20 years as it has found its niche in the industry and settled in for a long stay. ✳ The company, founded in 1919 by a British pharmacist named F.A. Upsher-Smith, manufactures

value-added, branded generic medications—off-patent prescription and nonprescription drugs in various forms. "We're positioned midway between the generic companies and the major branded pharmaceuticals," says Ken Evenstad, chairman and chief executive officer, whose wife is the granddaughter of the company founder.

The difference between Upsher-Smith and other generic companies is that Upsher-Smith often applies a bit of innovation in dosage formulation to tailor a drug to a specialized market that others overlook. Then it backs the product with the kind of sales support and record for quality and consistency that typically characterize a branded drug. Upsher-Smith sells the product for 30 to 50 percent less than what a major brand-name product would cost, although at a higher price than that charged by conventional generic companies. "We don't go after the blockbuster drugs when they come off patent because every other generic company in the world is doing that," says

THE UPSHER-SMITH FACILITIES, LOCATED IN SUBURBAN MINNE-APOLIS, INCLUDE A STATE-OF-THE-ART MANUFACTURING FACILITY, ADMINISTRATIVE OFFICES, AND QUALITY ASSUR-ANCE AREAS (RIGHT).

UPSHER-SMITH'S NEWEST PROD-UCT, PREVALITE®, A GENERIC ALTERNATIVE TO QUESTRAN, IS USED IN THE REDUCTION OF HIGH CHOLESTEROL (BELOW).

Evenstad. "Instead, we try to apply innovation, largely in terms of dosage form, that allows us to take advantage of smaller, less crowded market niches."

The company has a history of developing and bringing to market innovative dosage forms of pharmaceutical products. In 1919, its founder, a pharmacist, developed and marketed the first standardized potency for digitalis for use in heart disorders. In 1969, the company came under the leadership of Evenstad, who is also a pharmacist. The first innovative product developed under his direction was SSKI®, a stabilized preparation of potassium iodide that is used in the treatment of respiratory disorders. As the company grew, it continued to develop innovative dosage forms, especially in analgesic drugs and for the hospital unit-dose market.

One example of the company's innovation at work is the Klor-Con® brand of extended-release potassium chloride tablets, Upsher-Smith's major product. In the early 1970s, the FDA banned a potassium chloride

tablet used to replace potassium depleted by hypertension medication because the pill tended to create bowel ulcerations. So Upsher-Smith came up with the first low-priced liquid formulation, which dispersed the potassium chloride and prevented ulcerations. But the liquid also had an unpleasant metallic taste, so the company went on to develop a time-release pill that solved both the taste and the ulceration problems. Today, Klor-Con® is the fastest-growing brand of potassium chloride tablets and is among the top 200 prescription drugs dispensed in the United States.

Another example is acetaminophen, an analgesic that Upsher-Smith decided to aim at the infants' and children's market. Because it is so difficult to get small children to swallow a pill, and because the liquid form of the drug is bitter, the company came up with its Feverall® product in a suppository form to solve both problems. Feverall Suppositories holds the number one share in the retail and hospital markets. The company has also

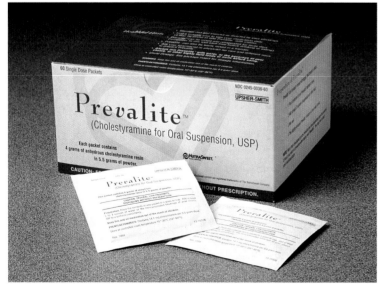

developed proprietary technology for the production of taste-free acetaminophen particles under its Medicoat™ system. This technology has potential application for many other drugs as well, especially in the pediatric and geriatric markets.

The People behind the Success

Upsher-Smith's commitment to innovation applies to its leadership and management style as well. With a strong vision and values-centered focus, the company manages its primary business functions through cross-functional teams. The dialogue developed in these processes results in highly integrated and effective operations. "The real strength of this company is its people," says Evenstad. "We have nearly 300 employees, but we still run our company like an old-fashioned family business in which respect, dignity, and sincerity are the guiding principles. Because of that, people are proud to be a part of this organization."

That sense of pride—along with a deep respect for Evenstad's business acumen—convinced Ian Troup, a native of Scotland with an impressive leadership track record, to join the company as its president in 1995. Troup had spent eight years as head of a German-based pharmaceutical company located near Milwaukee, and had helped expand the company's sales from $12 million in 1989 to $200 million in 1995. His goal at Upsher-Smith is to help the company reach and exceed $100 million in sales by 1999. Few doubt he will do it. "The company has built a solid foundation and we are poised and ready to take the next steps," says Troup. "We continue to develop products that provide significant growth opportunities for us, and the market is starting to notice."

The market is not alone. In the last four years, Upsher-Smith has twice been chosen by the National Wholesale Druggists' Association as the best overall pharmaceutical manufacturer with sales under $100 million. Upsher-Smith also was joint winner, with Upjohn Pharmaceuticals, of the 1995 Supplier of the Year award given by Bergen Brunswig, the nation's second-largest pharmaceutical wholesaler.

UPSHER-SMITH LABORATORIES HOUSES THE COMPANY'S SALES AND MARKETING DEPARTMENT AS WELL AS ITS NEW RESEARCH AND DEVELOPMENT LABS (ABOVE).

ONE EXAMPLE OF THE COMPANY'S INNOVATION AT WORK IS THE KLOR-CON® BRAND OF EXTENDED-RELEASE POTASSIUM CHLORIDE TABLETS, UPSHER-SMITH'S MAJOR PRODUCT. TODAY, KLOR-CON® IS THE FASTEST-GROWING BRAND OF POTASSIUM CHLORIDE TABLETS AND IS AMONG THE TOP 200 PRESCRIPTION DRUGS DISPENSED IN THE UNITED STATES (LEFT).

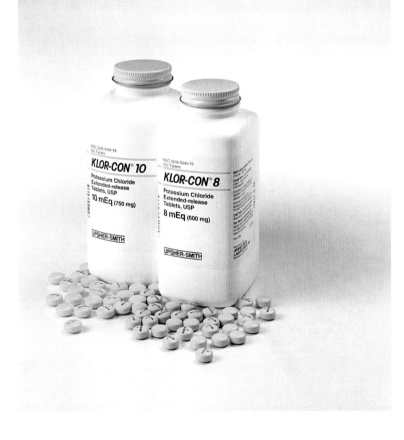

LAND O'LAKES, INC.

IN THE EARLY 1920S, A COOPERATIVE WAS FORMED THAT HAD NEW ideas about producing and marketing butter. Back in those days, most butter was made from sour cream and was sold in tubs. The quality of the butter was often erratic, distribution costs were high, and marketing efforts were nonexistent. ✳ As the story goes, most people who ate butter and cheese were forced to put up with dairy products that "smelt bad, tasted worse, and did not keep at all." Only

Clockwise from top right: Dairy farmers and cooperative creameries formed Land O'Lakes in 1921 in order to secure a better price for their butter.

More than 1,000 locally owned co-ops are served by Land O'Lakes.

In 1987, Land O'Lakes Ag Services joined with Cenex in an innovative joint venture that now provides feed, seed, agronomy, and petroleum products to more than 300,000 farmers in 19 states.

cooperation among dairy farmers could improve the quality of their product enough to fetch decent prices and attract more customers. The cooperative effort that resulted became today's Land O'Lakes.

THE SWEET SMELL OF SUCCESS

John Brandt, a dairy farmer from Litchfield, helped churn the "butter revolution." But Brandt was not satisfied with merely organizing small-town co-op creameries into more effective shipping units. He wanted all of the creameries to make their butter from sweet, unsoured cream since sweet cream butter tasted better and could be stored longer. He also wanted creameries throughout the state to join together in an effort to control the marketing, handling, and selling of butter on a large-scale basis. On July 8, 1921, Brandt helped create the Minnesota Cooperative Creameries Association.

In 1924 the association decided to expand its butter market, and a search was made for an appropriate brand name and trademark. A contest—with $500 in gold as first

Creamery Cokato, Minn k-1020

prize—was announced to choose a name. Two contestants offered the winning name: Land O'Lakes. The name became so popular that the association changed its corporate name to Land O'Lakes Creameries, Inc. in 1926.

Now, more than seven decades later, Land O'Lakes is still true to its roots. It is currently owned by farmers, ranchers, and local cooperatives in 19 states from the Midwest to the West Coast. More than 5,000 employees are dedicated to providing agricultural inputs to 1,000 local cooperatives supplying 300,000 farmers; serving more than 9,000 direct producer-members; and manufacturing and marketing a wide array of quality food and feed products sold around the country.

DAIRY AND A WHOLE LOT MORE

To many, Land O'Lakes will always be thought of as the "butter company." However, food production expertise at Land O'Lakes extends beyond products on grocers' shelves. Over the past 70 years, the company has grown to become a supplier of feed, agronomy, and seed products,

while still remaining a successful dairy-foods manufacturer and marketer.

Over the last three-quarters of a century, Land O'Lakes has become firmly established as the premier dairy food marketing cooperative in the United States. From member creameries and from more than 4,000 direct farmer members, the company collects and processes 4 billion pounds of milk a year. Land O' Lakes manufactures cheese, butter, and other dairy products, and it dries milk. It also dries whey, a by-product of cheese production, and produces various dairy-based ingredients, which then are further processed.

Because proper feed and feeding methods are essential for quality milk and butter production, it was a logical step for Land O'Lakes to get involved in the manufacture and distribution of feed. Today, Land O'Lakes is one of the foremost feed companies in the nation, involved in everything from cattle, hog, poultry, and specialty feeds to milk replacers.

Always looking for ways to improve its products and services, Land O'Lakes is currently expanding its Feed division, moving it toward a

Minneapolis ✳ *St. Paul*

complete animal-production system intent on helping livestock producers raise exactly the types of animals customers want. This move involves channeling significant amounts of research money into proprietary and branded products, with the focus on lean market animals in swine, and on high-producing cows in dairy.

Because of its commitment to providing a full range of top-quality products and services, the company has joined with Cenex, a St. Paul-based farm-supply cooperative, to form the Cenex/Land O'Lakes Agronomy Co. This unique joint venture allows Land O'Lakes to supply member cooperatives with plant food and crop protection products, as well as a host of technical services, including AgriSource, a computerized information management system.

Although smaller, in terms of annual sales, than either the Agronomy Co. or the Feed division, the Land O'Lakes Seed division plays an important role in providing Ag Service members with a full range of ag products. Concentrating on alfalfa, soybean, and corn varieties, the Seed division is committed to delivering the latest technologies as well as the top-performing genetics to its co-op members. Examples of such products include multileaf alfalfas, energy-dense corn, and new insect-resistant crop varieties.

"Our vision," says Land O'Lakes President Jack Gherty, "is to be one of the best food and agricultural companies in the world. If we do

this, we will be our customers' first choice for products and services, and our employees' first choice for work. We also will be responsible to our owners and to rural America, and a leader in our communities." Gherty points out that this vision was formed not by him, but by the company's employees and members. The Land O'Lakes heritage is rich in rural val-

ues, family, and respect for the land; its cooperative roots run deep. Gherty notes that these values were essential to the company's success over the past 75 years, and will continue to be integral to the company's future. "With these values as our guide, we believe we will succeed both individually and as a company today and into the future."

CLOCKWISE FROM TOP LEFT: AN AGGRESSIVE ADVERTISING CAMPAIGN ESTABLISHED LAND O'LAKES AS THE NATION'S NUMBER ONE BUTTER MARKETER BY THE LATE 1920S.

BUTTER REMAINS THE MOST FAMOUS FOOD PRODUCT MADE BY LAND O'LAKES. A NEW VARIANT IS LIGHT BUTTER WITH HALF THE FAT OF REGULAR BUTTER.

MOST OF THE MILK SUPPLIED BY LAND O'LAKES PRODUCERS TODAY GOES TO MAKE CHEESE.

FEDERAL **C**ARTRIDGE **C**OMPANY RECENTLY CELEBRATED ITS 75TH anniversary in the ammunition business. It is a history rich with tradition. And it all began with a few dedicated people who believed in themselves, their company, and their products. ✳ On a spring day in 1922 a dozen workers filed into a small-scale ammunition plant in the quiet little town of Anoka, Minnesota. They were there to manufacture shotgun shells. Although their numbers were not strong, their midwestern work ethic was.

Over the next several years, the company expanded its product line to include centerfire and rimfire ammunition, and constructed several new buildings in Anoka to make room for equipment, production, and product storage. The workforce grew steadily, as did the demand for Federal ammunition.

Federal ammunition became popular because it offered hunters good value for their money and because the company distributed it through unique channels. Hunters often would buy their Federal ammunition at the places where they gathered with friends to swap stories—barber shops, grocery stores, and service stations. And while the company manufactured its own line of ammunition, it also produced several lines of private label cartridges and shells for department store chains such as Sears, Roebuck & Co. This strategy paid off, and soon Federal became known nationally as one of the most dependable suppliers of quality ammunition.

Federal still adheres to the philosophy of giving customers what they want, where they want it. As

a result, the number of consumers served by Federal has increased significantly—and steadily—over the years. Today Federal develops products for three major markets: hunting, law enforcement, and recreational shooting.

"At Federal we have different kinds of customers with different kinds of needs," says Federal President Ron Mason. "The bottom line, however, is that they want from Federal what we all want from the companies we do business with—good value for our money. They want quality at a competitive price. They want reliable performance. And they want to do business with a company that treats them well, that conveys a

personal commitment to their satisfaction. Our goal is to meet those demands, with every customer, every day."

Federal's efforts have not gone unrewarded. Hunters who want high-end performance turn to Federal for "designer" bullets—like Nosler Partition and Trophy Bonded Bear Claw—in factory-loaded ammunition. For many years, the Federal Bureau of Investigation has made Federal's Hydra-Shok its round of choice.

And in 1991 Federal began development of a round that would forever end America's reliance on foreign countries for match-grade .22 ammunition. The result was Federal's UltraMatch .22 ammuni-

OLYMPIC CHAMPION KIM RHODE DISPLAYS THE 1996 GOLD MEDAL SHE WON WITH FEDERAL PAPER SHOT SHELLS (RIGHT).

RON MASON, PRESIDENT OF FEDERAL CARTRIDGE COMPANY (BELOW).

▼ MITCH KENZAR

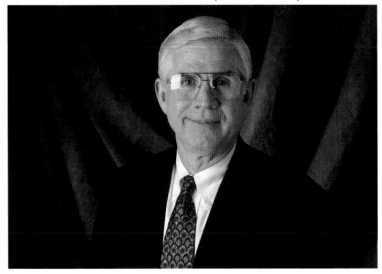

BOW

tion, which U.S. shooters Launi Meili and Bob Foth used to win gold and silver medals, respectively, in the 1992 Summer Olympic Games in Barcelona, Spain.

Following this achievement, American shooters fired Federal's "magic" international paper shotgun shells to gold, silver, and bronze medals at the 1996 Summer Olympic Games in Atlanta.

"There's a reason why we call them our 'magic bullets.' You put them in your gun and know you can win with them," says Olympic Shotgun Coach Lloyd Woodhouse. "There's no better shell out there. All my shooters have total confidence in Federal."

SUPPORTING THE SHOOTING SPORTS

Federal doesn't just look to its bottom line to measure success. The company has a long-standing tradition of responsibility and concern for conservation, wildlife management, and support of the shooting sports. As far back as 1934 Federal was teaming up with 4-H to sponsor Conservation Camps, which taught youngsters about the importance of gun safety and preserving wildlife and the environment.

In 1937 the company encouraged Congress to adopt the Pittman-Robertson Wildlife Restoration Act, which created a self-imposed

excise tax on ammunition and firearms. Billions of dollars raised through this act throughout the years have been used to help preserve the environment and give millions of people the opportunity to enjoy wildlife and the outdoors, and to participate in the shooting sports.

Today the company's dedication to wildlife and conservation is evident in Federal's Support the Shooting Sports initiative, a program created to foster support of shooting sports and conservation by hunters and shooters around the globe. Some of the groups benefiting from the initiative include Ducks Unlimited, Pheasants Forever, Becoming an Outdoors Woman,

the Rocky Mountain Elk Foundation, Minnesota Deer Hunters Association, National Wild Turkey Federation, and the U.S. Olympic Shooting Team.

THE SECRET: THE PEOPLE

The real secret to Federal's success, according to Mason, is the people who work there. The company has grown from eight employees in 1922 to nearly 1,000 employees today, the vast majority of whom are hunters and shooters themselves.

"One very telling statistic about Federal and its people is that the average length of service is almost 20 years," says Mason. "That kind of tenure means we enjoy our work. And people who enjoy their work do the highest-quality work and produce the highest-quality product."

Mason adds that there are many second-generation and even third-generation associates working at Federal, men and women whose parents and grandparents made ammunition with the same passion for excellence in craftsmanship.

"We're proud of our heritage. Yet, we really believe that the best is still to come," says Mason. "The Federal of the 21st century will continue to deliver good value, but will be even better known for its continuing commitment to quality and to advancing the state of the art in ammunition performance."

FEDERAL IS A NATIONAL SPONSOR OF BECOMING AN OUTDOORS WOMAN, A PROGRAM THAT ANNUALLY INTRODUCES THOUSANDS OF WOMEN TO THE HUNTING AND SHOOTING SPORTS.

MITCH KENZAR

ENGINEERS (FROM LEFT) SHAWN CALLAHAN, BOB KRAMER, AND BRUCE LAMBERTY LED THE DEVELOPMENT OF FEDERAL ULTRAMATCH .22, THE AMMUNITION AMERICAN SHOOTERS USED TO WIN GOLD AND SILVER MEDALS AT THE 1992 OLYMPICS.

▲ CHRIS FAUST

1925 - 1969

1928

SNYDER'S DRUG STORES, INC.

1929

CUMMINS POWER GENERATION

1929

NORWEST CORPORATION

1932

ST. PAUL PORT AUTHORITY

1938

CARLSON COMPANIES, INC.

1949

AUTOMATIC PRODUCTS INTERNATIONAL, LTD.

1949

KARE 11

1949

MEDTRONIC, INC.

1956

POLKA DOT DAIRY/TOM THUMB FOOD MARKETS

1957

OWENS SERVICES CORPORATION

1961

Minnesota Twins

1963

Regal Minneapolis Hotel

1966

AVR, Inc.

1966

Best Buy Co., Inc.

1967

Advance Circuits, Inc.

1967

Slumberland, Inc.

1967

Smarte Carte, Inc.

1967

TREND enterprises, Inc.

1968

Cuningham Group

1969

Robert Half International, Inc.

SNYDER'S DRUG STORES, INC.

FOR THE PAST 70 YEARS, SNYDER'S DRUG STORES, INC. HAS been building its own success story. As the leading drug chain in the Twin Cities and in Minnesota, the company has grown to become a major economic force in the upper Midwest. ✳ Snyder's history dates back to 1928 when Max P. Snyder had a cigar store in downtown Minneapolis, carrying a small variety of items to satisfy his customers. By 1931, the store was carrying pharmaceuticals as

CLOCKWISE FROM RIGHT: EACH YEAR SNYDER HOLDS AN ANNUAL GOLF TOURNAMENT TO RAISE MONEY FOR THE VARIETY CHILDREN'S ASSOCIATION AT THE UNIVERSITY OF MINNESOTA IN MINNEAPOLIS, AND RECENTLY DONATED THE COURTESY VAN FOR TRANSPORTATION TO AND FROM THE BIOTHERAPY INSTITUTE.

CORPORATE AND INDEPENDENTLY OWNED SNYDER'S STORES ARE LOCATED IN MINNESOTA, WISCONSIN, IOWA, SOUTH DAKOTA, AND MICHIGAN.

SNYDER'S HAS BEEN BUILT ON A CORPORATE PHILOSOPHY THAT HONORS ITS CUSTOMERS, EMPLOYEES, AND ASSOCIATES.

well and soon became known as a cut-rate drugstore rather than a cigar store. On June 30, 1939, Snyder's Drug Stores, Inc. was officially incorporated. The chain continued to grow steadily, numbering 12 stores by the 1950s.

Over a period of some 20 years, beginning in 1962, the lucrative Snyder chain was bought and sold by a series of larger companies. Don Beeler, chairman and CEO, developed the independent retailer program in 1969 and has led the company since 1980. Beeler and five other officers—Gary Hawley, Rich Oorlog, Michael Pan, Phil Perkins, and Bill Vidmar—purchased the company in a leveraged buyout in 1986.

Today corporate and independently owned Snyder's stores are located in Minnesota, Wisconsin, Iowa, South Dakota, and Michigan. Snyder's has been built on a corporate philosophy that honors its customers, employees, and associates. "We are very proud of what Snyder's has become," says Beeler. Snyder's offers the broadest selection of health care merchandise available in the upper Midwest, as well as beauty care

items, general merchandise, and related items and services.

HEALTH CARE LEADER

During its growth, Snyder's positioned itself as a community-based drugstore focused on meeting its customers' health care needs, establishing the Snyder Drug name as synonymous with health care. The company emphasizes health care information and additional services that provide quality pharmaceutical care to its thousands of valued customers. "Because Snyder Drug has locations in virtually every community, our pharmacists are often the most accessible health professionals," says Pan, president and COO. "Surveys repeatedly show that pharmacists are the most trusted health professionals. This is consistent with the long-standing relationship that many of our customers have with their Snyder pharmacist."

Snyder's offers telephone access to pharmacists 24 hours a day, seven days a week, and home delivery

Monday through Friday. Emergency delivery service is available 24 hours a day.

Snyder Drug has been a sponsor of many health care activities including flu shots, free blood pressure monitoring, cholesterol testing, and mobile mammography. The company's pharmacies have served as convenient sites for smoking cessation classes, immunization programs, maternal and child health centers, and well-baby clinics. "With its many locations, Snyder Drug can provide patients with convenient access to community-based primary and preventive care, using pharmacists as low-cost providers," says Pan.

COMMUNITY LEADER

"As a community-based drugstore, Snyder's cares deeply about its neighborhoods and the quality of life that makes them unique," says Beeler. Each year Snyder holds an annual golf tournament to raise money for the Variety Children's Association at the University of Minnesota in

Minneapolis. Snyder's is a major sponsor of the Multiple Sclerosis Society's 150-mile bike fund-raiser, donating kits containing sunscreen, lip balm, insect repellent, facial tissue, and gum to the bikers.

Snyder also participates in the "Adopt-a-High-Rise" program. Several times a year Snyder employees plan an event for the residents of its adopted high-rise residential building. Events for the residents, who are primarily low-income families or elderly men and women, have included a game night, a barbershop quartet, and picnics in the park. Approximately 50 Snyder employees volunteer their time to make these events successful.

Each year Snyder, in cooperation with the Sister Kenny Institute—a nationally renowned rehabilitation facility that offers a full range of services to help people with spinal cord, brain, and neuromuscular disabilities—produces a calendar featuring selected artwork of artists with disabilities, giving the artists much deserved exposure, recognition, and financial reward.

Other efforts to which Snyder stores and employees contribute donations and time include the Kidney Foundation's Annual Airplane Toss, the Annual Santa Anonymous Toy Drive, the Red Cross Blood Mobile, and the United Way.

Service Leader

Under a department called "Yes Express," Snyder's offers its customers much more than health care. Services include one-hour photofinishing, faxing, postage stamps, package shipping and mailing, money orders, key production, Western Union capabilities, and other services customized by the local store manager. Some Snyder stores even offer "Portrait Express," a professional studio photography service at an attractive price. "We think we truly differentiate ourselves," Pan remarks. "For example, the larger chains tend to look at how many 24-hour stores they can open, while we look at how we can service customers 24 hours a day. The consumer doesn't really care how many stores you have, as long as they have

access to around-the-clock service. Our goal is to say yes to our customers' needs and we train our people that way."

Beeler acknowledges that all of these services are part of the chain's ongoing efforts to enhance the appeal of its stores in order to set Snyder's apart from the myriad of competition that has cropped up in recent years. "The ability of Snyder's Drug Stores to remain a dominant retailing force for nearly 70 years stems from our willingness to embrace change and innovation," he says. "It's unrealistic to think we are going to win customers on price alone. We have to focus on convenience, health care, and strong customer service as means of attracting business."

CLOCKWISE FROM TOP LEFT: SNYDER'S OFFERS TELEPHONE ACCESS TO PHARMACISTS 24 HOURS A DAY, SEVEN DAYS A WEEK, AND HOME DELIVERY MONDAY THROUGH FRIDAY. EMERGENCY DELIVERY SERVICE IS AVAILABLE 24 HOURS A DAY.

"BECAUSE SNYDER DRUG HAS LOCATIONS IN VIRTUALLY EVERY COMMUNITY, OUR PHARMACISTS ARE OFTEN THE MOST ACCESSIBLE HEALTH PROFESSIONALS," SAYS MICHAEL PAN, PRESIDENT AND COO.

SNYDER'S OFFERS THE BROADEST SELECTION OF HEALTH CARE MERCHANDISE AVAILABLE IN THE UPPER MIDWEST, AS WELL AS BEAUTY CARE ITEMS, GENERAL MERCHANDISE, AND RELATED ITEMS AND SERVICES.

UNDER A DEPARTMENT CALLED "YES EXPRESS," SNYDER'S OFFERS ITS CUSTOMERS MUCH MORE THAN HEALTH CARE. SERVICES INCLUDE ONE-HOUR PHOTOFINISHING, FAXING, POSTAGE STAMPS, PACKAGE SHIPPING AND MAILING, MONEY ORDERS, KEY PRODUCTION, AND WESTERN UNION CAPABILITIES.

EVER SINCE THERE'S BEEN POWER, THERE'S BEEN POWER failure. And for almost 80 years, Onan Corporation, now Cummins Power Generation, has provided reliable emergency/standby, prime, and interruptible power—whenever and wherever necessary. In 1989, Onan power systems kept the phone lines open and the floodgates closed during Hurricane Hugo. Six years earlier, the company did the same thing when Hurricane

Alicia blew through Houston. Onan was in San Francisco during the World Series earthquake; Jackson, Mississippi, when the floods hit in 1979; Alaska during the 1964 Anchorage quake; and New York City during the blackout of 1965. When the power failed, Onan generator sets didn't.

"From brownouts to blackouts, from natural disasters to human error—Onan power generation systems have always stood for three things: reliability, quality, and performance," says Jerry E. Johnson, general manager. "Obviously, we don't know when a disaster will occur or how to stop it. But our products can do a lot to help avoid a disaster. We feel good about that, and so do our customers."

FOR ALMOST 80 YEARS, CUMMINS POWER GENERATION HAS PROVIDED RELIABLE EMERGENCY/STANDBY, PRIME, AND INTERRUPTIBLE POWER—WHENEVER AND WHEREVER NECESSARY (RIGHT).

THE ONAN BRAND QUIET DIESEL 7500 HAS A NEW, REVOLUTIONARY DESIGN THAT DRAMATICALLY LOWERS NOISE, VIBRATION, AND HARSHNESS. (BELOW).

A RICH MINNEAPOLIS HISTORY

Onan was originally founded by D.W. Onan in 1920 in Minneapolis. For the first 20 years, the company produced and sold increasing numbers of electric generator sets in the United States and overseas. During World War II, Onan served its country by producing vast quantities of generator sets for military application.

In 1947, the company discontinued private labeling and built its own distribution system. The same year Onan introduced the first U.S.-designed small diesel engine. That engine continued to evolve and eventually became part of the J Series engines, which were introduced in the 1960s and would become Onan's main line of gasoline and diesel engines for more than 20 years.

Through a series of acquisitions—both by and of Onan—the company continued to grow, and in 1989, total sales exceeded $500 million. In 1992, Onan became a wholly owned subsidiary of the Cummins Engine Company, Inc., a leading worldwide designer and manufacturer of diesel engines and related products.

Today, Cummins Power Generation systems and services are utilized in a wide range of emergency standby and prime power applications. The product line, which is the broadest in the industry, comprises generator sets from five kilowatts to 1,500 kilowatts, transfer switches, paralleling switch gear, communications networks, and related electrical and mechanical accessories.

Primarily, Cummins Power Generation products provide emergency standby power to commercial facilities such as banks, office buildings, retail stores, grocery stores, and data centers, as well as institutional and industrial facilities such as prisons, hospitals, schools, factories, wastewater treatment, agricultural processing, livestock housing, and public buildings. In many countries where utility power is unreliable or unavailable, Cummins power systems are used as a prime source of power in a variety of applications.

In terms of consumer products, Cummins has supplied more Onan brand generator sets for recreational vehicles and pleasure boats than all other competitors combined. There are also Onan brand portable generator sets for construction and for power generation in remote sites. "Our leadership in all of these markets results from extensive experience, and a focus on total customer satisfaction and ongoing quality improvements," says Johnson.

The company is unique in that it designs and manufactures all its power system components—from the engines and alternators all the way down to the interconnection points between the generator sets, transfer switches, and paralleling switch gear. "We are a fully integrated manufacturer, a single source of supply for all components of a generator set. No other power generation manufacturer offers this level of vertical integration," says Johnson.

Meeting Customer Demands

Cummins has become widely known as one of the highest-quality suppliers of power generation equipment and customer services. In addition to generator sets and total power systems, Cummins Power Generation also offers custom engineering for special customer applications, parts, service, maintenance, accessories, accessory upfit, and complete documentation for installation, wiring, operation, and service.

Before the power systems are shipped and installed, customers have the option to visit the factory in Minneapolis to see their systems perform and pass the required measures to assure field performance. All power generation products are designed, engineered, and tested in Minneapolis, and are manufactured in Minneapolis and in Adelaide, Australia. ISO 9001 registration verifies the quality of the products, as well as the company's commitment to exceed customers' expectations. The products are then sold and supported by an extensive network of 170 full-service distributors at more than 300 locations worldwide.

Over the years, these products and services have given the company a reputation for quality and support, and also made it one of the major suppliers to customers in the Americas and around the world. A large U.S. telephone company relied on Cummins Power Generation for custom-engineering capabilities to supply specialized power units for controlled environmental vaults containing highly sensitive communications transmission equipment. In South Africa, another telecommunications provider found it could count on Cummins Power Generation for fast delivery, as well as customer support from the local distributor for planning, managing, and installing 300 emergency systems at cellular sites within a three-month period. A government utility in South America selected Cummins power systems to provide power to villages in the rain forest.

"Today, over 85 of our power generation systems provide power for remote villages that are not serviced by the utility grid," says Johnson. "These are just a few applications of Cummins power systems that take special advantage of the reliability, efficiency, and performance Cummins provides."

NORWEST CORPORATION

THERE IS A SAYING THAT IS PART OF NORWEST CORPORATION'S vision statement: "We want to 'out local' the nationals and 'out national' the locals." That means the diversified financial services company is committed to offering a broader product line than its competitors, while staying close to customers, understanding their needs, and providing To The Nth Degree® service. ✳ Today Norwest Corporation, with its corporate headquarters in

Minneapolis, has grown to more than 53,000 employees in all 50 states, Canada, the Caribbean, Central America, and overseas. But Norwest's roots lie deep in the Twin Cities.

Norwest grew from a Minneapolis bank established in the late 1800s. In 1929 that bank took the lead in founding a regional bank holding company called Northwest Bancorporation. Renamed Norwest in 1982, the corporation has grown to more than 3,400 financial services stores offering banking, consumer finance products, insurance, investment, and mortgage services to consumers, small businesses, agricultural producers, and corporations. In the Twin Cities metro area, Norwest has about 9,500 employees at more than 100 banking stores and other Norwest entities.

COMMITMENT TO COMMUNITY

Through focus groups, meetings, and surveys, Norwest assesses community banking needs, then creates products, services, and delivery systems to meet those needs. The company provides financing to stimulate business and housing growth, and contributes time and money to community projects.

Norwest has made a concentrated effort to use new technology to give customers the products and services they want, when and where they want them. For example, a new Norwest Superstore on the St. Paul downtown skyway system is user-friendly, focusing on specific needs and events in customers' lives. The Norwest Phone Bank™ service answers more than 800,000 calls each month in the Twin Cities, allowing customers to get information and complete banking transactions 24

hours a day. And Norwest has added Spanish-speaking ATMs and hired multilingual employees to help serve its culturally diverse population.

Norwest Foundation contributes more than $4 million each year to the Twin Cities nonprofit community, and metro-area Norwest employees devote thousands of hours to projects such as the annual metro Paint-A-Thon, Habitat for Humanity, and Junior Achievement.

SPARKING THE GROWTH

Norwest recognizes that economic growth and development of the Twin Cities metro area depend on the vitality of business and the ability of government entities to service the people. For several years, Norwest Bank Minnesota has been rated Minnesota's top Small Business Administration (SBA) lender. Norwest Investment Services, Inc., the investment subsidiary, structures tax-exempt financing to metro governments, schools, and nonprofit organizations.

Norwest Mortgage originated and purchased more than $775 million in residential real estate loans in the Twin Cities area in 1995, including loans to low- and moderate-income individuals who otherwise would have had difficulty

purchasing homes of their own.

Norwest also gives major support to education in the Twin Cities area, underwriting bonds for school districts, providing student loans, and contributing to educational programs. Norwest sponsors numerous financial seminars to help area residents understand the fundamental importance of managing money.

In the Twin Cities, as in its other communities, Norwest is fulfilling its goal: To be an outstanding company known for its accessible financial products and services, and recognized for its good citizenship.

NORWEST FOUNDATION CONTRIBUTES MORE THAN $4 MILLION EACH YEAR TO THE TWIN CITIES NONPROFIT COMMUNITY, AND METRO-AREA NORWEST EMPLOYEES DEVOTE THOUSANDS OF HOURS TO PROJECTS SUCH AS THE ANNUAL METRO PAINT-A-THON, HABITAT FOR HUMANITY, AND JUNIOR ACHIEVEMENT (TOP RIGHT).

NORWEST CORPORATION, WITH ITS CORPORATE HEADQUARTERS IN MINNEAPOLIS, HAS GROWN TO MORE THAN 53,000 EMPLOYEES IN ALL 50 STATES, CANADA, THE CARIBBEAN, CENTRAL AMERICA, AND OVERSEAS (BOTTOM RIGHT).

Minneapolis ✳ St. Paul

*I*F INDUSTRIAL PARKS WERE ICE CREAM, THEY WOULD SURELY BE labeled "vanilla"—colorless and generally unexciting to the average person. But upon closer look, they have their own special appeal. Unlike the more glamorous types of corporate real estate, they very seldom leave a bitter financial aftertaste in the mouths of their investors. And in today's high-stakes environment of cities vying for new jobs and business growth, the proven, long-term success of targeted

industrial/business parks makes them a public investment that communities cannot afford to overlook.

In urban environments, the cost of such land redevelopment is never an easy or inexpensive proposition, to be sure. Activities such as acquiring land, environmental cleanup, financing, permits, and equipment turn new construction or expansion projects into seemingly overwhelming tasks. Thankfully, there's help available.

The Saint Paul Port Authority helps growing manufacturing and industrial companies gain a competitive advantage by providing sites, financing, customized job training, and professional services. Having financed local business growth since the 1960s, the Port Authority is committed to assisting established manufacturing and industrial firms with their expansion needs throughout the Twin Cities' Metro East community.

The state legislature originally founded the quasi-governmental agency in 1932 to handle commerce in and along the Mississippi River. In 1957 the Port Authority was reorganized to allow it to acquire land for industrial redevelopment anywhere within the Port District, which included most of St. Paul. A 1963 resolution established the first industrial financing plan and enabled the Port Authority to acquire recreational property; and a subsequent decision in 1965 gave the agency greater flexibility to issue industrial revenue bonds, after which the Port Authority's industrial parks began to grow rapidly. To date, the Port Authority has helped to create or retain more than 40,000 jobs and generated $210 million in tax revenues from projects it has assisted.

PARTNERING FOR SUCCESS

Hundreds of companies have chosen to partner with the Port Authority because of the development team's can-do attitude and extensive experience. "All thriving industrial businesses experience growing pains at some time," says Port Authority President Kenneth Johnson. "That's why the Saint Paul Port Authority has developed strategic services to help growing companies evolve into stronger, more profitable businesses which create living-wage jobs for St. Paul residents and expand the city's tax base."

In addition to providing financing and real estate assistance, Port Authority experts perform expansion needs analyses, complete site and building searches, secure permits and variances, consult on engineering issues, and coordinate soil and environmental remediation. "In each case, we determine a company's specific needs, find the site that best fits those needs, and work through the necessary issues to ensure the project goes smoothly. For growing businesses, we're a one-stop shop for expansion," says Johnson.

As part of its mission, the Port Authority has made its top priority the identification and reclamation of now-unusable parcels of land called brownfields. Port Authority experts have identified 1,000 acres suitable for manufacturing at 18 sites scattered throughout St. Paul's neighborhoods; they estimate that once developed, these sites would generate more than 13 million square feet of light manufacturing space. "We know the value industrial parks provide to a community," says Johnson, "and we're committed to helping industrial companies make their businesses the best they can possibly be."

CLOCKWISE FROM TOP LEFT: THE EXECUTIVE OFFICERS OF THE SAINT PAUL PORT AUTHORITY ARE (FROM LEFT) CHIEF FINANCIAL OFFICER LAURIE J. HANSEN, CHAIRMAN OF THE BOARD OF COMMISSIONERS W. ANDREW BOSS, AND PRESIDENT KENNETH R. JOHNSON.

THE PORT AUTHORITY DEVELOPMENT TEAM CONSISTS OF (STANDING LEFT TO RIGHT) PROPERTY MANAGER RICHARD A. GIERDAL, VICE PRESIDENT PATRICK E. DEAN, VICE PRESIDENT JOHN W. YOUNG; (SEATED LEFT TO RIGHT) VICE PRESIDENT GREGORY W. DREHMEL, VICE PRESIDENT STEVEN C. KING, DIRECTOR OF INDUSTRIAL DEVELOPMENT LORRIE J. LOUDER, VICE PRESIDENT CHARLES L. MCGUIRE; AND (SEATED, FOREGROUND) DIRECTOR OF REAL ESTATE WILLIAM M. MORIN.

HAVING FINANCED LOCAL BUSINESS GROWTH SINCE THE 1960S, THE PORT AUTHORITY IS COMMITTED TO ASSISTING ESTABLISHED MANUFACTURING AND INDUSTRIAL FIRMS WITH THEIR EXPANSION NEEDS THROUGHOUT THE TWIN CITIES' METRO EAST COMMUNITY.

ARLSON COMPANIES, INC. IS A MULTIFACETED, MULTINATIONAL, multi-billion-dollar corporation that grew out of a simple idea and a $55 loan. When Curtis LeRoy Carlson quit his job selling soap for Procter & Gamble in order to start his own business, no one expected him to build one of the world's largest privately held corporations. Few, in fact, held out any hope that he could persuade small grocers to give away his Gold Bond Stamps to boost sales, since up to then the

practice was common only to department stores. But, eager to capitalize on his idea, Carlson borrowed $55 from his landlord and began doing business from his dining-room table. He called his fledgling operation the Gold Bond Stamp Company.

After a slow start and meager gains during World War II (during which time merchants, confronted with widespread shortages, saw little reason to offer stamps), the Gold Bond Stamp Company hit the big time in the early 1950s, when Carlson and his aggressive sales force persuaded one of the nation's largest supermarket chains, SuperValu, to offer his stamps—and their sales skyrocketed. The ensuing rush to stamps revolutionized the way retail goods were marketed and eventually made Carlson a billionaire—and Carlson Companies (the name was

officially adopted in 1973) has been growing ever since.

The company expanded for the first four decades at an annual compounded growth rate of 33 percent and has doubled its revenues every five years since 1973. Today Carlson Companies comprises more than 100 corporations with a worldwide workforce of more than 130,000 per-

sons who collectively speak about two dozen languages and represent 125 different countries. Carlson Companies' systemwide revenues are expected to reach $20 billion by the year 2000.

THREE COMPANIES, ONE VISION

The trading stamp phenomenon was the forerunner of what has become Carlson Marketing Group, and provided the foundation for Carlson Companies' diversification into related businesses, including hospitality and travel. All three businesses, as well as Carlson Companies, Inc., the parent company, are headquartered in Minneapolis.

Carlson Marketing Group is a global marketing services company that maximizes individualized relationships between its clients and

CARLSON'S EXPANSION INTO THE HOSPITALITY INDUSTRY CAME WITH THE PURCHASE OF THE ORIGINAL RADISSON HOTEL IN DOWNTOWN MINNEAPOLIS IN 1962, WHICH IS NOW THE SITE OF THE NEW RADISSON PLAZA MINNEAPOLIS (TOP).

THE WORLD HEADQUARTERS OF CARLSON COMPANIES, INC. IS LOCATED IN MINNETONKA, MINNESOTA, A SUBURB OF MINNEAPOLIS (RIGHT).

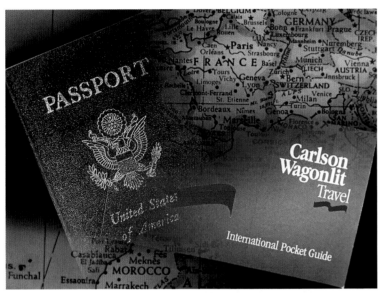

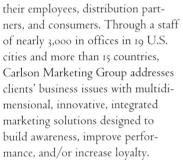

their employees, distribution partners, and consumers. Through a staff of nearly 3,000 in offices in 19 U.S. cities and more than 15 countries, Carlson Marketing Group addresses clients' business issues with multidimensional, innovative, integrated marketing solutions designed to build awareness, improve performance, and/or increase loyalty.

These solutions are backed by the most effective technologies and an extensive collection of integrated resources for implementation of successful marketing programs, and are followed with measures to track program performance and results.

Carlson's expansion into the hospitality industry came with the purchase of the original Radisson Hotel in downtown Minneapolis in 1962, and the construction of new Radisson facilities in Minneapolis-St. Paul and Duluth. This move was the genesis of Carlson Companies' hospitality businesses, which today encompass the globe with more than 1,100 hotel, cruise ship, and restaurant locations under the flags of Regent Hotels International, Radisson Hotels Worldwide, Radisson Seven Seas Cruises, Country Inns & Suites by Carlson, Country Kitchen, T.G.I. Friday's, and Italianni's restaurants, plus Friday's Front Row Sports Grills.

During the past two decades, Carlson Companies has made numerous acquisitions and extensive expansion of its retail and wholesale travel business, including the purchase of Ask Mr. Foster travel agencies in 1979, A.T. Mays (UK) in 1990, and a partnership with Wagonlit Travel, Paris in 1994. The growth has propelled Carlson Wagonlit Travel into position as one of the two largest travel management brand names in the world, with more than 4,100 travel locations in 125 countries around the globe. Currently, the Carlson family of travel agencies books more travel in a single week than 99.9 percent of U.S. travel agencies book in an entire year.

TRIED AND TRUE PRINCIPLES

Despite Carlson Companies' international scope and extensive diversification, it remains committed to the principles upon which it was founded—entrepreneurial initiative, goal setting, and excellence of performance—with the objective of being the best in each of its businesses. "A successful company must continually analyze society's needs, develop ideas that meet those needs, and carry the ideas to successful fruition in the global marketplace," according to Carlson.

Carlson continues to oversee the corporation's far-flung operations as chairman of its board. His right-hand man is actually a woman, daughter Marilyn Carlson Nelson, who is vice chair of Carlson Companies and cochair of Carlson Wagonlit Travel. "The Carlson Companies story has just begun to unfold. Curt's passion to serve the customer better than anyone else at the fairest price on the market will propel us to new markets, products, and services. We have great roots," Nelson says. "They will sustain our growth well into the 21st century."

CLOCKWISE FROM TOP LEFT: CARLSON WAGONLIT TRAVEL BOOKS BUSINESS AND LEISURE TRAVEL THROUGHOUT THE WORLD.

THREE GENERATIONS OF CARLSONS ARE INVOLVED IN THE OPERATIONS OF CARLSON COMPANIES, INC. THEY ARE (LEFT TO RIGHT) CURTIS L. CARLSON, CHAIRMAN AND CEO, CARLSON COMPANIES, INC. & CARLSON HOLDINGS, INC.; MARILYN C. NELSON, VICE CHAIR, CARLSON COMPANIES, INC. AND COCHAIR, CARLSON WAGONLIT TRAVEL; AND CURTIS NELSON, PRESIDENT AND CHIEF EXECUTIVE OFFICER, CARLSON HOSPITALITY WORLDWIDE.

CARLSON HOSPITALITY WORLDWIDE OFFERS MULTIPLE BRANDS AT ONE LOCATION IN THIS COUNTRY INN AND SUITES/ T.G.I. FRIDAY'S RESTAURANT AT THE MALL OF AMERICA IN BLOOMINGTON.

Since its inception in 1949, Automatic Products international, ltd. has focused on quality and reliability in the manufacturing of dependable automated vending machines. Such dedication has propelled the company to a leadership role in vending throughout the world. With more than 400,000 square feet of manufacturing capacity and a strong distribution network, Automatic Products international, ltd. (APi) is committed to designing

and manufacturing equipment that provides innovation, simplicity, selectivity, convenience, and reliability to customers in more than 35 countries around the world.

However, APi's growth and development did not occur overnight. The hard work of dedicated employees, innovative engineering, and a long-term commitment to the marketplace have allowed the company and its customers the best opportunity for success.

Growth of a Leader

APi was formed from a sheet metal job shop, and for the first few years the company focused its efforts on making sheet metal cabinets. In the 1950s and 1960s, APi expanded its product line to include candy and snack merchandisers, as well as cigarette machines. In 1966, the Pastryshop followed and demand for the company's machines soared.

Substantial growth continued through the 1970s, when the product mix was again expanded to include the Snackshop in 1976. Over the next

two decades there were four generations of glass-front merchandising machines; each generation resulted in a piece of equipment that provided increased convenience, selectivity, and ease of operation.

Current machines, such as those in the company's popular 110 Series Snackshop line, have the capacity to hold up to 1,260 items in 70 different selection spirals, and include chiller units to keep products fresh and automatic programming that directs the machine to turn itself off during designated time periods. And, for the customer's convenience, these machines will accept coins, dollars, or debit cards for payment.

In 1981, the company acquired RMi, a company in Warminster, Pennsylvania, that produced fresh brew and freeze-dry coffee machines. But making a high-quality cup of coffee was not enough. In 1986, APi introduced the first domestic vending machine to actually grind coffee beans and brew them one cup at a time.

Over the next 10 years, the company added options including dual cup capability, adjustable cup rings, and a unique "build-a-drink" menu system. APi's hot beverage merchandisers can vend any type of gourmet coffee—espresso, cappuccino, café mocha—as well as adding just the right amount of sugar, cream, or artificial sweetener. With the Model 213 Hot Beverage Merchandiser, customers can choose from several premium hot drink selections, two cup sizes, three strength options, and three additive strength options. Today, APi's coffee machines are the best-selling machine in the vending coffee market, and the company is a world leader in the production of innovative vending and merchandising machines.

President and CEO Alan J. Suitor (standing) is flanked by Vice President of Manufacturing Scott Edgerton (left) and Vice President of Total Quality Management Richard Gross (right).

Whether it's the sleek, new Model LCM3 Glassfront Snack Merchandiser and Model 213 Hot Beverage Merchandiser or the "Matching Pair" Candyshop and Smokeshop (circa 1972), APi has always produced contemporary, attractively styled machines (bottom).

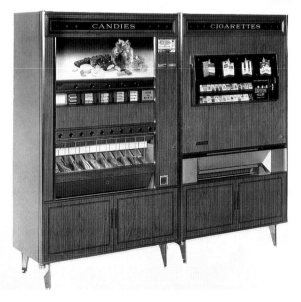

Worldwide Growth

By the 1980s, APi's leadership in the domestic marketplace was well known, and requests to expand its offerings outside the United States represented an opportunity and a challenge. "We couldn't just take the same machines we use in the United States and ship them over to Europe," says APi President and CEO Alan J. Suitor. "Often we're not dealing with the same types of products. For instance, the chocolate in Europe is much different than the chocolate available in the United States. That means that it melts at higher temperatures. We had to specifically design machines that would accommodate the snacks and beverages for European customer tastes."

Export machine requirements resulted in the development of chilled versions of the glass-front merchandisers with a scrolling display available in seven different languages, and the Model 402, a machine with a European design that delivered hot and cold beverages.

Strategies for Success

APi continues to aggressively pursue additional international markets, including South America, Latin America, Mexico, and the Pacific Rim. "Our goal is to double our sales in the next five years, and expanding our international business is a key factor in helping us achieve that goal," says Suitor.

The company's long-term growth strategy includes three elements. First, APi will increase its product offerings through the standard distribution channels. "We plan to release one new product each year for the next five years," says Suitor. The company will also look into nontraditional vending applications. For example, they may develop a merchandiser that vends overnight express envelopes or safety items such as goggles or latex gloves.

Finally, APi will look to changing demographics to tap into new customer markets. "People are looking for healthy, low-fat items when it comes to snacking," says Suitor. "They want their food to look good, and also be good for them. However, they are also looking for convenience and value, and that's where we believe vending comes into the picture. The potential for attracting new custom-

ers is enormous as long as we remain conscious of changing trends and continue to respond to what they are looking for."

Today, the third generation of family owners continues APi's commitment to its customers and the vending industry. Already known around the world for its quality products and post-sales service, the company recently became the only North American vending company to receive ISO 9001 certification for its quality manufacturing processes. "At APi, we will always strive to provide innovative and reliable equipment that is simple to service and operate, and convenient for people to use," says Suitor. "We have nearly 50 years of commitment to the vending industry, and we have a worldwide service network and 24-hour parts service to back up this commitment."

KARE 11 HAS A LONG AND RICH HISTORY IN THE MINNEAPOLIS-St. Paul community. Its seeds were planted almost 70 years ago when Minnesota fans first heard KARE 11's predecessor, WRHM, on their AM radio dial. ✳ The station changed hands numerous times over the next 30 years, at one point broadcasting on television Channel 4. In 1952 the station—known then as WTCN-TV and Channel 4—was sold to another broadcast company.

WTCN-TV and WMIN Radio were granted a license in 1953 for a joint operation on Channel 11, which the two stations shared until 1955 when they merged.

Throughout the next 10 years, WTCN went through many more changes. Chris Craft Industries bought the television station. The radio station was sold to another company and renamed. WTCN-TV became an independent. Due to its success as an independent television station, Channel 11 attracted Metromedia, Inc., a diversified media company that purchased it in 1971. Construction began on the modern studio facilities in suburban Golden Valley that same year.

A Gannett Broadcasting Station

On March 6, 1979, WTCN-TV became an affiliate of the NBC Television Network. The changing dynamics of the Twin Cities at that time provided WTCN-TV with significant growth opportunities. Over the next several years, Gannett Broadcasting—one of the largest diversified news and information companies in the United States—kept its eye on the station and the local marketplace. Gannett is the United States' largest newspaper group in terms of circulation, and publisher of USA Today, the nation's largest-selling daily newspaper. The company now owns and operates 16 television stations and cable television systems in major U.S. markets.

Seeing WTCN-TV's strength and potential for future development, Gannett purchased the station in 1983. Along with the purchase came the decision to bring some fresh faces into the newsroom, people who could grow with this new, forward-looking station. Enter Paul Magers and Diana Pierce as news anchors, and Randy Shaver in the sports department. A Twin Cities favorite, anchor Pat Miles, came on board in 1988, and Ken Barlow joined the team in 1990.

In 1985 the station's call letters were changed briefly to WUSA, but one year later those call letters were moved to Gannett's newly purchased station in Washington, D.C., and Channel 11 was renamed KARE 11.

Today KARE 11 serves nearly 1.5 million homes as the NBC affiliate in the Minneapolis-St. Paul area. It is carried by more than 250 cable systems, is satellite fed throughout central Canada via Canadian Satellite Communications, and is widely regarded as the market leader for news, information, and weather.

What's in a Name?

Although the station's call letters are no coincidence, few could have predicted how apropos the name would turn out to be. Adding a few new faces wasn't the only change the station undertook in 1983; rather, station executives developed a plan to reposition KARE 11 as the station that cares about the local community and its members, as well as the newsworthy events of any given day. From the very beginning, the members of the KARE 11 news team placed a great deal of importance on maintaining a strong presence throughout

THE KARE 11 NEWS ANCHORS MAINTAIN A STRONG PRESENCE THROUGHOUT THE TWIN CITIES AREA (RIGHT).

NEWS ANCHORS KEN BARLOW, PAT MILES, PAUL MAGERS, DIANA PIERCE, AND RANDY SHAVER KEEP THE TWIN CITIES UP TO DATE ON NATIONAL AND LOCAL NEWS (BELOW).

ANN MARSDEN

ANN MARSDEN

the Twin Cities area. If there was a local parade, food drive, charity fund-raiser, or banquet, KARE 11 was there, not only to cover the event but also to participate.

KARE 11's visibility at these events gradually helped to redefine the way that community and television were intertwined. "A station's newscast, particularly the personalities of the news team, helps shape the community's perception of a station as a whole," says Steve Thaxton, vice president and creative director for KARE 11. "In our case, the dedication and involvement of our news team outside of the daily broadcast helped reinforce the idea that we were in touch with the local community, and that we really do care about what's happening throughout the Minneapolis-St. Paul area."

Thaxton explains that the difference between KARE 11 and a lot of other stations is that the staff has taken on personal ownership of the station's image; they walk the walk, so to speak, not because they have to, but because they believe so strongly in what the station stands for. It's the individual members of KARE 11's team—not

the station's executives—who help organize, promote, and participate in the ongoing KARE 11-sponsored community events such as Health Fair 11, Food for Families, and the Volunteer Connection.

Since 1983, Magers and Pierce have hosted the "Eleven Who Care" awards, a televised program recognizing the contributions of grassroots volunteers and promoting the spirit of volunteerism in Twin Cities communities. KARE 11 presents winners with a $1,100 donation for the charity or community organization of their choice. The program has continued to gain recognition in large part because of the dedication

of the KARE 11 staff, who tirelessly work on the program like a social cause.

"The personalities and tenure of a station's news team are the most important factors in a station's long-term success," says Thaxton. "KARE 11 is fortunate because it is backed by a corporation that was willing to invest millions of dollars to build a solid foundation. But our current success—and what looks to be a bright future—is a result of the people who show up to work here every day. They are the reason KARE 11 News is, and will continue to be, the Twin Cities' top-rated newscast."

CLOCKWISE FROM TOP LEFT: SINCE 1983, DIANA PIERCE AND PAUL MAGERS HAVE HOSTED THE "ELEVEN WHO CARE" AWARDS, A TELEVISED PROGRAM RECOGNIZING THE CONTRIBUTIONS OF GRASSROOTS VOLUNTEERS AND PROMOTING THE SPIRIT OF VOLUNTEERISM IN TWIN CITIES COMMUNITIES. THEY ARE SHOWN HERE WITH RECIPIENTS JULES AND DORA ZAIDENWEBER.

METEROLOGIST KEN BARLOW ADDRESSES THE CROWD AT THE MINNESOTA STATE FAIR.

KARE 11 BROADCASTS LIVE FROM THE MINNESOTA STATE FAIR.

MEDTRONIC, INC. IS THE WORLD'S LEADING MEDICAL TECHnology company specializing in implantable and invasive therapies. During the company's 1996 fiscal year, Medtronic products and therapies benefited more than 1.3 million people worldwide as the company focused on its mission of alleviating pain, restoring health, and extending life in partnership with the medical community. Medtronic has placed a special

emphasis on leveraging its technology to address unmet medical needs, thereby fulfilling its mission while creating new markets and growth platforms for the future.

Guided by its mission statement, which includes a directive to focus on growth in the company's areas of "maximum strength and ability," Medtronic continually investigates medical conditions that have unmet patient needs for cures or more effective treatments. Management evaluates these needs within the context of the health care marketplace and the company's technological strengths, then moves forward in areas of greatest potential for a positive impact on patients' lives. Current initiatives include products and therapies for atrial fibrillation, heart failure management, minimally invasive cardiac surgery, and the treatment of stroke, restenosis, incontinence, sleep apnea,

aneurysms, tremor, spasticity, chronic pain, and neurodegenerative disorders such as ALS and Alzheimer's and Parkinson's diseases.

A COMMITMENT TO MEDICAL INNOVATION

A commitment to restoring lives through medical innovation has been integral to Medtronic's growth and success since 1949. That was the year Earl Bakken, then a 25-year-old electrical engineer, and his brother-in-law, lumberyard manager Palmer Hermundslie, set up shop in a northeast Minneapolis garage and began repairing electrical equipment for local hospitals.

Through their work, Bakken and Hermundslie became acquainted with Dr. C. Walton Lillehei, a pioneer in open-heart surgery at the University of Minnesota who was exploring the new frontier of applying electrical stimulation to control heart activity. In 1957—the same year that he and Hermundslie incorporated their venture under the name Medtronic—Bakken developed the first wearable, external, battery-powered, transistorized pacemaker for Lillehei.

Today, half of the world's pacemakers are manufactured by Medtronic and more than 2 million of the company's pacing systems have been implanted. The company has greatly expanded and diversified, and now has approximately 12,000 employees, one-third of whom work in the Twin Cities area. Medtronic's business sectors—Pacing, Vascular, Cardiac Surgery, Neurological, and Developing Businesses and Ventures—encompass 14 separate business units and nine ventures with product lines and therapies for bradycardia pacing, tachyarrhythmia

management, coronary and peripheral vascular therapy, and neuroradiology, as well as stents, ablation systems, heart valves, extracorporeal perfusion circuits for cardiac surgery, blood management systems, implantable neurological drug delivery and stimulation systems, and hydrocephalic shunts.

In addition to the emphasis on addressing unmet medical needs, Medtronic's growth strategies include continued market share gains in its core businesses, acquisitions designed to establish new platforms for growth, and global expansion in both established and developing markets.

International business growth has been a Medtronic priority for more than 30 years; today non-U.S. sales are approaching 50 percent of total revenues. In addition to the developed markets of North America, Western Europe, Japan, and Australia, Medtronic also is building a strong base for future growth in developing markets in India, China, Asia, Latin America, the Mediterranean, and Africa that account for more than 80 percent of the world's population. The company does business in more than 120 countries and its operations are organized into three global areas: Americas, Europe/Middle East/Africa, and Asia/Pacific.

Over the past 40 years, Medtronic has channeled major creative energies and financial resources into research and development. Nearly 2,300 U.S. and international patents have been awarded to Medtronic scientists and engineers since the company began. The company is a medical technology industry leader in the area of research and development, applying more than 10 percent of its annual revenues to R&D. Medtronic's

COMPUTER-GENERATED THREE-DIMENSIONAL MODELS OF THE HEART HELP RESEARCHERS LIKE SENIOR MEDTRONIC SCIENTIST AND RESEARCH FELLOW RAHUL MEHRA DETERMINE THE PATHWAYS OF ELECTRICAL CURRENT FLOW IN THE HEART WHEN IT IS STIMULATED BY ELECTRODES.

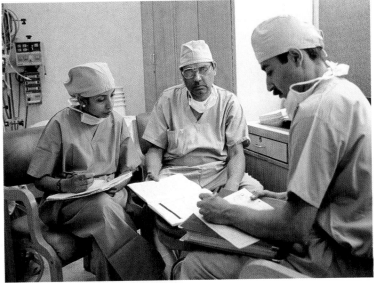

philosophy is to invest simultaneously in several alternate product designs or therapy approaches, increasing the odds of finding the highest quality, most cost effective solution to any given medical problem.

A COMMITMENT TO THE COMMUNITY

Thanks to the Medtronic Foundation, substantial resources also are channeled back into the communities in which Medtronic does business. Established in 1978, the Foundation makes grants that focus on education, health, and community, with priority given to programs that benefit the socioeconomically disadvantaged. Two programs in particular are designed to encourage young people's interest in scientific careers. Science and Technology Are Rewarding (STAR) grants are designed to stimulate and sustain students' interest in science. Medtronic scientists, engineers, and technicians involved in the Medtronic Masterminds program volunteer to take science and math workshops to Twin Cities-area schools and nonprofit groups, host student tours of Medtronic facilities, and serve as mentors for students who need science or health-related career guidance.

Philanthropic activities continue to expand both in the United States and other parts of the world. There are Medtronic Foundation grant recipients in Japan, Europe, Canada,

CLOCKWISE FROM TOP LEFT: THE TIME NEEDED TO COMPLETE FINAL ASSEMBLY ON IMPLANTABLE PULSE GENERATOR PRODUCT LINES HAS BEEN CUT SIGNIFICANTLY AS MEDTRONIC CONTINUES TO REFINE AND AUTOMATE GLOBAL MANUFACTURING OPERATIONS.

BECAUSE CUSTOMER EDUCATION IS CRUCIAL TO MEDTRONIC'S SUCCESS, THE COMPANY HAS 12 BAKKEN EDUCATION CENTERS AROUND THE WORLD.

MORE THAN 100 JUNIOR-HIGH-AGE STUDENTS FROM THE INNER-CITY AREAS OF MINNEAPOLIS AND ST. PAUL TOOK PART IN THE MINNESOTA ZOO MENTOR PROGRAM LAST SUMMER, FUNDED BY THE MEDTRONIC FOUNDATION'S STAR (SCIENCE AND TECHNOLOGY ARE REWARDING) INITIATIVE.

Asia, and even South Africa, where the foundation has supported the development of the nonprofit Medtronic Southern Africa Institute of Cardiovascular Medicine at Baragwanath Hospital in Johannesburg.

While Medtronic has grown and changed over the years, one

element has remained constant: the goal of saving lives and improving the quality of life for millions of people around the world. This mission continues to serve as both the ethical and practical framework for Medtronic's operations.

IN SEPTEMBER 1959, WHEN MILK SOLD FOR 50 CENTS A GALLON, bread was almost 20 cents a loaf, eggs were 53 cents a dozen, and coffee was a whopping 78 cents a pound, Wally Pettit decided to enter the growing retail convenience food business. Along with his partner, Herbert Koch, Pettit founded Tom Thumb Food Markets Inc. and opened the first store on the corner of St. Paul's Snelling and Larpenteur avenues. By the end of the 1960s, the two men oper-

ated 18 Tom Thumb locations, and in 1979 they had more than 100 stores throughout Minnesota and western Wisconsin.

The company sustained steady growth by opening new stores and acquiring regional convenience store chains such as Minit Mart, Miss Swiss, and Lil' General stores. In 1987, Pettit became the sole owner of Tom Thumb Food Markets and today, along with his wife, Penny, and his six children, operates more than 150 stores throughout the region. Pettit was named Minnesota's 1996 Grocer of the Year by Minnesota Grocers' Association.

ROOTED IN GOODNESS

In most people's minds, Tom Thumb stores are known for three things: good food, a friendly atmosphere, and—of course—the guy with the pointy hat and little red suit. Since the first store opened in 1959, Tom Thumb has targeted "family" consumers, providing them with an extended line of grocery items and a commitment to community service. "Our competitive edge is maintaining

a food orientation in the stores," says Derrell Deming, director of marketing. "We need to sell gasoline to compete in our market, but our edge is inside sales, particularly our grocery selection. We are a food-based convenience store that happens to sell gas, not a gas station with a few food essentials on our shelves."

Tom Thumb's food orientation stems back to the com-pany's roots in the dairy business. In 1946, Wally Pettit began his career in the dairy

industry as a driver for Dutch Mill Dairy in Loretto, Minnesota. After holding similar positions at other regional dairy operations and completing a two-year stint in the army, Pettit started Polka Dot Dairy with the help of Herbert Koch.

The business grew significantly by selling a variety of dairy products to neighboring supermarkets within a 150-mile radius of Minneapolis/St. Paul. But it was really the personalities of Pettit and his wife, Penny,

▲ MAC MCGOON

IT WAS THE PERSONALITIES OF WALLY AND PENNY PETTIT, AS WELL AS THEIR WORK ETHIC, THAT DIFFERENTIATED POLKA DOT DAIRY AND, SUBSEQUENTLY, TOM THUMB FOOD MARKETS, FROM OTHER RETAIL OPERATIONS (RIGHT).

TOM THUMB FOOD MARKETS OFFER MUCH MORE THAN AVERAGE CONVENIENCE MARKETS, INCLUDING FRESH PRODUCE AND A VARIETY OF DAIRY PRODUCTS (BOTTOM LEFT AND RIGHT).

as well as their work ethic, that differentiated Polka Dot and, subsequently, Tom Thumb, from other retail operations. "We really are a reflection of Wally and Penny and the family," says Deming. "And that family spirit pervades all of our stores to this day."

Although the dairy business was expanding, Pettit and Koch wanted to create more demand for their products. "We had to make up our minds at that time," says Pettit. "If you wanted an outlet to sell your products in the Twin Cities, you had to create your own." That's exactly what they did, and convenience store shopping would never be the same.

Meeting Customer Needs

Historically, Tom Thumb has devoted more space to groceries than most convenience stores. The stores are also known for their Double T Delis, which serve everything from doughnuts and muffins to pressure-fried chicken, hot entrées, fresh baked bread, and hotdogs. And, of course, there are the famous homemade sandwiches and hand-dipped ice-cream cones, which are considered the food-service cornerstones at Tom Thumb.

Deming admits that one of the challenges in the coming years will be striking the right balance in each store between an impressive array of food-service items and grocery square footage. "What you see in our stores

is an evolution of our grocery background," he says. "Where we're having our conflict is on the question of what do we do with the available footage? How much food-service do we include? Is a full-blown deli necessary or should we concentrate more on self-serve, which is less expensive and has a better return on investment?" Tom Thumb plans to address these challenges by keeping a close eye on its customers and their needs. Product offerings are constantly being reviewed, revised, and adjusted, depending on the location and customer base. And the company is not afraid to try new things to make its customers happy.

For example, the Tom Thumb store in downtown Minneapolis rivals just about any convenience store in the country in terms of giving customers what they want. Fancy muffins, gourmet crackers, cheeses, coffees, bottled water, and chocolate

truffles are just a few of the "convenience" items customers can pick up. Another example of the company's willingness to adapt is the recent conversion of 10 Tom Thumb stores into Bonkers Discount stores. "We found that customers in these neighborhoods were more interested in traditional convenience items and less interested in perishable produce, so we developed a store that better met their needs," says Deming.

Polka Dot Dairy and Tom Thumb Food Markets have been successfully meeting customer needs for almost 40 years. The Tom Thumb chain is consistently ranked as one of the top 50 convenience stores in the nation in terms of sales. And with Pettit at the helm, the sky's the limit. "We've been around longer than any other convenience store in this area," says Deming. "And we plan to maintain a major presence for many years to come."

CLOCKWISE FROM TOP LEFT: FOUNDED BY WALLY PETTIT, POLKA DOT DAIRY HAS GROWN SIGNIFICANTLY BY SELLING A VARIETY OF DAIRY PRODUCTS TO NEIGHBORING SUPERMARKETS WITHIN A 150-MILE RADIUS OF MINNEAPOLIS/ST. PAUL.

TOM THUMB FOOD MARKETS ARE KNOWN FOR THREE THINGS: GOOD FOOD, A FRIENDLY ATMOSPHERE, AND—OF COURSE—THE GUY WITH THE POINTY HAT AND LITTLE RED SUIT.

THE STORES ARE ALSO KNOWN FOR THEIR DOUBLE T DELIS, WHICH SERVE EVERYTHING FROM DOUGHNUTS AND MUFFINS TO PRESSURE-FRIED CHICKEN, HOT ENTRÉES, AND FRESH BAKED BREAD. AND, OF COURSE, THERE ARE THE FAMOUS HOMEMADE SANDWICHES AND HAND-DIPPED ICE-CREAM CONES, WHICH ARE CONSIDERED THE FOOD-SERVICE CORNERSTONES AT TOM THUMB.

"WE TREAT EVERY BUILDING AS IF IT WERE OUR OWN." THIS simple business philosophy permeates Owens Services Corporation and has propelled the 40-year-old company to regional and national prominence. Owens has provided the right answers for thousands of commercial, industrial, and institutional customers, helping them to run a better building. The company continues to be the right team to help design, construct, operate,

A DEEP AND ABIDING COMMIT-
MENT TO QUALITY RUNS
THROUGHOUT OWENS SERVICES
CORPORATION'S 100-PLUS EM-
PLOYEES (BOTTOM LEFT).

OWENS HAS PROVIDED THE
RIGHT ANSWERS FOR THOUSANDS
OF COMMERCIAL, INDUSTRIAL,
AND INSTITUTIONAL CUSTOMERS,
HELPING THEM TO RUN A BETTER
BUILDING (BOTTOM RIGHT).

and maintain its customers' mechanical and electrical systems.

Whether through engineering, construction, building services, or control systems, Owens' three main measures of performance have remained unchanged. Reliability: Will a customer's mechanical and electrical systems perform consistently and when they are needed the most? Comfort: Are a company's employees comfortable and productive in their indoor environment? Are there indoor air quality problems lurking beneath the surface? Cost-Effective Operation: Is a company's building consuming more cash than it should?

Does the money saved with a low-first-cost solution result in bloated energy bills and costly maintenance headaches?

Because of its dedication to providing reliability, comfort, and cost-effective operation, Owens was named Contractor of the Year in 1996 by *Contracting Business* magazine.

SINGLE-SOURCE RESPONSIBILITY FOR ABSOLUTE ACCOUNTABILITY

Owens' ability to provide single-source responsibility allows it to deliver outstanding customer service. Its broad range of abilities and skills gives Owens the right perspective to help in any heating, ventilation, air-conditioning, and refrigeration (HVACR) situation. Owens' integrated disciplines enable it to produce results, not excuses.

Owens personnel analyze a facility's needs, engineer solutions to the problem found, implement

the work to achieve comfort and efficiency improvements, and live with the results through guaranteed performance. The company provides ongoing equipment service and maintenance, system monitoring, and building operation. Owens can finance, and even own, a client's energy assets—taking them off the company's balance sheet and reducing liability.

Over the years, as its list of satisfied customers has expanded from local facilities to multilocation national corporations, Owens' mission has never wavered. "We achieve our goals by making sure you achieve yours," says CEO and company founder Robert Owens.

A COMMITMENT TO QUALITY

A deep and abiding commitment to quality runs throughout Owens. "We work very hard and will go to the wall for our customers," says John Owens, Robert Owens' son

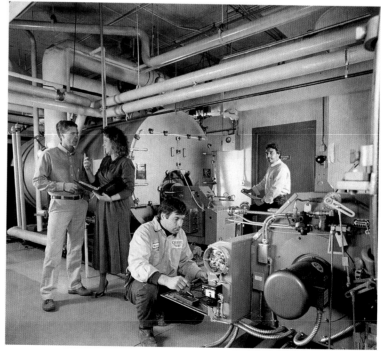

and the company president. "I believe contractors have the greatest impact on customer buildings and productivity, so it's absolutely essential that Owens has no bad jobs." This attitude is reflected by the 100-plus employees at Owens. In fact, employees list their home phone numbers on their business cards so customers can always reach them.

More evidence of this commitment is hung in the entrance of the Owens Training Center and printed on the back of employees' cards. It is the Owens Quality Commitment: "To meet or exceed customer requirements every time; to provide an environment for our employees, which fosters personal growth, professionalism, and team effort; to be good corporate and individual citizens of our communities."

To ensure that employees have everything they need to get the job done right, Owens fosters an environment for growth and development through extensive employee training and involvement in management decisions. All employees have a voice in company committees making decisions on training, safety, the chlorofluorocarbon (CFC) issue, and Owens' quality improvement process.

It is no surprise that this kind of commitment extends to corporate citizenship as well. Owens is one of a select group of Minnesota companies that has been recognized for more than a decade with Keystone Awards for donating more than 5 percent of

pretax profits to charitable and civic organizations.

A History of Innovation

Innovation has been a key element in Owens' success from the very start. To become a better service provider, the company began searching for ways to better predict equipment breakdown and failures. What it developed as a result of its search set the standard for Predictive Maintenance today. For example, in the 1960s, Owens pioneered the use of refrigerant oil analysis as a standard diagnostic tool in the industry, saving building owners thousands of dollars in costly breakdown service or premature equipment failure.

Prompted by the 1973 oil embargo, Owens began providing extensive building energy audits and programs to help customers lower operating costs. Out of this service developed the Owens Leasing Company in 1975, established to enable customers to finance energy retrofits through future energy cost savings. Today, this practice is widely used and most commonly referred to as Performance Contracting.

When the Environmental Protection Agency and the U.S. Congress enacted the Clean Air Act, Owens was prepared. John Owens had formed a committee within the company in 1989 to study the CFC issue. Owens has become a recognized authority on the issue, continuing to guide companies through the

phaseout of CFCs, and again taking the lead by helping companies navigate through the volatile and confusing Indoor Air Quality process.

For 40 years Owens has been on the leading edge of the HVACR industry. The company's core ideologies—customer service, single-source responsibility, concern for employees, innovation, and integrity—continue to provide the foundation and compass for Owens. "We continuously seek new opportunities, better ways to solve customer comfort problems, and smarter ways to do business," says John Owens. "We plan to adapt to industry changes, while also staying ahead of and creating change as we grow. What will not change are the core ideologies upon which this company is built."

CLOCKWISE FROM TOP LEFT: OWENS CONTINUES TO BE THE RIGHT TEAM TO HELP DESIGN, CONSTRUCT, OPERATE, AND MAINTAIN ITS CUSTOMERS' MECHANICAL AND ELECTRICAL SYSTEMS.

KEEPING OWENS ON THE LEADING EDGE OF THE HVACR INDUSTRY ARE (FROM LEFT) JOHN OWENS, ROBERT OWENS, AND JIM OWENS.

OWENS PERSONNEL ANALYZE A FACILITY'S NEEDS, ENGINEER SOLUTIONS TO THE PROBLEMS FOUND, IMPLEMENT THE WORK TO ACHIEVE COMFORT AND EFFICIENCY IMPROVEMENTS, AND LIVE WITH THE RESULTS THROUGH GUARANTEED PERFORMANCE.

Linked to the Future

THERE ARE SEVERAL DEFINING MOMENTS IN THE HISTORY OF a state. For Minnesota, October 25, 1987—the day the Minnesota Twins beat the St. Louis Cardinals 4-2 to win the World Series—is one of those dates. "People often tell me they still remember where they were and what they were doing the day the Twins won the Series," says Twins President Jerry Bell. "There is such a strong sense of community and pride associated with the team, and that win really embodied a lot of those feelings."

Winning the World Series was so much fun that the team did it again in 1991, defeating the Atlanta Braves 1-0 in 10 innings in the seventh and deciding game. "Certainly the players on those two championship teams deserve credit for playing outstanding baseball," says Bell. "But I know that most players would say the support and enthusiasm of the fans was a strong driving force behind the victories. There are few teams whose fans are as enthusiastic and loyal as the fans of the Minnesota Twins."

LAYING THE FOUNDATION

On October 26, 1960, Calvin Griffith, president of the Washington Senators, announced the historic decision to move his American League baseball franchise from the nation's capital to the Twin Cities, giving birth to the Minnesota Twins. In 1961 well over 1 million fans turned out during the team's first season at Metropolitan Stadium in Bloomington. They saw a struggling team that finished seventh out of 10, but the fans kept coming back. In 1962 the Twins jumped from seventh to second, the first of many pennant runs in the 1960s—a decade in which Minnesota led the American League in attendance.

Fans turned out to watch such players as Harmon Killebrew, Tony Oliva, Bob Allison, Zoilo Versalles, Jim "Mudcat" Grant, Al Worthington, Jim Kaat, and Jimmie Hall win the American League Championship in 1965 and Western Division crowns in 1969 and 1970. The '70s brought leaner days for Minnesota, but there were plenty of memorable moments, such as Oliva's and Killebrew's last

KIRBY PUCKETT EARNED THE DISTINCTION AS MINNESOTA'S ALL-TIME MOST POPULAR ATH-LETE WITH A HISTORIC CAREER, BOTH ON AND OFF THE FIELD (ABOVE).

THE TWINS CELEBRATE THE FIRST OF THEIR TWO WORLD CHAMPIONSHIPS IN OCTOBER 1987 (FAR RIGHT).

home games, and Rod Carew's run at the untouchable .400 mark. In the later years of the decade, attention increasingly turned to the new era to be initiated on opening day, 1982, in the new Hubert H. Humphrey Metrodome.

In 1984 Carl Pohlad purchased the team; two years later Tom Kelly became team manager and the foundation for success was in place.

NAMES TO REMEMBER

Each year brings the chance for fans to greet a few new faces, support their favorite veterans, and bid farewell to a few cherished friends.

During the 1996 season, fans shared the experience of Paul Molitor's becoming the 21st player in baseball history to collect 3,000 or more career hits. They also shared their disappointment when Kirby Puckett, the Twins' all-time leader in hits, runs, and doubles, and Minnesota's most-loved athlete, was forced to retire. Puckett will become the fifth Minnesota Twin—along with Killebrew, Carew, Oliva, and Kent Hrbek—to have his number retired as a sign of respect and thanks for all the great moments he and all the other past and present Twins have given to their fans.

ADVANCE CIRCUITS, INC.

WHEN IT CAME TIME TO LAUNCH THE FIRST SPACE shuttle, NASA called on Minneapolis-based Advance Circuits, Inc. The payloads the shuttle carried into space extensively utilized circuit technology—and NASA knew that Advance Circuits was the company to go to if only the best would do. ✳ A Johnson Matthey Company, Advance Circuits, Inc. was organized in 1967 to produce

multilayer circuit boards, which at the time was the ultimate in printed wiring density. Until the early 1980s, the company's product was used by electronics firms primarily in the defense industry for communications and aerospace applications. In fact, the U.S. Air Force relied on Advance Circuits products to attain the extreme accuracy demanded in missile guidance and control.

The year 1983 saw the introduction of the personal computer and the birth of Advance Circuits' commercial division. Electronic hardware was in great demand, and Advance Circuits responded by producing the high-technology multilayer and double-sided boards needed by the commercial market. By the mid-1980s, the company was selling to international markets, including Asia and Europe, and commercial sales accounted for more than 50 percent of total sales.

In the early 1990s, to meet the needs of an ever-competitive marketplace, Advance Circuits acquired Florida-based Targ-it-Tronics and Minneapolis-based Acsist as part of its strategy to become the number one supplier of printed circuit board solutions to the leading telecommunications, computer, and semiconductor companies.

In 1995 Advance Circuits was acquired by London-based Johnson Matthey, a world leader in advanced materials technology with 175 years of experience and operations in 37 countries worldwide. "Since the early 1990s, we have tried to position ourselves as a one-stop-shopping resource for our customers," says Benoit Pouliquen, Advance Circuits president. "Customers look to the technology leaders, and we want to be one of those leaders. Johnson

Matthey gives us the financial backing and electronic expertise to help further solidify our leadership position." Pouliquen adds that the acquisition has also created good growth opportunities for Advance Circuits in the mobile communications, high-end computer, and semiconductor materials markets.

WORTH THE INVESTMENT

Quality has always been a top priority at Advance Circuits. In 1988 the company started preparing for the Malcolm Baldrige Quality Award; in 1992 the company was a Malcolm Baldrige site finalist; and in 1996 all four of the company's manufacturing facilities achieved ISO 9002 registration. The company also prides itself on nurturing growth opportunities for its employees. "Our industry is obviously very capital intensive," says Pouliquen. "But we recognize that, just as we need to invest in new technology to ensure that we produce the high-quality product, we also need to invest in our people, since they are our greatest asset."

With more than $200 million in sales in 1996, Advance Circuits

is the fourth-largest printed circuit board manufacturer in the nation, ranking among the 20 largest in the world. Pouliquen attributes the company's success to its ability to remain focused and customer-driven. "We've paid close attention to the trends, we've taken advantage of growth opportunities, and we've concentrated on doing what we do best. Other companies may brag about the large number of customers they have; we prefer to focus on a few key customers and let the high quality of our product do the bragging for us."

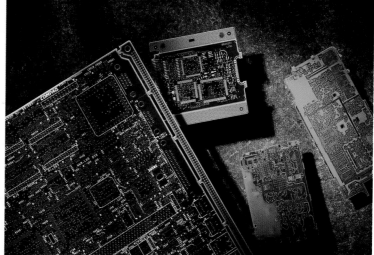

CLOCKWISE FROM TOP: ADVANCE CIRCUITS MANUFACTURES SEVERAL SPECIAL PRODUCT LINES FOR THE LEADING TELECOMMUNICATIONS AND COMPUTER COMPANIES.

ADVANCE CIRCUITS PRODUCES HIGH-TECHNOLOGY MULTILAYER AND DOUBLE-SIDED BOARDS FOR THE COMMERCIAL MARKET.

THE COMPANY SUPPLIES PRODUCTS TO SEMICONDUCTOR MATERIALS MARKETS WORLDWIDE.

Linked to the Future

HAVING FIRST OPENED ITS DOORS TO GUESTS ON JULY 1, 1995, as the Regal Minneapolis Hotel, this property may be considered a newcomer to the downtown Minneapolis area. But a second glance will show the Regal's impressive structure to be a familiar face. Originally constructed in 1963 and named Capp Towers after its owner, Marty Capp, the hotel has undergone three name changes on its way to becoming the

Regal. As part of the latest enhancement, the hotel has spent nearly $1 million renovating several of the guest rooms as well as the 14th-floor meeting facility. The efforts have resulted in a first-class hotel that is as regal in feel as it is in name.

LOCATION, LOCATION, LOCATION

When purchasing a house, buyers are told to consider three features: location, location, location. The same adage should hold true when one is choosing a hotel for business or leisure. With its superb central location, the Regal Minneapolis Hotel offers the perfect base from which to explore the many treasures of the Twin Cities area. Connected by a skyway to the Minneapolis Convention Center, the Regal is also

just steps away from the city's countless cultural, shopping, sports, and entertainment attractions including Orchestra Hall; Guthrie, Orpheum, and State theaters; the Hubert H. Humphrey Metrodome; and the Target Center. Because the Regal is located on the fashionable 12-block, pedestrian-transit-only Nicollet Mall, guests can take to the streets or enclosed skyway to reach some of the nearby shopping areas, featuring such stores as Dayton's, Neiman Marcus, and Saks Fifth Avenue. And the world-famous Mall of America is only minutes away aboard a convenient express bus.

Of course, once guests have checked into the Regal, they may find themselves hard pressed to find reasons to leave. The hotel's 325 guest rooms, including five suites, were

created to meet the needs of every guest, including those who require nonsmoking or handicapped-accessible rooms, or who prefer the added amenities and services of Regal Class accommodations. Express check-in and check-out, complimentary breakfast, free local calls, long-distance access, and inbound fax service in each room are just a few of the services and luxuries that make Regal Class more than good news—it's good business. All guests can also enjoy a leisurely swim in the hotel's indoor heated pool, work out in the health club, or relax their tired muscles in the sauna.

The hotel's restaurant, George's, is accessible from the skyway or the Nicollet Mall, and caters to travelers and residents of the Twin Cities alike. No ordinary hotel restaurant,

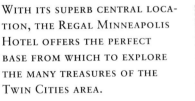

WITH ITS SUPERB CENTRAL LOCATION, THE REGAL MINNEAPOLIS HOTEL OFFERS THE PERFECT BASE FROM WHICH TO EXPLORE THE MANY TREASURES OF THE TWIN CITIES AREA.

George's offers the finest cuisine for breakfast, lunch, and dinner, including delectable pastas, salads, entrées, and desserts that are beyond compare. The menu changes every two months, allowing diners to let their taste buds travel the United States and abroad.

When it is time to get down to business, the Regal houses an impressive array of facilities to handle virtually any group, business, or social function. In addition to the 334,000-square-foot Convention Center, the hotel offers 20,000 square feet of meeting, exhibit, and banquet space, including a vehicle-accessible ballroom that can accommodate groups of up to 700. A full line of audiovisual equipment and a creative, detail-oriented catering staff are all part of the total package.

On the Regal Horizon

One of the Regal's most notable—and recognizable—features is the glass dome perched high atop the hotel. For more than three decades guests have been awed by the floor-to-ceiling city views from the Horizons meeting room—the original location of the hotel's pool—or any of the four smaller meeting rooms on the 14th floor.

In terms of the bigger picture, the future looks bright for the Regal Minneapolis Hotel. Its parent company, Regal International Holdings Limited, is a growing force in the international lodging market. In addition to owning and operating four hotels in Hong Kong and one in Toronto, it also operates 12 properties throughout the United States.

Future expansions are likely to occur on the West and East coasts as the company continues to fuse its transglobal relationships.

Regal Minneapolis Hotel General Manager Robert Rivers points out that the idea of fusion is central to the hotel chain's success: "What makes Regal Hotels so unique is that each hotel has its own distinctive flavor and style, reflective of its geographic location. Yet we all share a sense of the overall Regal culture, which is a part of everything we do, from the food and beverages we serve to the services and amenities we offer." For Rivers and the rest of the staff at the Regal Minneapolis Hotel, Regal culture translates into a service-driven attitude that helps to set the Regal apart from its competitors. "Our slogan says it all: 'Where the Regal Treatment Is Reserved. For Everybody.' We really take that to heart," Rivers says. "We want guests to come to the Regal Minneapolis Hotel and come back to us again, because of how we treat them while they're here." From all indications, the strategy seems to be working.

THE HOTEL'S 325 GUEST ROOMS, INCLUDING FIVE SUITES, WERE CREATED TO MEET THE NEEDS OF EVERY GUEST, INCLUDING THOSE WHO REQUIRE NONSMOKING OR HANDICAPPED-ACCESSIBLE ROOMS, OR WHO PREFER THE ADDED AMENITIES AND SERVICES OF REGAL CLASS ACCOMMODATIONS (TOP).

NO ORDINARY HOTEL RESTAURANT, GEORGE'S OFFERS THE FINEST CUISINE FOR BREAKFAST, LUNCH, AND DINNER, INCLUDING DELECTABLE PASTAS, SALADS, ENTRÉES, AND DESSERTS THAT ARE BEYOND COMPARE (BOTTOM).

AVR, Inc.

PEOPLE WALKING ALONG THE STREETS OF DOWNTOWN MINNEAPOLIS may not have heard of AVR, Inc. But, in fact, those people are literally surrounded by outstanding examples of AVR's solid reputation. For more than 30 years, AVR has been supplying ready-mix concrete to some of the best-known contractors in the industry. To that end, AVR has had a hand in helping to erect some of the most well known buildings in the city—the Dain

Bosworth Tower, Lincoln Center, Norwest Center, Target Center, and the Mall of America, just to name a few. As company owner and president Mathias Fischer says, "There's not a building over 30 stories in downtown Minneapolis that we haven't supplied product to." AVR is a family company that includes Fischer; his wife, Ann; son Peter; and daughter Liza.

CONSTRUCTING A SUCCESSFUL BUSINESS

In 1957 a present subsidiary company of AVR, Inc., Fischer Sand & Aggregate, began commercial mining and aggregate production in Lebanon Township, renamed Apple Valley, Minnesota, upon its incorporation in 1969. Operating out of a gravel mine on the site of Fischer's parents' farm—in the family since 1924—Fischer Sand & Aggregate slowly grew its business. As the aggregate business became more successful and a need for higher-production equipment became necessary, the Fischer family decided to expand into the

ready-mix concrete business on a very limited and localized scale.

Apple Valley Red-E-Mix, known today as AVR, was formed in 1966 and consisted of one small dry batch (transit mix) plant and six trucks. Designed to serve primarily the local communities of Apple Valley, Lakeville, and Farmington, AVR's early customer base was residential and light industrial contractors. As the years passed, AVR and Fischer Sand & Aggregate enjoyed a slow but steady growth.

In an effort to expand its marketing area, AVR purchased additional plants and trucks from Western Concrete and Suburban Ready-Mix in the early 1970s. The company continued to grow in size and prosper until 1978, when a major cement shortage became evident in the upper Midwest. During the two-year shortage, construction was at a high point and demand for concrete could not be met by local producers. In order to continue to supply its ever expanding customer base, the company made arrangements to import concrete from Canada, Spain, and the southern United States.

Customers have not forgotten Fischer's dedication and commitment to serving their needs. Since 1980, AVR has enjoyed increasing levels of success. Today the company consists of 115 trucks of the latest design at seven permanent locations, including a Robacks Modular Plant, which is considered one of the most advanced such plants in Europe and the United States. Although the nature of the business is seasonal,

CLOCKWISE FROM TOP RIGHT: MATHIAS FISCHER IS FOUNDER AND CHIEF EXECUTIVE OFFICER OF AVR, INC.

AVR WAS HIRED TO SUPPLY CONCRETE FOR THE NORWEST CENTER PROJECT, MARKING THE FIRST TIME A READY-MIX SUPPLIER HAD TAKEN COMPLETE RESPONSIBILITY FOR THE PUMPING AND SUPPLY OF LIGHTWEIGHT CONCRETE.

AVR IS ONE OF THE TOP READY-MIX PRODUCERS IN THE TWIN CITIES.

Minneapolis ✳ St. Paul

during peak times AVR employs as many as 400 people, including a team of veteran dispatchers and a full-time quality control engineer, making AVR the largest private employer in the city of Apple Valley.

In addition to its role in the business community, the Fischer family is actively involved in community service as members of the Rotary Club, the Chamber of Commerce Board, and the local cemetery board, as well as several industry organizations such as the Associated General Contractors of Minnesota.

KEEPING ON THE CUTTING EDGE

Fischer has taken a deliberate and steady approach to growing AVR, but acknowledges that success rarely comes without taking a few risks. For AVR one of those risks was purchasing a cement pump truck to literally pump concrete to the upper floors during construction of the Dain Bosworth Tower. Traditionally, cement was sent up in buckets. "We were the first in the industry to pump up that high," says Fischer. "We were able to see which direction the technology was heading and decided to establish ourselves as a leader in that technology."

The company's gamble paid off. AVR was hired to supply concrete for the Norwest Center project. That project signified the first time a ready-mix supplier had taken complete responsibility for the pumping

and supply of lightweight concrete. AVR pumped lightweight to the 57th floor, a vertical height of 780 feet with a total line layout of 1,280 feet. Not one yard of lightweight was rejected or lost due to mix specifications or the inability to pump. Today AVR owns four concrete pumps that are used for both commercial and residential construction. This innovation, coupled with AVR's use of imported and high-strength concrete, has made the company one of the top ready-mix producers in the Twin Cities.

STEADY AND SURE

When you're in the gravel business, you need to go where the gravel is. Several years ago Fischer had the foresight to buy approximately 1,000 acres in Dakota County—of which substantial portions are aggregate reserves—adjacent to the company's

current location. In addition to land, he is currently involved in large-scale development and reclamation projects, including the reclamation of the gravel pit where his office is currently located. "We're set for at least the next 25 years on this current vein, and we're in the process of developing a number of additional mining opportunities," Fischer says. "Our business philosophy is that a project, no matter how large or how small, how simple or how complicated, deserves our complete dedication in doing the best job possible, with all of our company's talent, integrity, and quality ingredients in every yard of concrete we formulate and deliver. We believe in working hard, and in doing right by our people and our customers. That philosophy has served us well in the past and I believe it will continue to serve us in the future."

CLOCKWISE FROM TOP LEFT: AVR, INC. AND FISCHER SAND AND AGGREGATE CO. COVER APPROXIMATELY 450 ACRES IN APPLE VALLEY, MINNESOTA.

AVR HAS HAD A HAND IN HELPING TO ERECT SOME OF THE MOST WELL KNOWN BUILDINGS IN THE CITY, INCLUDING THE MALL OF AMERICA.

A LOOK AT THE SKYLINE OF MINNEAPOLIS REVEALS SEVERAL AVR PROJECTS, INCLUDING CITY CENTER, NORWEST CENTER, PILLSBURY CENTER, LINCOLN CENTER, AND TURNER TOWER.

AVR PROVIDED THE READY-MIX CONCRETE FOR THE BLOOMINGTON FERRY BRIDGE.

W HEN 24-YEAR-OLD ST. PAUL NATIVE DICK SCHULZE started his own company, he thought $100 million in sales would mean he'd "made it." Today, Best Buy, is the nation's leading volume specialty retailer in its combined product categories. With 40,000 employees nationwide, Best Buy's sales surpassed $8 billion in 1997. By the year 2000, Schulze plans to operate stores in every major market.

RETAIL INNOVATION

Schulze credits his success to implementing the right strategy at the right time. "My strength is marketing and the ability to add spin to what's already been done," says Schulze. "I look for market opportunities and find out how to use efficient, productive techniques and technologies in different and more exciting ways." This method has established Best Buy as the consumer's first choice for the purchase of consumer electronics and home office products.

In 1989 Best Buy introduced a new retail format known as Concept II. This concept placed all inventory on the sales floor and, with the help of noncommissioned product specialists (Best Buy was the first major retailer to move from commissioned sales to salaried product specialists), offered consumers great prices with less pressure.

Schulze describes Concept II as his "attempt to differentiate Best Buy from a sea of sameness" in consumer electronics and major appliance retailing. One industry analyst describes Concept II as "the most innovative thing to happen in this industry—ever."

However, Concept II was just the first in a long series of innova-

tions for Best Buy. The company was the first in its sector to introduce personal computers and music into its product mix. Today Best Buy's extensive assortment of 60,000 CDs is one of the strongest in the industry.

Best Buy was also the first to provide interactive capability throughout its stores. Known as

Concept III, this strategy allows for more product selection, more information, and more fun for the customer. In 1994 Best Buy increased the size of its stores to 45,000 square feet and began using hands-on displays to increase the consumer's knowledge of the product features. The company also introduced its internally developed, touch screen

FOUNDER RICHARD M. SCHULZE SERVES AS CHAIRMAN AND CEO OF BEST BUY, THE NATION'S LEADING VOLUME SPECIALTY RETAILER IN ITS COMBINED PRODUCT CATEGORIES.

SPECIALTY RETAILER BEST BUY SELLS CONSUMER ELECTRONICS, PERSONAL COMPUTERS, HOME OFFICE PRODUCTS, ENTERTAINMENT SOFTWARE, AND APPLIANCES IN MORE THAN 30 STATES NATIONWIDE.

kiosks, featuring product information through full-motion video. Recent research shows that, in new markets, consumers prefer Best Buy's store format over its closest national competitor by a margin of two-to-one. In markets where the company has operated three years or longer, customers prefer Best Buy more than four-to-one.

Recently Best Buy unveiled a strategic plan to establish itself in the housewares and gourmet businesses; significantly increase its volume of major appliances; and continue to drive its mix to higher-margin upscale goods. To that end, Best Buy stores added approximately 200 SKUs in small electrics, cooking supplies, cookbooks, and spices.

GIVING SOMETHING BACK

As a major retailer, customer service is central to Best Buy's business strategies; however, Schulze feels strongly about giving something back through a wide range of community programs. Nonprofit organizations receive financial or merchandise support through Best Buy's corporate contribution programs. Best Buy employees contribute hundreds of volunteer hours to assist with a variety of other community projects, as well.

In 1996, the company gave nearly half-a-million dollars to orga-

nizations across the country. A priority for Best Buy's charitable efforts is supporting programs and services that benefit children and youth.

The Best Buy Children's Foundation, established in 1994, targets leadership and personal growth programs. More than $250,000 has been donated to organizations in Best Buy markets through the Foundation. Best Buy's strong commitment to leadership is demonstrated by managers volunteering in Junior Achievement programs. Management volunteers teach Project Business and Applied Economics classes to local high school students in more than 50 classrooms.

MEETING THE CHALLENGES

Although Schulze has made retailing look easy, he emphasizes that it is neither easy nor automatic. "There are many challenges in the retail industry, from changing customer demographics to new competition," says Schulze. But he remains undaunted, asserting, "We believe our retail strategy is right for today's consumers and expect to improve our execution in all product categories. And we are confident that the initiatives we are implementing will strengthen our market-leading position as we celebrate our 30th year of business."

BEST BUY'S HANDS-ON ENVIRON-MENT IS PREFERRED FOUR TO ONE BY CONSUMERS (ABOVE).

RECENTLY BEST BUY UNVEILED A STRATEGIC PLAN TO ESTABLISH ITSELF IN THE HOUSEWARES AND GOURMET BUSINESSES AND TO SIGNIFICANTLY INCREASE ITS VOLUME OF MAJOR APPLIANCES (LEFT).

KENNETH LARSON, PRESIDENT OF SLUMBERLAND, INC., BELIEVES wholeheartedly in the philosophy of customer service. "Our mission is to give our customers the quality, value, and service they seek in furnishings for their homes, while constantly finding new ways to exceed their expectations," says Larson. "And the best way we know to find out what they're expecting is to listen to them." ✴ Originally begun as an all-purpose mattress store,

Slumberland today sells mattresses and box springs, brass and metal beds, daybeds, bunk beds, bedroom case goods, sleep sofas, sofas, love seats, reclining chairs, occasional chairs, glider rockers, leather sofas, chairs, reclining motion sofas and love seats, occasional tables, and other specialty items and accessories.

A FOCUSED APPROACH

Slumberland was founded in 1967 by E.G. Graham and his son, James, and was acquired by Larson in the early 1970s. Under his direction, the company targeted customer satisfaction and focused merchandising as its two main guidelines.

With its emphasis on the customer, Slumberland implemented a revolutionary guarantee policy, now called the Mattress Plus program. The policy guarantees that Slumberland's prices are the lowest in the area. The company also offers a full refund or an exchange within 120 days of purchase if customers believe they have made the wrong mattress choice. Finally, Slumberland offers a full year's guarantee on material and workmanship—

even if the manufacturer offers none.

In recent years, the company has expanded its policy even further, adding a guarantee to deliver the next day on any in-stock sleep set, to pick up the old mattress set with a delivery of any new mattress and box spring, and to set up the new mattress and box spring set free of charge.

Slumberland's customers are not the only beneficiaries of the company's policies. Through an agency representing community nonprofit groups, Slumberland donates an average of 15 semitrailer loads of used mattress sets each month for use by others.

EMPLOYEE TRAINING AND MERCHANDISING

Slumberland has implemented intensive employee training programs to educate sales associates about the products it sells. Following each purchase, sales associates send a handwritten note thanking the customer for his or her business. "Our mission is a difficult one that requires a day-in, day-out, ongoing, never-ending commitment by each of us," says Larson.

Slumberland has grown steadily in recent years. Sales have grown 19 percent per year for the last 15 years, with total sales revenue for corporate-owned and franchise stores exceeding $114 million in 1995. Based on a recent America's Research Group study, Slumberland has earned the number one market share in the Minneapolis-St. Paul area in mattress and box springs, sofa beds, reclining chairs, brass beds, and daybeds. Even more impressive, despite the fact that Slumberland is a specialty retailer, the company has the number one market share position in the Twin Cities for the entire home furnishings category. And, this past year, Slumberland was awarded the Retailer of the Year, the highest award its industry confers.

"Our goal is always to be the first company that comes to people's minds when they think of home furnishings," says Larson. "We believe that our combination of convenient, high-profile store locations; high-quality, name-brand merchandise; and a value-added approach to serving the customer will continue to serve us well in the years to come."

IN TODAY'S SPECIALIZED BUSINESS ENVIRONMENT, COMPANIES ARE relying more on specialists to meet their staffing needs, especially in financial services. That's why more and more companies are turning to Robert Half International (RHI), the world's first and largest accounting, financial, banking, administrative, and information technology staffing service. Founded in 1948, the company now has more than 200 offices in the United States, Canada, and Europe,

including four offices in the Twin Cities area where it has had a presence since 1969.

"A key element of our success is our reputation for customer service excellence and value-added service," says Pat Boen, vice president, area manager, Minnesota region. "We provide companies with a sense of trust, integrity, and commitment that they won't find anywhere else."

Robert Half International operates six separate divisions, each serving distinct markets. They include Accountemps®, Robert Half®, OfficeTeam®, RHI Consulting™, RHI Financial Consulting™, and The Affiliates®.

ACCOUNTEMPS

As the world's first and largest accounting and financial temporary service, Accountemps is well situated to help organizations staff more cost effectively and competitively. Accountemps has the specialized expertise, leadership standing, and network to attract the most qualified temporaries and offer them the most rewarding assignments.

ROBERT HALF

For nearly 50 years, Robert Half's expertise has helped clients strategically build their accounting, finance, bookkeeping, banking, and information systems departments with the right mix of skills and personnel, while helping them avoid the inefficient, often protracted and costly process of performing their own candidate searches.

OFFICETEAM

OfficeTeam specializes only in administrative staffing. The division provides companies with qualified

administrative temporaries at all skill levels, including executive secretaries, office managers, word processors, receptionists, and other office support positions. OfficeTeam is the only administrative staffing service that enjoys a strategic alliance with Professional Secretaries International, the preeminent professional trade association for administrative and office support personnel.

RHI CONSULTING

RHI Consulting offers high-quality contract consultants for assistance ranging from multiple platform systems integration to end-user support, including specialists in programming, networking, systems integration, database design, and help desk support. To keep ahead of the ever changing information technology environment, the division makes an ongoing commitment to industry research on technology developments, workplace trends, and employment issues, and then shares its findings with companies and candidates.

RHI FINANCIAL CONSULTING

RHI Financial Consulting provides, for a specified engagement period, an individual consultant or special-

ized team who will take on operational responsibilities within the framework of a corporate project. This includes financial professionals to fill senior and executive level financial management positions while companies conduct a search for a permanent candidate.

THE AFFILIATES

The Affiliates is the recognized leader in specialized legal staffing. The division provides the legal community with specialists for legal secretaries, paralegals, and word processing technicians on a temporary and full-time basis.

"As the pioneer and leader in temporary and permanent professional staffing, RHI has remained committed to providing service beyond the expectations of our clients and job candidates," says Boen. "Our mission—to be the premier provider of specialized staffing services to the accounting, financial services, information technology, legal, and office automation industries while adhering to the highest professional standards of excellence—has become a self-fulfilling prophecy, leaving us well positioned to remain the industry leader."

PRODUCTS SUCH AS THESE HAVE SERVED THE MANY CLIENTS ROBERT HALF INTERNATIONAL HAS WORKED WITH SINCE ITS FOUNDING IN 1948.

TREND ENTERPRISES, INC.

IN TERMS OF EXCITEMENT AND ANXIETY, FEW EXPERIENCES RIVAL a child's first day of school. His stomach is full of butterflies, and his eyes grow wide as he approaches the classroom filled with desks, books, games, other children—and a four-foot-tall emperor penguin? Once inside, he finds colorful bulletin boards, inspirational posters, math and language arts games, and stickers to reward him when he accomplishes a goal. Does this sound like a place in which

a child would be delighted to spend some time?

Kay Fredericks hopes so. Fredericks, founder of New Brighton-based TREND enterprises, Inc., wants to help create classrooms that foster the spontaneity and curiosity that are so important to learning. "We want to show parents, teachers, and students that learning can be fun," she says.

It would seem the message is hitting the mark. TREND, an industry-leading designer, manufacturer, and supplier of educational materials, exceeded $25 million in sales some time ago and continues to grow. Focusing on four areas—room environment, learning games/skill builders, incentives/motivators, and teacher helpers—TREND develops products that teach, reward, and inspire children of all ages and nationalities.

Yet Fredericks isn't ready to claim success. "When our products are in the hands of children all over the world, then I'll be satisfied," Fredericks says.

PURSUING A DREAM

When Fredericks emerged from college, her focus was on teaching in a way that made learning fun and encouraged children's natural curiosity, inquisitiveness, and self-confidence. She made bulletin board cutouts and classroom games for her own kindergarten classroom. "Based on teaching themes, I created large colorful cutout figures that were about two and a half feet high," says Fredericks. "Teachers from the school district and around the country visited my classroom and they all asked the same question, 'Where did you get those bulletin board characters?' "

A car accident and subsequent

hospitalization gave Fredericks the opportunity to think more seriously about the teachers' question. While continuing to teach, she started TREND in 1968 with $700. Working in a relative's basement, she and her former husband built a silk screen press about the size of a dining room table. Fredericks used an old typewriter her father had given her in seventh grade to create mailing labels from State Department of Education lists.

Fredericks took a two-pronged marketing approach. She presented TREND's product to teachers and educational catalogers and retailers, showing them what they could do and how it could benefit them. "I believed that if teachers could see our products they would eventually start asking for them in their area stores," says Fredericks. "Some catalogers and retailers took on the products while others said to come back once they were successful. Teachers loved the colorful products and what they accomplished with children. Children were instantly attracted to them and thought they were fun to play with while they were learning."

TREND grew steadily, and by the early 1970s Fredericks made the transition from teaching to full-time businesswoman. TREND had become a multimillion-dollar company with 65 employees, leading its industry as an innovative designer, manufacturer, and distributor of educational materials. As the company approaches the end of the 1990s, it has undergone a substantial plant and office expansion; added to its employee force; formed alliances with major national retailers such as OfficeMax, Staples, and Michael's; and also built a strong private-label business.

Setting the Trends

TREND's name conveys the company's vision. "We were innovative from the start. We created whole new categories of materials for educating children," says Fredericks. "In that sense, we saw ourselves as trendsetters, and so did teachers and educational catalogers and retailers. We created many product lines which didn't exist previously, but have since become classroom staples, such as bulletin board sets, Terrific Trimmers® scalloped borders, Ready Letters®, recognition awards, and Scratch 'n Sniff Stinky Stickers®. Our company takes innovation seriously, and we continue to introduce brand-new educational products that we believe are ahead of industry trends."

For instance, in 1979 TREND introduced Scratch 'n Sniff Stinky Stickers®, stickers with a variety of scents that caught the attention of teachers and kids everywhere. The result was a national sticker craze. By 1983, TREND had sold more than 1 billion Stinky Stickers®. TREND was also the first company in its industry to design brightly colored packaging for instructional products. Until that time, school supply dealers basically were carrying commodity products that did not require eye-catching, creative packaging. However, when retail businesses began capitalizing on the demand for instructional materials, TREND's packaging became a positive point of distinction for the company.

Fredericks is very proud of TREND's involvement in helping to create a product category that emphasizes rewards and incentives for students. In her own classroom, Fredericks' philosophy was to motivate children by rewarding them for good work and behavior, rather than punishing them for poor performance. She brought that same philosophy with her to TREND. Over time, TREND was instrumental in developing a variety of incentives that focused on positive feedback to encourage good behavior and reward good work and progress.

Today, Fredericks' vision "to educate the children of the world" is shared by the company's 200 employees. An Equal Opportunity Employer, TREND has always employed differently abled people in sheltered workshops to assist with product packaging. TREND prod-

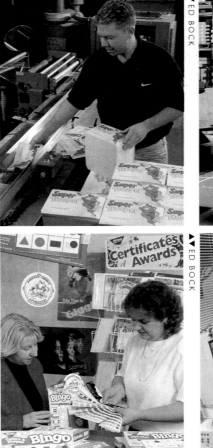

ucts can be found in 37 countries including Canada, Mexico, England, Japan, Korea, Greece, Australia, New Zealand, and South Africa. And major growth worldwide is on the agenda.

"If you look at our entire product line, you will see basic themes that run through all of our products," says Fredericks. "Multiethnic, multicultural, promotion of self-esteem, environmentally friendly, gender balance, and so on. Our materials are bright, colorful, visual, and easy to use. We believe these ideas and products transcend national boundaries. Our goal is to reach children everywhere, and reach them early in their lives, to show them that learning is fun and that they can succeed. That's where TREND products make a real difference."

CLOCKWISE FROM TOP LEFT: QUALITY CONTROL IS MAINTAINED BY ON-SITE MANUFACTURING AND PACKAGING.

TREND PRODUCTS ARE SHIPPED TO 37 COUNTRIES WORLDWIDE, INCLUDING JAPAN, AUSTRALIA, AND SOUTH AFRICA.

PACKAGING AND DISPLAY MATERIALS ARE COORDINATED FOR MAXIMUM VISUAL IMPACT.

ALL PRODUCTS ARE DEVELOPED AND DESIGNED BY TREND'S CREATIVE TEAM.

SMARTE CARTE, INC.

TRAVEL IS MOVEMENT—THE MOVEMENT OF PEOPLE AND baggage from one place to another. Whether baggage is small and precious, or awkward and cumbersome, its movement needs to be efficient and convenient. As the number of travelers increases each year, airports look for new ways to minimize congestion and get people and their bags through the terminal. Smarte Carte provides an easy solution to keep travelers and their belongings

on the move.

Since its inception in 1967, St. Paul-based Smarte Carte has grown from a fledgling start-up company to a global market leader in airport baggage cart management. Smarte Carte's dedication to professional service, leading-edge technology, and customer satisfaction has set the company apart from its competition and has resulted in substantial growth each year.

MAKING TRAVEL EASIER

Hughes Industries, in Littleton, Colorado, had just begun manufacturing the first airport baggage carts in 1967 when Jim Muellner was contracted to streamline the company's design. After setting up nine baggage cart dispensers, now known as cart management units, in Salt Lake City and just over a dozen in Minneapolis, Hughes Industries went bankrupt trying to produce a large order of carts for the Los Angeles International Airport.

In order to recoup his losses from the Hughes bankruptcy, Muellner bought the company, taking the advice of a friend who had once told him, "If you see a product with national or international market possibilities, hold on to it." Muellner also was excited about the product because the carts really did make travel easier. And so, Smarte Carte was born and officially incorporated in August 1970.

Today, Smarte Carte designs, operates, and maintains cart, locker, and stroller management systems in airports, train and bus terminals, shopping centers, and entertainment facilities around the world. There are more than 60,000 baggage carts in the Smarte Carte network providing continuous service to more than 35 million travelers 365 days per year in more than 160 airports worldwide. "Service, technology, and innovation have always set Smarte Carte apart as the industry pioneer and leader in baggage cart management," says Conrad Solberg, chief operating officer of Smarte Carte. "Our commitment is to exceed our customers' expectations by providing unsurpassed service and technology customized to solve their unique needs."

INNOVATIVE PRODUCTS AND SERVICE

With dozens of patents on the books, Smarte Carte cart systems are, by far, the most advanced in the world.

WITH DOZENS OF PATENTS ON THE BOOKS, SMARTE CARTE CART SYSTEMS ARE, BY FAR, THE MOST ADVANCED IN THE WORLD (BOTTOM LEFT).

ELECTRONIC LOCKERS PROVIDE THE SECURITY AIRPORTS NEED BECAUSE LOCKER DOORS CAN BE OPENED IMMEDIATELY AND REMOTELY FROM THE CENTRALIZED COMPUTER THAT CONTROLS THE SYSTEM (BOTTOM RIGHT).

Cart management units provide a variety of conveniences and advanced features. Units are customized to meet specific needs, including change making, instructions in multiple languages, and the acceptance of major credit cards for cart rental. Smarte Carte has recently developed technology that will network its cart management units into a central control data network, and then interpret and report cart availability and usage along with system diagnostics. After experimenting with different alternatives, all Smarte Carte baggage carts are made of stainless steel because they last longer and stay cleaner.

In addition to airport baggage cart management systems, Smarte Carte operates computerized electronic storage lockers that feature unmatched security with keyless entry and provide conveniences such as the option to pay for locker rental with major credit cards. Smarte Carte entered the locker business in 1992 with the realization that airports around the world were focusing on tightening security. Electronic lockers provide the security airports need because locker doors can be opened immediately and remotely from the centralized computer that controls the system.

Currently the company manages electronic and mechanical lockers in more than 300 airports, train stations, and bus depots. Smarte Carte also provides stroller rental services at more than 200 shopping malls, zoos, and amusements parks, including the famous Mall of America, located in Bloomington, Minnesota.

Smarte Carte is first and foremost a service company. Anywhere there's a Smarte Carte cart, locker, or stroller service, Smarte Carte personnel are nearby to help ensure customer satisfaction. Since 1991 the number of frontline service personnel has risen from 260 to nearly 1,000. "Our location managers are key to our success," says Solberg. "They are trained and coached to provide the best possible customer service." Smarte Carte also provides a 24-hour, toll-free customer service line. Its customer service representatives utilize a sophisticated database to quickly identify and resolve customer questions. The database also functions as an internal quality control tool.

SMARTE GROWTH STRATEGY

In 1993, company founder Jim Muellner cashed in on his foresight and success in building Smarte Carte into a well-known industry leader when he sold the company to New York merchant bank Castle Harlan, Inc.

Smarte Carte is now entering a new era, having recently been sold to Haas Wheat & Partners Incorporated, a private investment firm based in Dallas, and known for its strategic investing in leading companies in niche markets. "Smarte Carte's seasoned management has been extremely successful in establishing a strong leadership position in a well-defined market niche," says Chairman Robert Haas. "The company is continuing to expand at domestic airports and shopping malls, but the most exciting opportunities for dramatic growth in its services are international."

Haas Wheat is expected to provide capital for Smarte Carte's aggressive international expansion plans, as well as provide domestic customers with more advanced services and equipment. Haas Wheat will also support opportunities for Smarte Carte to add new services through acquisitions of complementary businesses.

"Smarte Carte has the systems, the expertise, and the financial resources to expand our scope internationally," says Solberg. "We look forward with enthusiasm to meeting the needs of airports, airlines, travelers, and others around the world."

CART MANAGEMENT UNITS ARE CUSTOMIZED TO MEET SPECIFIC NEEDS, INCLUDING CHANGE MAKING, INSTRUCTIONS IN MULTIPLE LANGUAGES, AND THE ACCEPTANCE OF MAJOR CREDIT CARDS FOR CART RENTAL.

T

RIBE . . . VILLAGE . . . TOWN . . . CITY. WHAT IS COMMUNITY? Community is a tapestry of experience, a weaving together of earth and soul over time. Community is a place, informed by arrivals and departures, the subtle interplay of tradition and transformation, a dialogue between the past and the future. Community is myth, binding people together in stories.

PLACE

It is a story of place. The character of this place is shaped by the river. Its power first used to nourish the spirit—later to drive great machines. The river is a passage through both space and time, connecting people to the past, to each other, to the world.

HISTORY

It is a story of people. They came to hunt, fish, and gather food from the land. They came to raise grain and mill it into flour, log the forests, mine the earth, manufacture, and trade. They built monuments to their success. Some remain, some decay.

The roots of the community run deep into the richness and ruin of their legacy. Listen to the echoes of their experience.

TRADITION

It is a story of traditions. Many people have come here from different

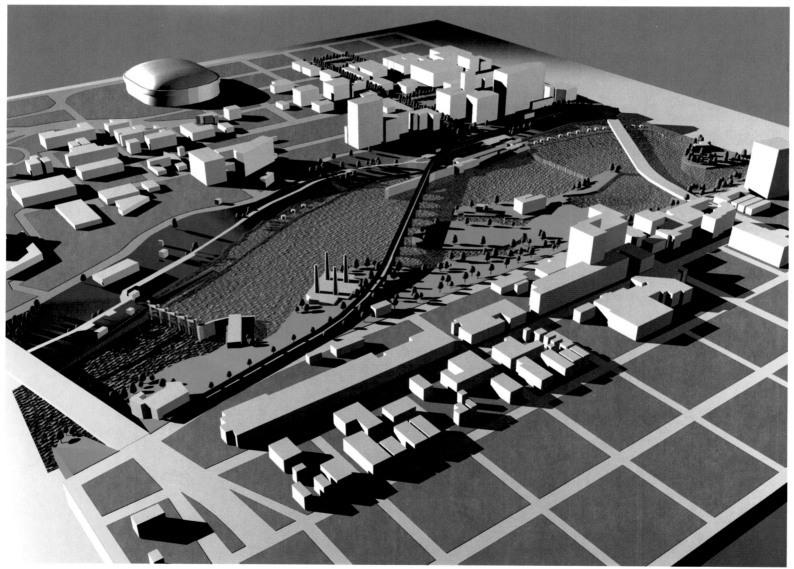

MISSISSIPPI RIVERFRONT

EDEN PRAIRIE HIGH SCHOOL

cultures and different backgrounds—people of many races and spiritual beliefs with a multitude of skills and ideas to apply to the craft of living in this place. Interpreting the meaning in this brings respect to the many and makes from the many a whole.

RESPONSIBILITY
It is a story yet to be told. To be part of a place is to give back for what predecessors have provided—to build on their successes and learn from their failures; to learn and to teach; to serve the interests of both those who are here now and those who will follow.

CUNINGHAM GROUP
Cuningham Group is a Minneapolis-based provider of architecture, interior design, planning, and construction services. Committed to meeting the needs of the community, Cuningham Group works together as a team with each client to transform imaginative ideas into practical realities.

GRAND CASINO TUNICA

MILLE LACS CEREMONIAL BUILDING

HOLLYWOOD ROOSEVELT HOTEL

RAINFOREST CAFE—MALL OF AMERICA

Linked to the Future

▲ CHRIS FAUST

1970 - 1997

1971
Landscape Structures Inc.

1972
IDS Center, a Heitman Property

1972
Innovex

1973
Norstan Inc.

1975
Lawson Software

1977
Hines

1978
Centex Homes/CTX Mortgage

1978
ROI Systems, Inc.

1979
Katun Corporation

Minneapolis ✳ *St. Paul*

1980
DOTRONIX INC.
1980
INTERACTIVE TECHNOLOGIES, INC.
1984
MEDTOX LABORATORY INC.
1984
THE RAMADA PLAZA HOTEL
1985
DYNAMARK, INC.
1985
JAY PHILLIPS CENTER FOR JEWISH-CHRISTIAN LEARNING
1988
AUGSBURG FORTRESS, PUBLISHERS
1989
ANDERSEN CONSULTING
1989
MIDWEST GUEST SUITES
1992
FISHER-ROSEMOUNT SYSTEMS, INC.

FROM THE COLORFUL SLIDES OUTSIDE FAST-FOOD RESTAURANTS TO the playground equipment beckoning schoolchildren out of doors, chances are good that Delano-based Landscape Structures Inc. had something to do with it. With more than $59 million in sales in 1995, Landscape Structures has become a major player in the playground equipment industry. And no one is more proud of that fact than Landscape Structures' President Barbara King or her husband, Steve,

Landscape Structures' chairman and landscape architect.

The Kings founded the company in 1971 with little more than a shoestring budget and a desire to enhance the lives of children. Steve had been working as a park and playground planner with a Minneapolis landscape architecture consulting firm and Barbara as a home economist with Pillsbury. Steve had been doing a fair amount of custom design for playground equipment, but too often the custom designs he was preparing would be cut from budgets simply because the whole project had been overbid. Steve's frustration led him to question whether he should start to manufacture the equipment himself, which would allow him to use mass production to get the quality up and the price down.

The couple borrowed $1,000—just enough to pay for a single saw and the attorney fees needed to incorporate—and they were in business.

BUILDING A BETTER PLAYGROUND

In the past, playground equipment often consisted of freestanding metal-framed jungle gyms, slides, teeter-totters, and swings grounded in asphalt. Beyond the obvious safety issues, each piece of equipment was separated from the next, resulting in a more isolated play experience. The first thing the Kings did with their playground equipment was to develop the continuous play concept in which all the playground equipment at a given location is connected together. "The current technology is connective play, which lets the child experience a number of different challenges that are all together rather than separate," says Barbara. "In terms of developing socially and physically, it has proved to be a much better option to integrate the playground equipment."

Landscape Structures has gained the reputation in the playground industry as the company that innovates. Landscape spends between 3 and 5 percent of its total budget on

BARBARA AND STEVE KING, FOUNDERS AS WELL AS PRESIDENT AND CHAIRMAN, RESPECTIVELY, STAND IN FRONT OF THE PLAYBOOSTER—THE BEST-SELLER AT LANDSCAPE STRUCTURES, INC. (RIGHT).

THE PLAYSHAPER PLAY STRUCTURE IS DESIGNED TO MEET THE SPECIFIC NEEDS OF TWO- TO FIVE-YEAR-OLDS (BELOW).

research and development. "Product positioning and proprietary products have definitely been our number one opportunity," acknowledges Barbara. "We've always tried to stay ahead of everybody else. We don't just try to make the mousetrap a better one, but to make a unique mousetrap before anybody else does."

The company's commitment to innovation influences not only the design, but also the choice of material used to build the equipment. Steve, who is in charge of product development and marketing, began by building his play structures out of redwood. When that material grew too scarce and expensive, he began experimenting with aluminum posts. More recently, the company has developed products made from recycled or reclaimed industrial and post-consumer waste, and Steve continues to work on developing even more effective—and post consumer—materials with which to build the playgrounds.

Creating playgrounds that are safe is a primary concern for Landscape Structures. Although the company likes to focus on the fun it creates for children around the world, the downside to the business is that children can get hurt on playground equipment. Steve, a member of the National Standards Setting Committee for playground safety,

THE PLAYBOOSTER PLAY STRUCTURE WITH SULTAN'S PALACE ROOFS IS AN EXAMPLE OF A CONTINUOUS PLAY STRUCTURE, COMBINING IMAGINATIVE PLAY WITH PHYSICAL DEVELOPMENT.

believes that only 5 to 10 percent of playground injuries have anything to do with design flaws or equipment failure. Still he has changed his designs over time to make them safer. Landscape Structures also promotes customer education. "We don't just want our sales representatives to go out and sell," says Steve. "We have to educate customers and let them know what the new guidelines are. We have an obligation to tell them how the equipment should be used."

Although customers are the primary benefactors of Landscape Structures' innovative, quality-driven way of doing business, the company has also been noticed by industry organizations. In 1994 Barbara won the Small Business Administration's Small Business Person of the Year award. This year Landscape Structures earned ISO 9001 certification, an achievement that both Barbara and Steve feel is essential if they hope to maintain and improve the quality of their products and also increase their overseas market share. Currently about 20 percent of the company's business comes from international markets. Long-term plans include exploring additional international markets.

But even as Landscape Structures continues to grow, the company culture is still very much driven by the friendly, hardworking husband-and-wife team that started it all 25 years ago. Company decisions are not based solely on the bottom line, but on what is best for the employees who make the products, the customers who buy them, the representatives who sell them, and the children who play on them. "More and more companies seem to be striving to achieve a 'corporate culture,' " says Barbara. "That's just really not our style. We have a very practical management style and we're very hands-on. We plan to continue that way for as long as people keep buying our products."

THE PLAYVENTURE PLAY STRUCTURE, DESIGNED FOR FIVE- TO 12-YEAR-OLDS, IS MADE FROM UP TO 85 PERCENT RECYCLED MATERIALS.

TO A TOURIST PASSING THROUGH THE TWIN CITIES, THE Minneapolis skyline provides an impressive array of handsome architectural landmarks to admire. But ask any Minnesotan which of these truly embodies the heart and soul of downtown Minneapolis, and the answer will be quick and unanimous: the IDS Center. ✳ It was a quarter of a century ago that Minnesota's most venerated landmark first opened its doors. At one point, in

1963, the IDS Center was conceptualized as a simple 12-story, quarter-block building. By 1969, the project was formally announced as a mixed-use complex occupying an entire city block and consisting of a 774-foot-tall, 57-story office tower; an eight-story annex; a luxury hotel; and a two-story retail complex—all surrounding a magnificent eight-story central plaza known as The Crystal Court. To this day, the IDS Center continues to be the tallest building in Minneapolis. The transformation of the building was due in part to the involvement of the world-famous architectural team of Philip Johnson and John Burgee. As a writer at the *Minneapolis Star* wrote in 1969, "[They] may not have started their project with the intent of building a monument, but before they were through, they knew they had created a monumental building." Amid a series of changing designs, Johnson and Burgee decided to trim the corners of the tower, giving it a revolutionary octagonal shape. Each edge was then further trimmed, creating "zogs" that allow for up to 32 corner offices per floor. These changes, together with a newly developed reflective glass skin, helped

to create the elegant, shimmering form on the Minneapolis skyline that everyone instantly recognizes as the IDS Center. The structure is consistently voted Minnesota's favorite building by architects and local citizens. According to architecture writer Larry Millett of the *St. Paul Pioneer Press*, "The Star of the Twin Cities Skyline is the IDS Tower, a building that simply looks better with each passing year."

A CITY WITHIN A CITY

Today more than 4,500 professionals are located at the IDS Center's impressive business address. Blue-chip corporate tenants, financial institutions, prestigious law firms, and a host of other companies occupy the 1.2 million square feet of prime office space. The naturally lit, 20,000-square-foot Crystal Court serves as a gathering place or "town square" for many of downtown Minneapolis' 20,000 residents and 135,000 commuters. In addition to major banking and service facilities, the Crystal Court is also the center of downtown's retail district and proudly offers a wide spectrum of retail shops, including The Gap,

Banana Republic, Godiva Chocolates, Starbucks, and Williams-Sonoma. Parking space for 640 cars is located on three levels below ground, and visitors to the center can easily travel to any point downtown through one of the IDS Center's four prominent skyway connections. It's no surprise, then, that downtown pedestrians consistently rank the Crystal Court as one of Minneapolis' most heavily traveled skyway connections.

Also part of the IDS Center is the 19-story Marquette Hotel, operated by Hilton International. The hotel's design takes advantage of the distinctive architectural pattern to transform each of the 278 oversized guest rooms into a luxurious corner accommodation. Hotel management thinks of every little detail when it comes to meeting the needs of business travelers who stay in their guest rooms. From high-tech room amenities, such as computer modem access and speaker phones, to simple touches like full-length mirrors and ironing boards, the Marquette Hotel provides everything a guest could need or want. The Marquette also offers 21 function rooms, accommodating

CRYSTAL COURT HAS BECOME THE "TOWN SQUARE" OF DOWNTOWN MINNEAPOLIS (LEFT).

ALSO PART OF THE IDS CENTER IS THE 19-STORY MARQUETTE HOTEL, OPERATED BY HILTON INTERNATIONAL (RIGHT).

DON F. WONG PHOTOGRAPHY

Minneapolis ✳ St. Paul

receptions for up to 1,000 people. Windows on Minnesota, located on the 50th floor of the IDS Center, offers luxury meeting space and banquet accommodations while affording panoramic views of the entire metropolitan area.

Because of its location at the crossroads of four bustling thoroughfares, the IDS Center serves as the natural center of downtown. Over the years, the center has hosted two presidential visits, a mayoral debate, and the annual Aquatennial Festival kickoff; has served as headquarters for the Final Four and Super Bowl festivities; and has been used in the filming of two major motion pictures. And who could forget the now-famous image of Mary Tyler Moore riding up the Crystal Court escalator at the beginning of each show? Whether people come for work or for play, the IDS Center is the crown jewel of downtown Minneapolis and truly is a city within a city.

WORLD-CLASS MANAGEMENT FOR A WORLD-CLASS BUILDING

Since 1991 the center has been run by the knowledgeable staff of Heitman Properties Ltd., a subsidiary of Chicago-based Heitman Financial Ltd. For more than 70 years, privately held Heitman Financial has served as an intermediary for a broad range of institutional real estate investors around the world. Clients include pension funds, government employee retirement systems, life insurance companies, foundation and endowment funds, commercial banks, and individual real estate investors.

Heitman Financial's three subsidiaries—Heitman Properties Ltd., Heitman Financial Services Ltd., and Heitman Capital Management Corporation—offer a complete range of real estate investment services. The companies are designed to provide in-depth experience and a high degree of professionalism in all phases of property investment and operations, including property management and leasing, construction

management, property valuation, property and investment analysis, professional acquisition and analysis, financing and mortgage banking, and property advisory and consulting services. For more than 25 years, Heitman Properties Ltd. has been building expertise in the supervision, management, and leasing of commercial properties. Today, Heitman manages more than 175 million

square feet of property in 36 states and the District of Columbia. The company's real estate advisory firm, Heitman Capital Management Corporation, manages total gross assets valued at more than $12 billion on behalf of institutional investors.

Under Heitman's management, the IDS Center continues to dazzle visitors, delight its tenants, and win the hearts of Minnesotans.

THE IDS CENTER TRULY EMBODIES THE HEART AND SOUL OF DOWNTOWN MINNEAPOLIS.

HEINRICH PHOTOGRAPHY

NNOVEX CHAIRMAN AND CHIEF EXECUTIVE OFFICER THOMAS W. Haley could have called it quits in 1973 when, one year after his needle-wire assembly company was founded, the computer industry did an about-face. That was the year that solid-state computer memory devices were introduced—and the year that needle-wire assemblies became obsolete. But instead, Haley decided to refocus. He and his seven employees capitalized on their micro-welding and miniature assembly expertise to move into related areas of manufacturing. Soon the company was manufacturing small electromagnetic products—including fine wire lead assemblies—at a quality and price with which few could compete.

Twenty-three years later, what is now known as Innovex's Precision Products Division is the world's largest supplier of thin film lead wire assemblies to the computer disk drive market. As a primary or secondary supplier to virtually all of the disk drive market and magnetic head manufacturers, Precision Products shipped more than 366 million lead wire assemblies in 1996, and has opened plants in Thailand and China in order to meet the growing demand for its products.

To further promote Innovex's long-term growth, the company added two divisions in 1993 and 1994. InnoMedica redirected the company's acknowledged expertise in the area of fine wire manufacturing into the medical products industry, manu-facturing and selling its own proprietary line of implantable medical products, primarily cardiac pacing leads, adapters, and accessories.

The Iconovex Division was formed in 1994 as a result of the 1993 purchase of a technologically advanced natural language processing software engine. Software products subsequently developed and based upon this engine include AnchorPage™, a hypertext indexing and summarizing product for use on Web sites, and Echosearch™, a

search engine booster that can query multiple search engines simultaneously. Each of these products has received *Byte* magazine's Best of Comdex award, which is presented at the biannual industry trade show of the same name.

In 1996 Innovex acquired Litchfield Precision Components, Inc., a leading designer and manufacturer of fine line flexible circuitry and precision metal components. The addition of Litchfield Precision Components positions Innovex to successfully handle anticipated technology changes, broaden its product lines to current customers, and expand its customer base outside of the hard disk drive industry.

Currently, Innovex is headquartered in Hopkins, Minnesota, with additional manufacturing facilities in Bloomington, Montevideo, Litchfield, Thailand, and China.

In just 25 years, Innovex has transformed itself from an eight-person company without a viable product into a multinational employer that hopes to reach $100 million in sales in 1997. Innovex's outstanding performance was recognized in 1996 by both *Forbes* and *Business Week* magazines, which included the company in their lists of Best Small Companies in America and 100 Hot Growth Companies, respectively. Haley thinks the best is yet to come. "Innovex's competitive advantage," he says, "is a highly skilled, internally trained labor force that readily accepts new challenges. Our continued success in the future will be predicated upon our willingness to explore these challenges with our customers and develop successful solutions to their increasingly complex needs. I believe we are more than up to the task."

THE ACQUISITION OF LITCHFIELD PRECISION COMPONENTS POSITIONED INNOVEX TO BECOME A COMPETITOR IN THE GROWING FLEX CIRCUIT MARKET (RIGHT).

THE LEAD WIRES MANUFACTURED BY INNOVEX ARE APPROXIMATELY ONE-FOURTH THE SIZE OF A HUMAN HAIR.

THE RAMADA PLAZA HOTEL

OR MANY YEARS, DOWNTOWN MINNEAPOLIS HAS HAD A monopoly on business hotels and meeting facilities since so many major businesses were located downtown. In recent years, however, many companies have chosen to locate or expand in nearby suburbs, with the western suburbs in particular becoming home to a number of major corporations. The Ramada Plaza Hotel, conveniently located just eight miles west of downtown Minneapolis, is ready to capitalize on this

growing market by providing top-quality lodging and meeting facilities for business and leisure travelers alike.

Only at The Ramada Plaza Hotel can guests be in the hub of west Minneapolis' business community, yet watch a deer graze in the morning mist right outside their window. Surrounded on one side by the Crane Wildlife Preserve and on the other by Ridgedale Shopping Mall, one of the four famous "dale" retail centers, The Ramada Plaza Hotel provides access to the best that the Twin Cities has to offer.

A RANGE OF AMENITIES

Built in 1984 and updated in 1996, The Ramada Plaza Hotel meets the needs of both its corporate and leisure travelers. More than 220 gracious guest rooms and suites provide comfort and elegance at its best. All rooms feature individual-control heat and air-conditioning; oversized bathrooms with built-in hair dryers; in-room coffeemakers; and 25-inch remote-control televisions with ESPN and free Showtime and Disney channels. Six one-bedroom suites, perfect for long-term stays, provide extra amenities such as microwave ovens and refrigerators.

For the meeting planner, more than 10,000 square feet of flexible meeting space is available for meetings, banquets, conferences, training, and seminars. In addition, the hotel's pool atrium can accommodate up to 250 for a banquet and up to 400 for a reception. For more intimate banquets or receptions, the hotel's private dining room—Wellington's—can accommodate up to 125 people. One of the hotel's vans is available to transport guests to and from off-site meetings within the area.

Whether staying for work or pleasure, guests will enjoy the many health and leisure facilities provided by The Ramada Plaza Hotel, including the indoor swimming pool, exercise room, whirlpool, and sauna. Dining facilities include Kristy's Restaurant, a casual American-style bistro featuring a variety of healthy delicious entrées, salads, and sandwiches, and Winners Bar & Grill, which serves burgers, appetizers, and a full selection of beverages.

At The Ramada Plaza, guests enjoy all of the quality of staying downtown without all of the hassles. Over the past several years, The Ramada Plaza has built a number of significant relationships with local businesses that it hopes will continue to grow. The hotel also handles a good deal of state and association business. Once people stay at The Ramada Plaza, they come back because of the service they receive. It's that service that has earned The Ramada Plaza Hotel a reputation as an upscale, first-class hotel for business and meeting travelers.

ONLY AT THE RAMADA PLAZA HOTEL CAN GUESTS BE IN THE HUB OF WEST MINNEAPOLIS' BUSINESS COMMUNITY, YET WATCH A DEER GRAZE IN THE MORNING MIST RIGHT OUTSIDE THEIR WINDOW.

THE HOTEL'S POOL ATRIUM CAN ACCOMMODATE UP TO 250 FOR A BANQUET AND UP TO 400 FOR A RECEPTION.

BACK IN 1973, SIMPLY GETTING ACCESS TO A LONG-DISTANCE LINE could be a time-consuming experience for many corporate employees. Today, businesspeople have come to expect easy access to voice mail, teleconferencing, call centers, and interactive voice processing. Before long, videoconferencing and the integration of telephone and computer networks will be commonplace. How can a corporation keep abreast of the

ever changing, increasingly complex communications technologies available? The simple answer: Norstan.

BEST-OF-BREED PRODUCTS AND SERVICES

Norstan is a Minneapolis-based, full-range provider of integrated voice, video, and data communication solutions. The company is unique in the sense that, unlike many of its competitors, Norstan does not maintain its own network or manufacture anything. Rather, the company develops strategic partnerships with the best technological companies in the telecommunications industry. As a result, Norstan is able to choose which vendors' products it wants to represent and create a "best-of-breed" telecommunications system to match individual customer's needs. Also, because Norstan is not wedded to any specific vendors, the company is free to replace products if they are

no longer competitive. As new products become available, Norstan adds them to its list of offerings. Customers are guaranteed access to the most advanced communications products on the market.

More than a product distribution company, Norstan is a service company, providing communications systems integration services and full turnkey communication management outsourcing. Currently, 45 percent of Norstan's revenues come from services and 55 percent from product

NORSTAN IS A MINNEAPOLIS-BASED, FULL-RANGE PROVIDER OF INTEGRATED VOICE, VIDEO, AND DATA COMMUNICATION SOLUTIONS (TOP RIGHT).

NORSTAN OFFERS THE BREADTH OF TECHNOLOGIES, EXPERTISE, AND EXPERIENCE NEEDED TO HARNESS THE POWER OF THIS NEW AGE. THE COMPANY'S CAPABILITIES ENCOMPASS THE FULL COMMUNICATIONS AND INFORMATION TECHNOLOGY SPECTRUM (BOTTOM RIGHT).

Breadth

sales. "The convergence of voice, video, and data communication systems isn't simply the coming together of the historically disparate modes of communication delivery—telephony, data, video," says Norstan CEO Paul Baszucki. "It is also the integration of those technologies in the workplace. We want to be the single source for the full range of our customers' communication needs."

To deliver the full breadth of its capabilities, Norstan is organized around five businesses. The first group, Communication Systems, is responsible for providing customers with the full range of communication equipment, systems, and services drawn from strategic partnerships with leading communication systems and equipment manufacturers. Customer Services provides Norstan customers with systems maintenance, moves, adds and changes, troubleshooting, and repair. This group also supports the service requirements of the systems management teams for customers who choose to outsource their communication systems.

The third group, Integration Services, offers the in-depth analysis, consultation and systems design, Internet services, and cabling services customers need to merge their voice, video, and data communication into fully integrated systems. This group has developed important strategic partnerships with the industry's hardware and software leaders. Financial Services offers Norstan customers a comprehensive array of custom-tailored, highly flexible financing programs for communication equipment and systems. Finally, Resale Services offers Norstan customers previously owned, reconditioned, and fully warranted communication equipment. At its heart is Rolm Resale Systems, a partnership between Siemens Rolm and Norstan—the only authorized North American reseller of previously owned Siemens Rolm systems and equipment.

Norstan extends the full range of its services to more than 13,000

customers through 64 offices throughout the United States and Canada. Products and services sold to Norstan customers annually total more than $320 million in revenues.

PROVIDING LEGENDARY SERVICE

Baszucki attributes this impressive growth to the company's commitment to providing "legendary service," a style of service that works on two levels: first, responsive delivery of products and solutions to problems; and second, seeking out the best possible communications solutions, regardless of the products or technologies involved. "We recognize in our mission statement that to be successful we must provide solutions that satisfy both today's and tomorrow's needs," says Baszucki. "Even more than providing specific products, that means listening to our customers' concerns, and building long-term customer relationships based on integrity and our ability to deliver on our commitments."

Baszucki continues: "Our success comes not only from what we provide, but from how we provide it. We have confirmed that, through ethical, responsible, and profitable actions, and by providing a fulfilling work environment for our employees, legendary service for our customers, enhanced value for our shareholders, and a spirit of shared responsibility with our community, Norstan will grow and prosper. The greatest measure of our success is our ability to translate those values into strong, profitable business relationships."

To reflect its commitment to ethical, responsive, and profitable actions, the company has created the Norstan Values Cycle. "At the center of the cycle is our commitment to developing these values among all Norstan employees," says Baszucki. "The successive concentric circles represent the company's commitment to personify these values in its actions with customers, shareholders, and respective communities. Our values-

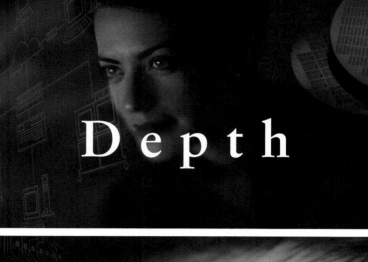

based approach to management is the cornerstone of what Norstan is and we believe it will continue to provide returns for our shareholder groups long into the future."

LOOKING TO THE FUTURE

Norstan's path to continued growth is well laid out. Customers are rapidly increasing their demand for specialized and complex communications solutions. As their desires exceed their ability to manage, they will come to depend on the one-stop source that promises legendary service: Norstan. "As the telecommunications industry continues to change and adapt, we believe Norstan will be the model that proves most effective. As a result, Norstan will be a premier integrator of telecommunications products and services long into the future," says Baszucki.

NORSTAN HELPS ORGANIZATIONS MEET THE CHALLENGE OF BUSINESS COMMUNICATIONS WITH THE DEPTH OF EXPERIENCE AND TECHNICAL KNOW-HOW REQUIRED TO INTEGRATE COMMUNICATION SYSTEMS (TOP).

WITH AN EYE FOR DETAIL, NORSTAN'S FIVE MAJOR BUSINESS UNITS WORK IN TANDEM TO SERVICE ITS CUSTOMERS, WORKING FROM 64 OFFICES THROUGHOUT THE UNITED STATES AND CANADA (BOTTOM).

F ONE WERE ASKED TO NAME MINNESOTA'S LARGEST AND MOST successful companies, it's possible—even likely—that Lawson Software would be left off the list. Never mind that Lawson is, in fact, Minnesota's largest software company, or that the privately held firm more than doubled in size between 1994 and 1996. Often called "one of the best-kept secrets in the industry" by analysts, Lawson has kept a fairly low profile during its more than 20 years in business.

But the fact that many Minnesotans aren't yet familiar with Lawson Software doesn't really bother the company's three founders: Chairman of the Board Richard Lawson, Chief Executive Officer and President Bill Lawson, and former Chairman John Cerullo. "Where it really counts, with our customers, the recognition is there," says Richard Lawson. "Our goal has never been to be the most widely known software company. Our goal has been to provide innovative software solutions that meet the changing business needs of our clients. We continue to achieve that goal, and that's what is most important."

Yet, when a company excels the way Lawson Software has, recognition eventually follows. The company is consistently ranked among the leading client/server business application vendors by the Gartner Group and International Data Corporation, and was listed among the top five vendors of client/server financial applications by Price Waterhouse LLP and *Information Week* magazine.

ADAPTING TO CUSTOMERS' NEEDS

Lawson Software specializes in enterprisewide accounting, human resources, procurement, and supply chain management business application solutions. By incorporating leading-edge technologies like Web deployability, client/server, and workflow enablement, Lawson's latest release, LAWSON INSIGHT™ Business Management System, assists companies in the management of financial and capital resources, personnel-related information, and the distribution of materials and inventory.

Lawson owes much of its success to its founders' decision to develop and offer a variety of products, rather than focus all its energy on one particular technology. As client/server technology has evolved,

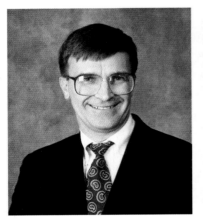

RICHARD LAWSON IS THE CHAIRMAN OF THE BOARD OF LAWSON SOFTWARE (ABOVE).

A SOPHISTICATED, THREE-TIERED CLIENT/SERVER STRUCTURE ENABLES CUSTOMERS TO PLACE THE THREE MAIN COMPONENTS OF THE LAWSON SYSTEM—APPLICATION LOGIC, DATA MANAGEMENT, AND PRESENTATION MANAGEMENT—WHERE THEY WILL BE MOST EFFECTIVE IN ADDRESSING BUSINESS PROBLEMS (RIGHT).

so have Lawson's products. A sophisticated, three-tiered client/server structure enables customers to place the three main components of the Lawson system—application logic, data management, and presentation management—where they will be most effective in addressing business problems.

Lawson's open-platform, open-database, object-oriented technology is incorporated into its suite of fully integrated products, allowing them to operate across disparate systems in heterogeneous environments. This openness meshes well with the ever changing structures of Lawson's customers, and allows Lawson to serve larger-scale organizations. "Our open-systems technology allows us to make our products available on all popular platforms, from AS/400 midrange computers to nearly any type of UNIX or Windows NT-based network," says Lawson. "This, in turn, allows our customers to be more flexible, which is crucial in this fast changing industry."

A policy of providing continuous upgrades has also been important to Lawson's success and the company promises to continue improving its software. "We have also kept up technically, adapting to whatever hardware our customers are buying as the computer industry continually reinvents itself," says Lawson, who proudly points out that in 20 years, the company has never had to rebuild its core product. "Because we're committed to our customers, and not to a specific technology, we can spend our time and energy improving our product to serve their needs."

In addition, Lawson staffs two 24-hour hot lines—one in Minneapolis and one in London—that provide after-sale customer support. Lawson affiliates in other countries provide support in their own languages, a task made somewhat simpler because the software has been designed to be multilingual and accommodate multiple currencies.

To serve its customers worldwide, Lawson maintains offices in Atlanta, Boston, Calgary, Chicago, Columbus, Dallas, London, Los Angeles, New York, San Francisco, Seattle, Toronto, and Washington, D.C., with affiliates in Europe and Africa.

Lawson's heritage of combining extraordinary customer service with the very latest technology continues to provide the company with a loyal and growing customer base. H. Brooks & Company, Lawson's first customer, is still a Lawson customer, 20 years and three hardware platforms later. And recent surveys show that 95 percent of Lawson's 2,000-plus customers—which include Sears, Roebuck & Co.; Dean Foods; Dayton Hudson; Piper Jaffray, Inc.; Polans Corp.; Byerly's; and Vincent Metals—would buy Lawson products again.

Delivering on its Mission

Although Lawson's primary focus will always be on its customers, the company goes to considerable lengths to make sure its employees are satisfied as well. Employees have been offered profit sharing for most

of the company's tenure, and in 1994 management established an employee stock-ownership plan. Each year in June, at the beginning of the company's fiscal year, Lawson Software stages a kick off event for all of its employees around the world to allow them to celebrate their successes as they look to the future. "We recognize that a company survives because of the talents of its people," says Lawson.

The future of Lawson is indeed bright, with the increased use of the Internet adding an entirely new arena to the client/server business application industry. Just as Lawson has been there to help its customers navigate through the technological advances of the past 20 years, so will it be there to help implement the coming changes as customers connect their businesses with the World Wide Web. And given that the company's annual revenue and employee growth rates have averaged nearly 35 percent, Lawson Software is sure to continue making a name for itself both inside and outside the computer industry.

LAWSON SOFTWARE SPECIALIZES IN ENTERPRISEWIDE ACCOUNTING, HUMAN RESOURCES, PROCUREMENT, AND SUPPLY CHAIN MANAGEMENT BUSINESS APPLICATION SOLUTIONS.

ERALD D. HINES STARTED AS AN INVESTMENT BUILDER IN 1957 by borrowing $52,000 from a bank to build a 5,000-square-foot office building in Houston. His firm, Hines, now controls a real estate portfolio of more than 460 properties representing in excess of 120 million square feet of office, mixed-use, industrial, retail, and residential properties, as well as large master-planned communities and land

developments all over the world. Although headquartered in Houston, Hines is a driving force in the Twin Cities area.

Once considered exclusively a building development company, Hines is now a full-service, vertically integrated real estate firm, ready to take on the competition in areas such as asset management, property management, acquisitions, and building renovation. "We are not just a developer anymore," says President Jeffrey C. Hines, son of the company founder. "We are a much more

broadly oriented firm. The skill sets we have developed are applicable to a much larger set of issues and real estate problems."

BUILDING A CITY

It was during the early 1970s that the Hines Banking Group identified the Twin Cities as an ideal market for development opportunities because of its strong demographics, quality of life, and large number of banking and corporate clients. To get the ball rolling, Hines made contact with the First National

Bank of Minneapolis and the Pillsbury Company, eventually bringing the two companies together in one development, Pillsbury Center. The year was 1977.

Set in the midst of Minneapolis' distinctive downtown, Pillsbury Center was designed to make an architectural statement while enhancing notable surrounding structures. Dynamic in scope and design, the center includes dual office towers containing more than 1.8 million square feet. A spectacular glass-enclosed atrium that steps up to a height of eight stories creates a large, open public space between the two towers. Pillsbury Center created a new business/financial complex that promoted the growth and vitality of downtown Minneapolis.

Subsequent to Pillsbury Center, Hines was chosen in 1985 by the Norwest Corporation to rebuild its banking headquarters building after the old building burned in one of the worst office fires in U.S. history. The impact that Norwest Center has on the Minneapolis community began with its inception, where it has been characterized as a phoenix rising from the ashes. The elegant 57-story Norwest Center, designed by Cesar Pelli, contains a full-block indoor pedestrian promenade that houses a 100-foot-high domed ceiling rotunda on one side and a 33-foot-high formal lobby on the other.

Upon its completion in 1987, the structure became a powerful new landmark property and redefined the skyline, creating a dramatic and glowing invitation to downtown Minneapolis. The center won the Urban Land Institute Award for Excellence for Large-Scale Office Development in 1989, the Building

THE ELEGANT 57-STORY NORWEST CENTER, DESIGNED BY CESAR PELLI, CONTAINS A FULL-BLOCK INDOOR PEDESTRIAN PROMENADE THAT HOUSES A 100-FOOT-HIGH DOMED CEILING ROTUNDA ON ONE SIDE AND A 33-FOOT-HIGH FORMAL LOBBY ON THE OTHER.

Owners and Managers of Minneapolis Office Building of the Year Award in 1993, and the BOMA Midwest Northern Region Office Building of the Year Award in 1994. The center is also home to Hines' Minneapolis office.

In August 1995 Hines acquired First Bank Place in Minneapolis. Designed by the world-renowned firm of Pei Cobb Freed & Partners, the 53-story office tower, which contains First Bank System, American Express, and additional tenants, is located at the vital intersection of the city's business, financial, and government districts. Virtually every major downtown building is within blocks of First Bank Place. The city's finest shopping and hotels are a skyway stroll away. Arteries leading to Freeways 94, 35W, and 394 pass close by, making it as convenient to come and go as it is to do business there.

In addition to its Minneapolis properties, Hines manages the Piper Jaffray Plaza in downtown St. Paul and the Minnesota Center in Bloomington. Both buildings are designated as Class A office space and provide tenants with unparalleled amenities and service.

Service Is Job One

A service-oriented company, Hines' philosophy is to maintain property and tenant services at the highest level, enabling tenants to focus on business rather than occupancy issues. Each Hines project reflects a commitment to long-term ownership and an overriding emphasis on quality from inception through continued management of the projects. A low turnover rate among the firm's senior management and its more than 2,500 employees worldwide creates the continuity for a corporate culture rich with seasoned, knowledgeable professionals. And tenant focus remains the top priority day in and day out.

Hines maintains regional offices in New York, Chicago, Atlanta, Aspen, Houston, and San Francisco, and additional branches in more than

46 U.S. cities. However, part of the company's corporate growth strategy is globalization of its product and services. To that end, the company has international offices in Germany, France, Italy, Spain, Russia, China, Mexico, England, and the Czech Republic.

Despite the fact that Hines is one of the largest real estate organizations in the world, it manages to maintain a close relationship with each and every one of its properties. "We don't have a whole group of tiers of people," says Hines. "In each region, we trust the experience and judgment of our employees to make decisions based on what's best for the tenants in that area. This allows us to service our tenants quickly and personally." Hines goes on to say, "The thing that really distinguishes us is the quality of the people we have and the fact that they have been

together as a team for 10, 15, 20 years. There is a culture here. Everyone understands our corporate way of treating tenants. They understand the corporate view of integrity and how to treat relationships. They understand the value of the franchise—in other words, the reputation we have."

 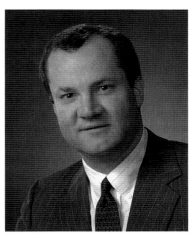

LEADING HINES INTO THE 21ST CENTURY ARE (ABOVE FROM LEFT) GERALD B. HINES, CHAIRMAN, AND JEFFREY C. HINES, PRESIDENT.

DESIGNED BY THE WORLD-RENOWNED FIRM OF PEI COBB FREED & PARTNERS, FIRST BANK PLACE IS A 53-STORY OFFICE TOWER, WHICH CONTAINS FIRST BANK SYSTEM, AMERICAN EXPRESS, AND ADDITIONAL TENANTS (LEFT).

MANY CORPORATIONS TALK ABOUT THEIR DEDICATION TO BUILDing strong communities. Centex Corporation is doing something about it. Since its inception in 1950 in Dallas, Texas, Centex Corporation has become the nation's premier company in construction-related businesses. Centex, through its subsidiaries, is one of the nation's largest builders of single-family homes (Centex Homes), one of the largest general building contractors (Centex

Construction Group), and a leading retail mortgage originator (CTX Mortgage). The company also owns 49 percent of Centex Construction Products, Inc., one of the largest U.S.-owned cement producers.

Centex Corporation is a Fortune 500 company and is touted by *Fortune* magazine as one of America's Most Admired Corporations. What is the secret behind the corporation's success? "Our people," says Connie McGuire, marketing director of the Minnesota division of Centex Homes. "Our people are committed first to creating the best homes and buildings, and providing the best financial services in the nation. But, also, to creating strong and positive human relationships between employees, between the company and our customers, and between the company and our neighbors in the communities where we work and live."

BUILDING STRONGER COMMUNITIES

Centex Homes established its Minnesota division in 1978. That first year, Centex Homes built approximately 20 homes in the Twin Cities area; today, the number is reaching 500. McGuire explains the company's success with two words: customer satisfaction. Although

Centex Homes is not the largest builder in the Twin Cities area, it is well known for its dedication to quality and customer service. "One of our strengths is our commitment to taking care of our customers," says McGuire. "We have built our business so that the customer remains the primary focus. One example of that commitment is our Homeowner Satisfaction Program."

As part of this program, Centex customers are surveyed at four different stages of the home-building process: first, when the home is started; second, at the drywall stage; third, at the time of move-in; and, finally, six months after they have moved in. If a customer expresses any dissatisfaction with the home or with the building process, a Centex representative is assigned to resolve the problem to the customer's satisfaction. "When you purchase a Centex Home, we are totally dedicated to your complete satisfaction. Nothing is more important to us," says McGuire.

"It's our goal to make your home-buying experience so satisfying that you will recommend Centex Homes to anyone without hesitation or reservation."

In addition to taking care of its customers, Centex employees do an outstanding job of taking care of their neighbors. Centex employees across the nation participate in a wide variety of activities aimed at strengthening their communities. The centerpiece of Centex's community service program is its relationship with Habitat for Humanity International. Since 1991, the company has built and donated more than 100 homes nationwide. The Minnesota Division of Centex Homes, with its subcontractors, vendors, and more than 200 employee volunteers, just completed its third Habitat home in the Twin Cities area. "At Centex, we use our building expertise to improve the quality of life in America, giving back to the communities that support us by doing what we do best,"

THE POPULAR CARRIAGE HOME DESIGN SUITS THE NEEDS OF FIRST-TIME HOME OWNERS AS WELL AS EMPTY NESTERS (LEFT).

THE BORDEAUX DESIGN AFFORDS TOWN HOME LIVING WITH ALL THE COMFORTS OF HOME AND NO YARD WORK (RIGHT).

says Centex Homes President and CEO Tim Eller. "We understand that building community goes beyond assembling materials. It is a human imperative demanding our involvement and trust and concern."

McGuire agrees: "Centex strives daily to construct homes and buildings that have enduring structural integrity and also please the eye. But our greater goal is that these structures will encompass places appealing to the mind and to the heart, where families can be nurtured, relationships strengthened, and, ultimately, community will be built."

CTX Mortgage

CTX Mortgage was originally established to provide mortgages for buyers of Centex Homes, and its geographic growth has generally paralleled that of the home builder. Today, more than 70 percent of Centex Homes buyers nationwide choose CTX as their mortgage provider. In addition, CTX has been able to attract and retain many high-production loan officers that have helped expand the company's mortgage business beyond the

financing of Centex homes. Based on retail production (company-originated mortgages), CTX currently ranks eighth in the nation but is second largest among independent (non-bank-affiliated) retail originators.

"It was once very easy to obtain a loan," says Kris Hoaglund, CTX Mortgage division vice president/ branch manager. "You would go to your local bank and apply for a 30-year fixed-rate mortgage. Times have changed since those days and

so have your choices. It's important to choose a mortgage company that you can count on." Hoaglund points out that CTX has been providing financing for thousands of customers for more than 20 years. And as a wholly owned subsidiary of Centex Corporation, CTX has more than 40 years of success and financial stability behind it. "Our customers are our first priority," says Hoaglund. "Our goal is to provide customers with the products and services they need to achieve their dreams."

DELIGHTFULLY DESIGNED EXTERIORS ENHANCE THE LOOK AND FEEL OF EACH CENTEX NEIGHBORHOOD.

WARM AND GRACIOUS INTERIORS ARE A HALLMARK OF CENTEX HOMES.

ROI Systems, Inc.

OUR MISSION IS TO BE THE BEST MANUFACTURING SYSTEMS AND services provider in the world," says ROI Systems, Inc. President and CEO Paul Merlo. ✳ Once companies find ROI, a Minneapolis-based provider of business information software, they rest easy. ROI's excellent track record of client retention proves that the company has satisfied the information technology needs of manufacturers for nearly 20 years. ROI's story dates back

to the mid-1970s, when Founder Michael Carnahan saw a need for manufacturing systems for small- and medium-sized manufacturers. Carnahan had gained hands-on experience in manufacturing, applied his experience to software, and gone on to direct the development of an on-line software system for Scientific Computers, Inc.

Carnahan founded ROI in 1978. After two years of research and development, he introduced ROI's original Material Requirements Planning (MRP) software. In 1985, Automatic Data Processing (ADP) purchased ROI, renamed it the ADP Manufacturing Systems Division, and continued investing heavily in R&D efforts. Carnahan remained active in the business.

In 1990 Merlo, then general manager of ADP's manufacturing systems division, and Carnahan took the company private again. Merlo brought his experience in sales, marketing, and general management at IBM, Xerox, and ADP to the table. Two other managers at the ADP division, Chris Holm and Bill Pisarra, also joined the team. All are active in the business today.

Meeting Client Needs

Since the early 1980s, ROI's MRP system has grown into a fully integrated production planning and control, engineering, finance, and sales and service management system. ROI offers more than 35 applications including forecasting, master production scheduling, material requirements planning, repetitive manufacturing, inventory, purchasing, serial number tracking, shop floor control, and configure-to-order. Integrating applications such as sales order processing, service management, general ledger, fax, and E-mail make this a truly companywide system.

Today, ROI clients represent virtually every type of manufacturer operating in one or multiple locations. "The majority of our clients use more than one manufacturing process: rules-based configure-to-order, just-in-time, high-volume repetitive, make-to-stock, and make-to-order," says Chairman Carnahan, who also leads ROI's research and development. He adds that the manufacturing processes used today by many ROI clients are different than those used by

ROI clients a decade or more ago.

Protecting Clients' Investments

Manufacturing companies that make large capital investments in hardware and software to support their business systems are understandably cautious about the long-term business partners they select. They want assurances that a system can be adapted to their needs and won't have to be replaced a few years down the line. And they look for a proven history of success as a strong foundation for future performance.

Merlo says, "We are committed to constantly evaluating advancements in hardware and software technologies and protecting our clients' investment by incorporating the best ones into our existing applications."

Satisfying Clients Equals Growth

Merlo points out that client feedback is the key to keeping ROI's solutions current. "We collect input via surveys, an on-line client suggestion system, focus groups, ROI/client development teams, and user groups

ROI'S SENIOR MANAGEMENT TEAM—(FROM LEFT) PAUL MERLO, BILL PISARRA, CHRIS HOLM, ROBERT GARBUTT, AND MICHAEL CARNAHAN—ARE COMMITTED TO ROI'S MISSION STATEMENT, WHICH IS TO BE THE BEST MANUFACTURING SYSTEMS AND SERVICES PROVIDER IN THE WORLD.

ROI SOFTWARE INTEGRATES MANUFACTURING PLANNING, PRODUCTION, PURCHASING, SALES, SERVICE, ACCOUNTING, AND ENGINEERING FOR ITS CLIENTS.

meetings," he says. "Our development strategy is definitely influenced by client priorities. This ensures that ROI's products continue to meet the changing needs of our clients."

The numbers suggest that ROI Systems has succeeded in meeting those needs. The company averages 20 percent annual growth and maintains an extraordinarily strong balance sheet. Regional offices and business partners around the globe serve the company's growing client base, which encompasses more than 200 U.S. cities and cities in Australia, southern Asia, Canada, the United Kingdom, Mexico, and Germany.

Most impressively, ROI boasts a 90 percent client retention rate. "We simply don't lose clients," says Merlo. "Our clients have never had to experience a painful, costly conversion in order to take advantage of the newest technology. That's a significant, tangible benefit they will always enjoy with ROI."

ROI SOFTWARE SUPPORTS DISCRETE MANUFACTURERS FROM START-UP COMPANIES TO LARGE, MATURE ENTERPRISES.

LIKE MANY BUSINESS SUCCESS STORIES, THE HISTORY OF KATUN Corporation begins with a vision. In the late 1970s, T. Michael Clarke recognized that although Japanese original equipment manufacturers (OEMs) such as Canon, Sharp, Ricoh, and others were dominating the market for lower-speed plain paper copiers, they were not as effectively meeting the demand for reliable delivery of replacement parts and supplies. Clarke founded Katun to better fill this demand

and bring the fundamental benefits of competition into the parts-and-supplies segment of the office equipment industry.

Today, under Clarke's guidance as president and CEO, Katun is the world's leading aftermarket distributor of toners and developers, photoreceptors, and parts for Japanese-designed office equipment. The company now operates sales and distribution facilities in strategic locations around the world, and employs more than 750 people dedicated to providing the best possible products and service to more than 15,000 customers in more than 140 countries.

FORMING PARTNERSHIPS FOR GROWTH

In its early years, Katun concentrated on forming and strengthening strategic partnerships with world-class manufacturers, building its own research and development capabilities, and establishing a broad customer base. These solid beginnings

created a company with a unique role in its industry. Whereas many other aftermarket companies simply procure and distribute parts and supplies, Katun is extensively involved in the development and testing of its products. While OEMs focus on new machine designs, Katun delivers the high-quality, cost-effective products that make service of existing machines more efficient and profitable.

Investigating and understanding the real-world service problems and requirements of its customers, Katun has responded with practical, cost-effective solutions. A groundbreaking example was Katun's introduction of a "blue-response" photoreceptive drum. In the early 1980s, drums coated with pure selenium couldn't

copy the blue-colored print on commonly utilized carbonless forms. Katun and its suppliers resolved this problem by pioneering the incorporation of tellurium into photoreceptive drum coatings, earning the respect—and the business—of many distributors and dealers.

This spirit of innovation has continued with introductions of other technologies that have become industry standards, such as Katun MICROSLEEVE lower pressure rollers for improved copy quality and extended life in duplexing copiers. Machine-specific problems such as gear breakage and developer leakage have been successfully resolved by Katun-designed modification kits. Today a wide range of OPTIMA parts are engineered to provide improved performance and longer life in comparison to standard OEM parts.

In a fast-paced, highly competitive industry, many distributors and dealers are most interested in dependable products that are priced to reduce their service expenses. "Wall Street analysts refer to Katun as the 'NAPA' of the office equipment industry," says Clarke. "For all the same reasons NAPA parts

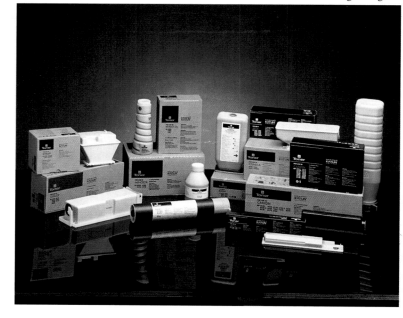

are installed in automobiles and other vehicles with great confidence, high-quality Katun products are installed in plain paper copiers, facsimiles, and printers. We have earned and upheld a reputation for consistently providing toners, developers, photoreceptors, and parts that meet or exceed all OEM standards for quality and performance. In addition, our products provide outstanding value, enabling our customers to increase their service profits."

Rapid, dependable product delivery is another critical aspect of Katun success, and one especially notable partnership illustrates the company's resourcefulness in transporting its products to wherever they are required. In January 1990, Clarke was in Saudi Arabia when Operation Desert Storm commenced. An embargo on all commercial air and sea shipments was making it extremely difficult for U.S. military units to obtain replacement parts and supplies for their Japanese-made copiers and printers. Katun answered the emergency call, delivering the necessary parts, supplies, service manuals, and tools. Both the U.S. Department of the Navy and the

U.S. Marine Corps formally recognized Katun and its leader for exemplary determination and professionalism.

Building for the Future
Katun shows no signs of relaxing its intensity or settling for current levels of success. In recent years, the company has expanded its capabilities by investing in its own U.S.-based manufacturing facility for top-quality fuser rollers. Minco Manufacturing, Inc. employs state-of-the-art instrumentation and computerized automation to produce fuser rollers specifically designed to meet the demands of today's advanced office equipment.

To enable the introduction of more new products, faster and more efficiently than ever, the research and development laboratory located at Katun World Headquarters in Minneapolis underwent a major physical expansion in 1996 and 1997. A wide range of new state-of-the-art testing and measuring equipment was added to the already impressive array of instrumentation. The practical applications lab, containing more than 400 copiers, printers, and facsimile

machines used for real-world product testing, was significantly expanded and equipped throughout with precise environmental controls.

Katun's strong presence in the office equipment industry provides distributors and dealers worldwide with a respected alternative supplier, and compels Japanese OEMs to remain competitive. Katun customers benefit from reliable protection against back orders, delivery delays, OEM product performance problems, and monopoly pricing. As rapid change in the office equipment industry continues, Katun will remain focused on meeting these critical needs of its customers. This commitment has led to more than 17 years of success, and will successfully lead Katun into the 21st century.

CLOCKWISE FROM TOP LEFT: KATUN ENGINEERS AND TECHNICAL SPECIALISTS EMPLOY STATE-OF-THE-ART INSTRUMENTATION IN THE DEVELOPMENT, ANALYSIS, AND ONGOING QUALITY ASSURANCE OF KATUN PRODUCTS.

IN A PRACTICAL APPLICATIONS LABORATORY CONTAINING MORE THAN 400 COPIERS, FACSIMILE MACHINES, AND PRINTERS, TECHNICAL SPECIALISTS EVALUATE THE REAL-WORLD PERFORMANCE OF ALL KATUN PRODUCTS.

MINCO MANUFACTURING, INC., A U.S.-BASED SUBSIDIARY OF KATUN CORPORATION, UTILIZES COMPUTER-CONTROLLED AUTOMATION IN PRODUCING FUSER ROLLERS OF THE HIGHEST QUALITY.

DOTRONIX, INC.

THE IDEA ORIGINATED WITH A MODEL AIRPLANE WHEN BILL Sadler was 14 years old. "When I was about 14, I wanted to radio control a model airplane, so I built a little radio transmitter," Sadler says. A Federal Communications Commission inspector saw him using the radio transmitter and told Sadler he couldn't operate it without a license. Sadler asked the inspector where he could get one, took some classes, and received his license. Two years later

he got his commercial radio operator's license and was on his way to a successful future in electronics. Today, Sadler is founder and president of Dotronix, Inc., an international CRT (cathode-ray tube) display company in New Brighton.

THE MAN BEHIND THE COMPANY

Sadler is a born entrepreneur. After studying college engineering throughout high school, he graduated during World War II and served as a young Coast Guard communications officer. During the next four years he made more than 30 trips to Europe, visited 35 countries, and went around the world three times. After the war,

while teaching and studying in San Francisco, Sadler built that city's first amateur experimental television station in the basement of his home— two years before San Francisco had commercial television. "I bought war-surplus equipment and assembled it into a television station," he says. "During World War II we were experimenting with an iconoscope camera so we could have a television-controlled flying bomb. I found some of those cameras and converted them to live cameras."

That feat led to jobs at the Bay City's KPIX and KRON commercial television stations, and, later, as chief engineer for Stanley E. Hubbard's video empire, particularly KSTP-TV

in the Twin Cities. In fact, it was Sadler's engineering that permitted the station to carry the December 10, 1953, edition of *Dragnet* in glowing color, a full decade ahead of competing stations.

Despite his tremendous accomplishments, Sadler was convinced there was much more he could be doing. "Because of my association with the broadcast industry, I became aware of the need for various products," Sadler says. "So I cashed in $1,000 in savings bonds and started a little company called Miratel, which comes from Minnesota Radio and Television. I had three employees and we operated out of a radio service garage." Miratel was the first company to supply solid-state displays to Complex 39, the moon launch project, and NASA's Manned Space Flight Center. Even Gary Francis Powers' ill-fated U2 carried a Miratel viewfinder for its high-resolution camera when it was shot down in 1960 over the USSR.

Sadler absentee-managed the company until 1959 when sales hit $1.25 million and he decided to devote his full attention to the endeavor. The company doubled sales every year for the first 15 years; then in 1967, Sadler decided to sell Miratel to Ball Brothers Research Corp., a subsidiary of Ball Corp. Ball Brothers persuaded Sadler to remain with the company as a vice president and general manager, which he did until 1976, when he felt the urge to drop out of the business and regroup. In 1980, Sadler incorporated Dotronix, Inc., and with support of friends, colleagues, and customers who had been with Sadler since the 1960s, he was again on his way.

DOTRONIX STACKABLE VIDEO WALL MONITOR SERIES OFFERS THREE CATHODE RAY TUBE SIZES DESIGNED FOR "CONTINUOUS ON" APPLICATIONS THAT REQUIRE VERSATILITY, HIGH PERFORMANCE, AND TRUE COLOR WITH SHARP, BRIGHT, DEPENDABLE IMAGES.

COMPETING WITH THE BEST

Today, Dotronix is a publicly held, $16 million firm with nearly 250 full- and part-time employees in manufacturing plants at New Brighton and at Eau Claire, Wisconsin. The company designs, manufactures, and markets monochrome and color CRT displays and closed-circuit television (CCTV) monitors for a broad range of applications. CRT displays are used to display alphanumeric information and graphics in market quotation systems, word processing systems, computer-aided design, manufacturing and engineering systems, desktop publishing systems, and other computer-based information systems. CCTV monitors are used to display video images generated by medical diagnostic imaging systems, closed-circuit surveillance systems, studio monitor systems, and other video-based systems.

What does all that mean in plain English? "We make lots of dots," says Sadler. "Dots that are vital to displays on medical imaging systems, to high-tech industrial processes, and absolutely essential to the airlines and their passengers who must get to the correct gates before their planes leave." In fact, Dotronix is the only significant U.S. manufacturer of the flight information displays (FIDs) found in airports around the world. "We're always head to head with giants like Sony and NEC," Sadler explains. "I'm proud that the airport at Seoul, Tokyo's brand of the Bank of America, and the railroad station in Taipei all use our imaging equipment. Each is in a so-called 'homeland' of low-cost TV monitors. We must be doing something right."

In the United States, Dotronix has been a major player in flight information and derivative (FID) large-screen color displays. Its FIDs are a fixture at most major U.S. terminals, including Minneapolis-St. Paul International Airport, one of its initial customers. Twin Cities' residents will also find evidence of Dotronix at the Target Center and several local retail complexes, including the Mall of America. The company was among the first to produce video walls, multiple monitors stacked to create a "wall" on which video images are displayed. The Dotronix Stackable Video Wall Monitor Series offers three CRT sizes specifically designed for "continuous on" applications that require versatility, high performance, and true color, with sharp, dependable images.

Sadler sees strong demand for information display—in medicine, with supersensitive diagnostic equipment; in enhanced video walls; in programmable outdoor signs; and in flat panels, featuring televisions that hang on a wall, similar to a picture. According to Sadler, Dotronix will be around to meet the demand. "We have proven that we can compete with—and often beat—our foreign competitors. Our customers know they'll get better customer service and the highest-quality products available," he says. "We've traditionally been a niche market supplier, but in the last several years we've broadened our capabilities, and now we're optimistic about the opportunities for growth in the larger, international markets." Dotronix is an ISO 9000 certified company.

CATHODE RAY TUBE DISPLAYS ARE USED TO DISPLAY APLHANUMERIC INFORMATION AND GRAPHICS IN MARKET QUOTATION SYSTEMS, WORD PROCESSING SYSTEMS, COMPUTER-AIDED DESIGN, MANUFACTURING AND ENGINEERING SYSTEMS, DESKTOP PUBLISHING SYSTEMS, AND OTHER COMPUTER-BASED INFORMATION SYSTEMS.

WHAT DO THE NATIONAL PARK SERVICE, U.S. Department of Transportation, U.S. Department of Justice, U.S. Postal Service, Veterans Administration, and Drug Enforcement Administration have in common? Along with dozens of additional governmental agencies, they have all purchased Interactive Technologies, Inc. (ITI) wireless security systems to protect their facilities and personnel.

Uncle Sam is not the only one placing trust in ITI systems. Since its inception in 1980, the company has become the leading designer and manufacturer of supervised wireless security systems in the United States. ITI security systems are used by families in their homes, by business owners worldwide, and by individuals who may need a personal emergency response system to remain independent and active. In 1995 those three consumer groups helped to generate annual sales exceeding $80 million, which represented a 34 percent increase over 1994.

THE GROWTH OF WIRELESS SYSTEMS

There are two primary types of security systems: hardwire systems, consisting of a control panel and sensors that communicate through wires; and wireless systems, which utilize sensors that communicate with a central control panel using radio signals. ITI was founded in 1980 with the specific goal of commercializing supervised wireless security systems. Although wireless security systems have existed since the early 1970s, it has only been since ITI's introduction in 1983 of the first supervised system that any significant market developed for this product.

The reasons for the growth are clear: wireless systems can be installed in less time and with less labor and other installation resources than hardwire systems require, thereby decreasing consumer installation costs.

A wireless system was not as simple as merely adding a radio to a hardwire system, however. A typical ITI wireless security system consists of four basic components: a control panel, which coordinates and controls all security and home automation system functions and automatically reports emergency conditions and service information to a remote central monitoring facility; touch pads, which enable the user to arm, disarm, and give other commands to the system, including panic buttons to alert the central monitoring facility to police, fire, and medical emergencies; a wide variety of sensors that detect intrusion, fire, and other environmental conditions, and report them to the system's control panel; and sirens designed to frighten away an intruder while alerting the user to the particular alarm condition by audible signal or digitized voice. Simultaneously, the control panel reports the condition to the central monitoring station. And some ITI systems can be controlled by Touch-Tone phone from the home, at work, or anywhere.

But the key component of each ITI wireless security system is, of course, the technology. ITI's technology is one of the best in the industry. Its patented Learn Mode Technology enables systems to automatically "learn" the identity and type of each factory-preprogrammed sensor at the time of installation. This eliminates programming errors in the field and other problems associated with the wireless systems of other manufacturers. Also, ITI's wireless products use a crystal-controlled narrowband radio technology. Crystal control radios are less subject to frequency fluctuations due to temperature or humidity, thereby further enhancing the system's reliability.

ITI President, Chief Executive

ITI'S INNOVATIVE ENGINEERING HAS BEEN THE KEY TO THE COMPANY'S SUCCESS AND WILL CONTINUE TO DRIVE ITS FUTURE GROWTH. THERE ARE ALMOST 80 PEOPLE IN ITI'S ENGINEERING DEPARTMENT, MOST OF WHOM ARE DEDICATED TO NEW PRODUCT DEVELOPMENT.

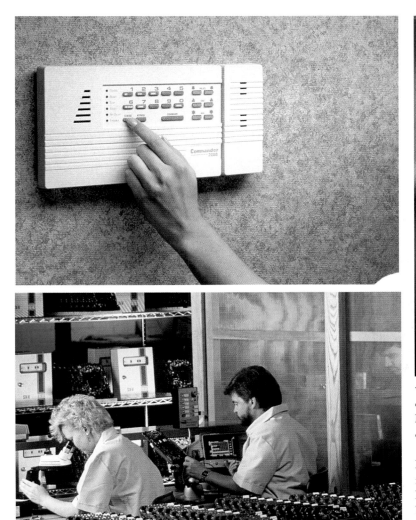

Officer, and Director Thomas Auth points out that ITI was not only the first to successfully market the technology, but its continued perfection is the company's primary focus. "At ITI, we've made innovation our way of life," says Auth. "ITI's innovative engineering has been the key to our success and will continue to drive our future growth." Auth adds that there are almost 80 people in ITI's Engineering Department, most of whom are dedicated to new product development. ITI is projected to spend $6 million in 1996 on product development efforts, which is a testimony to ITI's commitment to produce innovative, effective solutions for today's ever changing market.

BUILDING SUCCESSFUL RELATIONSHIPS

Another key component of ITI's success is its tradition of bypassing distributors and selling its products directly to dealers. This way of doing business gives ITI a clearer and more personal understanding of each dealer and what their customers' needs are, which allows ITI to develop products to fulfill those needs. "Currently, through our independent dealer network, ITI's products—including SX-V Special, CareTaker® Plus, Commander® 2000, LifeGard®, and VuFone®—are sold in virtually every major city in the United States and Canada," says Auth. "We know that our success is directly related to the success of our customers, so

we focus a good deal of energy on developing and growing successful, long-term relationships with our dealers."

Over the years ITI has established a reputation for excellence in consumer-oriented materials that help reduce false alarms. ITI has been recognized by the security industry for system design, user videos, owner's manuals, and demonstration kits that make ITI systems easy to operate and reduce false alarms caused by system users.

These components, together with increased concern about crime, the availability of insurance discounts to home owners who purchase security systems, improved technology, and lower-cost systems, present ITI with significant opportunities for growth and success. "Wireless systems represent the fastest-growing segment of the security industry," says Auth. "Industry sources expect wireless security systems to continue rapid growth in terms of share of future professional residential installations. As the leader in wireless security, we believe ITI is well positioned to benefit from the projected growth in this segment of the industry."

CLOCKWISE FROM TOP LEFT: THE COMMANDER® 2000 SYSTEM IS AN ENTRY-LEVEL SYSTEM DESIGNED FOR SMALL BUSINESSES, HOMES, AND APARTMENTS, AND CAN ACCOMMODATE UP TO 17 SENSORS.

INTERACTIVE TECHNOLOGIES, INC. IS THE LEADING DESIGNER AND MANUFACTURER OF SUPERVISED WIRELESS SECURITY SYSTEMS IN THE UNITED STATES.

ITI'S TECHNOLOGY IS ONE OF THE BEST IN THE INDUSTRY. ITS PATENTED LEARN MODE TECHNOLOGY ENABLES SYSTEMS TO AUTOMATICALLY "LEARN" THE IDENTITY AND TYPE OF EACH FACTORY-PREPROGRAMMED SENSOR AT THE TIME OF INSTALLATION.

MEDTOX Laboratories, Inc.

WHEN COMPANIES LOOK FOR COST-EFFECTIVE, SPECIALIZED toxicology laboratory testing, comprehensive employee drug testing, or a quality testing program to measure toxic substances in the body, St. Paul-based MEDTOX Laboratories, Inc. is the obvious choice. ✳ Under the direction of Founder, President, and Clinical Director Dr. Harry G. McCoy, MEDTOX first opened its doors in 1984 with a

ST. PAUL-BASED MEDTOX IS THE ONLY FEDERALLY CERTIFIED LABORATORY TO DEVELOP, MANUFACTURE, AND MARKET ON-SITE TESTING PRODUCTS FOR DRUGS OF ABUSE.

commitment to improving and saving lives by providing the most accurate testing coupled with the highest level of customer service. Today, the commitment is stronger than ever and has made MEDTOX a leader in the specialized toxicology industry. "Maintaining a leadership position takes qualified, dedicated people; state-of-the-art technology; and excellent laboratory practices," says McCoy. "From the very start, we have worked to ensure the presence of those three elements here

at MEDTOX. Our highly skilled laboratory scientists and trained client services staff utilize today's advanced technology to provide comprehensive toxicology and pharmacology, encompassing rapid, reliable results with dependable, customized service."

RAPID GROWTH

From four employees in 1984 to more than 350 employees today, MEDTOX has grown in size as well as scope. Currently, the com-

pany applies its unique technology to several different areas, including therapeutic drug monitoring, emergency toxicology, clinical analyses for toxins from occupational or environmental exposure, drugs of abuse screening and confirmation, and research and forensic analyses.

Hospitals and clinics rely on MEDTOX for clinical toxicology testing such as therapeutic drug monitoring. Drug therapy can be optimized by monitoring concentrations of various drugs, and this approach improves drug effectiveness, minimizes risk of toxicity, shortens the time required to ensure proper dosages, and reduces overall health care costs. The professional staff at MEDTOX utilizes state-of-the-art analytical instrumentation to ensure medications are being used at optimum levels. MEDTOX provides results to clinicians within a desirable turnaround time to facilitate useful and timely clinical decisions.

Hospitals and clinics also use MEDTOX for emergency toxicology screening, including unidentified but suspected toxins such as street drugs or prescription overdoses. Emergency toxicology service is available any hour of the day or night, seven days a week. This reliable and rapid laboratory support service is designed to provide the medical community with clinically useful information in the shortest time possible.

Industrial companies rely on MEDTOX for biological monitoring of toxins. Biological monitoring is the direct measurement of hazardous substances and markers in biological specimens. Anyone exposed

◀ WALTER DEPTULA

Minneapolis ✳ St. Paul

to heavy metals, trace elements, solvents, or other hazardous materials should be monitored for overexposure or toxic levels of the substance. Timing of the test can be critical. Therefore, MEDTOX has a dedicated staff of medical technologists and uses analytical instrumentation in order to provide clients with the fastest turnaround times in the industry.

In addition, MEDTOX has invested in the most up-to-date analytical robotic technology that can process customized menus of hazardous substances for analysis. When combined with environmental testing, biological monitoring provides definitive information on the level of toxic exposure to individuals. As a result, companies create a safer working atmosphere while reducing employee sick time, insurance premiums, and latent exposure claims.

Finally, MEDTOX's expertise in toxicology also includes identifying and confirming drugs of abuse. Currently, MEDTOX is the fifth-largest drug testing lab in the country. "Companies today demand fast, accurate, and legally defensible results from their toxicology labs," says McCoy. "At MEDTOX, a positive result is a confirmed one."

MEDTOX operates its forensic laboratories under meticulous and detailed procedures. Security is paramount; the building is secured, the lab area is secured, and the specimen processing area is secured. MEDTOX opens each specimen package individually to ensure accuracy and specimen integrity. The latest in robotic analytic instrumentation and computer technology is used for guaranteed results. The company also participates in the strictest certification and accreditation programs. "We believe these are the protocols necessary to ensure data that can undergo technical scrutiny and legal challenge," says McCoy.

For example, even when a test result is negative, it is reviewed three times: first by a medical technologist,

then by a supervisor, and finally by a certifying scientist. All positive results are reviewed by professional staff at least six times: three times during the screening process and at least three more times during confirmation testing. Furthermore, although the federal government requires each batch of specimens to have a minimum 10 percent quality control, MEDTOX exceeds this requirement by performing quality control up to a 30 percent rate.

It is no surprise that MEDTOX is the only federally certified laboratory to develop, manufacture, and market on-site testing products for drugs of abuse.

A SECOND DECADE OF SERVICE

To service clients' future needs, MEDTOX has a dedicated research and development laboratory. The research and development team provides assay validations, development of new methodologies, bioequivalency studies, and new assays for drugs just entering the market. In addition, the research and development staff is continually working on assays for other drugs of abuse, therapeutic drugs, and environmental toxins. "MEDTOX will maintain its leadership position in specialized toxicology by systematically delivering its proprietary technologies and procedures through its professional staff," says McCoy. "We believe we are the best choice for organizations concerned with reliable test results, specialized toxicology testing, and the highest quality available in the industry."

HOSPITALS AND CLINICS THROUGHOUT THE TWIN CITIES RELY ON MEDTOX FOR TOXICOLOGY LABORATORY TESTING.

▲ WALTER DEPTULA

DynaMark, Inc.

I F A COMPANY NEEDS DIRECT MARKETING SERVICES THAT GET THE right message to the right group of people at the right time, who should it turn to for help? Industry leaders—including Chase Manhattan Bank, Damark International, State Farm Insurance, and Dahlberg Inc.—turn to St. Paul-based DynaMark, Inc. And with good reason. ✳ DynaMark and its parent company, Fair, Isaac and Company, Inc., offer direct marketers a full scope of services to meet

their database marketing needs, including list processing, address hygiene, database design and management, predictive modeling, response analysis, postal optimization, demographic profiling and analysis, and list rental fulfillment. DynaMark's expertise extends to a wide range of markets, including financial services, catalog, insurance, fund-raising, advertising, retail, and publishing.

A Higher Level of Service

DynaMark first opened its doors in 1985, when Founder and President Ken Rapp saw the need for a data management company that could offer more than just data processing. Rapp proudly admits that he founded the company because he wanted to provide customers with a higher level of service than was currently available in the data management industry. "Most data managers were so focused on accounts that they forgot about the customers behind those accounts," Rapp says. "The most important element of establishing a successful customer retention program through direct mail is building customer trust. And that only happens when you have an understanding and a sense of connectedness with your customers."

In the beginning, DynaMark services included merge/purge, presort, and other mail list prep services, plus impact printing. In 1989 Dyna-Mark formed its Financial Division to service the data processing needs of its growing client list of financial institutions.

At the end of 1992, DynaMark was acquired by California-based Fair, Isaac and Company, the leading provider of decision support systems

in the consumer credit industry. By joining together DynaMark's data processing skills with Fair, Isaac's analytic and risk assessment expertise, the combined organization is uniquely positioned to provide products and services that fully support all direct marketing strategies.

Along with the products and services DynaMark provides, customers also appreciate the company's innovative approach to system design. "At DynaMark, the customer is first and foremost in our business," says Rapp. "To achieve true customer satisfaction, we must provide innovative database solutions that come from understanding a customer's business and surpassing their expectations."

While most marketing service companies strive to differentiate themselves from their competition by emphasizing small, incremental improvements in technology,

THE EMPHASIS DYNAMARK PLACES ON CUSTOMER AND EMPLOYEE RELATIONS IS WHAT MAKES THE COMPANY STAND OUT FROM THE COMPETITION (TOP).

DYNAMARK RECOGNIZES ITS CUSTOMERS' NEEDS TO TURN DATA INTO INFORMATION, AND INFORMATION INTO DECISIONS (BOTTOM).

DynaMark does more. "Good tools certainly are important for direct marketing data processing, data management, and analytical and consultative services," says Rapp. "And we've got those tools. But what really makes DynaMark stand out from its competition is the emphasis we place on customer and employee relations."

This emphasis is reflected in the company's philosophy, high standards, and corporate structure. DynaMark maintains a flat, accessible organizational structure to better meet the needs of a diverse client base. A dedicated account management and technical team works in partnership with each customer to assure responsive, exemplary service that reflects a comprehensive understanding of a customer's data as well as its business. By getting to know a customer's challenges and strengths, a DynaMark team can design and build a database solution that fits the customer's current needs, and anticipates future growth and requirements, notes Rapp.

DynaMark employees are empowered to make decisions on behalf of their customers. "The people designing and implementing a customer's solution know best what is required for that customer's success and satisfaction. That's why our management philosophy champions entrepreneurship and encourages people to continually explore better solutions," says Rapp. Since Dyna-Mark employees are expected to consistently deliver quality solutions, the company prepares them for success through extensive training. Employees receive training in leading-edge tools and techniques that allow them to design, develop, test, and deliver database solutions. They also receive quality processes training that prepares them to plan, execute, and measure project success.

QUALITY AND INNOVATION
Today DynaMark and Fair, Isaac provide clients with more than 40

years of experience and the expertise of more than 800 employees. In recent years the partnership has yielded significant growth. Meanwhile, the company's reputation for quality and innovation continues to grow with the introduction of new products, including the Marketing Strategy Control System, which provides the technology and techniques needed for true one-to-one marketing. "Each year since the company's founding, DynaMark has adapted its products, services, and corporate focus to better serve the evolving requirements

of its customers," says Rapp. "What has not changed since then is our constant commitment to producing the highest-quality results, providing excellent customer service, and being an unwavering strategic partner for our customers' business growth and success."

CLOCKWISE FROM TOP: ACCOUNT MANAGEMENT TEAMS DESIGN AND BUILD DATABASE SOLUTIONS TO FIT A CUSTOMER'S UNIQUE NEEDS.

DYNAMARK SPECIALIZES IN INNOVATIVE DATABASE SOLUTIONS.

DYNAMARK USES THE LATEST TECHNOLOGIES TO MAKE DATA USABLE FOR DIRECT MARKETERS.

JAY PHILLIPS CENTER FOR JEWISH-CHRISTIAN LEARNING

IN 1983, TWO MEN—SIDNEY COHEN, A JEW, AND TOM COUGHLAN, a Catholic—shared a dream. They envisioned a special place on the campus of the College of St. Thomas where Jews and Christians could come together to learn about each other's traditions and beliefs. In discussion with Monsignor Terrence J. Murphy, president of St. Thomas, and Rabbi Max A. Shapiro, soon to retire as senior rabbi of Temple Israel in Minneapolis, they determined it would be

much more than an academic enterprise; rather, it would be a place where Jews and Christians could meet for frank discussions of all aspects of their religious and cultural lives.

The initial idea was explored and finalized in 1984. Cohen and Coughlan, two St. Thomas board members, and their wives invited Monsignor Murphy, Rabbi Shapiro, and his wife to accompany them on a trip to Rome and Jerusalem. There the four men developed the idea for the Center for Jewish-Christian Learning.

FROM DREAM TO REALITY

Figuring out the "what" and "how" aspects of the center came first. Monsignor Murphy asked Rabbi Shapiro to write a proposal that would design a plan for St. Thomas. Rabbi Shapiro suggested a center that would go far beyond the scope of Jewish-Christian centers at other colleges. He recommended a center that would feature formal courses

in Judaism taught at St. Thomas and that would extend into the community; lectures at St. Thomas in the history, theology, and sociology of Judaism; lectures in Catholic high schools; talks by Catholic speakers at Jewish institutions; two symposia each year by leading Jewish and Christian scholars, theologians, and writers; and establishment of an interfaith library at St. Thomas.

Meanwhile, Cohen was taking care of the "how" part of the center

by leading a fund-raising campaign. Rabbi Shapiro was offered the post of director of the center, and a new era of understanding had begun. The Center for Jewish-Christian Learning opened in the summer of 1985 and conducted its inaugural symposium, "Jews and Christians in Dialogue," in November of that year.

A new chapter in the center's history was recently added with the help of the Jay and Rose Phillips Family Foundation. In 1969 Jay

CLOCKWISE FROM TOP RIGHT: POPE JOHN PAUL II GREETS SIDNEY R. COHEN, MONSIGNOR TERRENCE J. MURPHY, AND RABBI MAX A. SHAPIRO.

THE REVEREND DENNIS DEASE ADDRESSES THE 26TH ANNUAL SCHOLARS' CONFERENCE ON THE HOLOCAUST AND THE CHURCHES.

ELIE WIESEL DISCUSSES "THE ETERNAL QUESTION OF SUFFERING AND EVIL."

Minneapolis ✳ St. Paul

Phillips, well-known philanthropist, had established a Chair of Jewish Studies at Saint John's University in Collegeville, Minnesota. By the mid-1990s, the program was without a director, and the Phillips family appealed to the center at St. Thomas for help. A joint committee was formed, spearheaded by Edward Phillips, grandson of the late Jay Phillips, and Richard Cohen, son of Sidney Cohen. With the help of Rabbi Shapiro, Dr. John Merkle, professor of theology at St. John's University/College of Saint Benedict, and Karen Schierman, who joined the center in 1989, the idea of merging the Jay Phillips Chair and the Center for Jewish-Christian Learning was developed. Brother Dietrich Reinhart, O.S.B., president of Saint John's University, and Reverend Dennis Dease, president of the University of St. Thomas, approved the collaboration.

In July 1996, Rabbi Shapiro was named emeritus of the center. Succeeding him as the first director of the joint venture is Rabbi Barry D. Cytron. He was ordained from the Jewish Theological Seminary and holds a Ph.D. from Iowa State University in Jewish-Christian studies. As director, he also occupies the Chair of Jewish Studies at Saint John's University.

AN OVERWHELMING SUCCESS

By all accounts, the center has developed beyond anyone's wildest dreams. The first major public program organized by the center was an outstanding success. Nearly 800 people came to hear a series of six lectures focused on *Nostra Aetate*, a document of the Second Vatican Council that illuminated the relationship of the Catholic Church to non-Christian religions and mandated guidelines between Catholicism and Judaism. Three internationally recognized authorities—a Jew, a Catholic, and a Protestant: Rabbi Marc Tanenbaum, the Rev. Michael B.

McGarry, C.S.P., and Dr. Paul M. Van Buren—delivered the talks.

When Nobel Prize recipient Elie Wiesel came to speak, nearly 2,400 people attended. Nearly 1,800 were present to hear two of America's most popular authors, Rabbi Chaim Potok and the Rev. Andrew Greeley, talk about the novel as a teaching device. Joseph Cardinal Bernardin reflected on "25 years of Jewish-Catholic Relations" in 1989. In 1993, the center sponsored the series "Jews and Christians Speak of Jesus," featuring eight of the most renowned scholars in the field, which was published by Fortress Press under the same title. In 1996, the center hosted the 26th Annual Scholars' Conference

on the Holocaust and the Churches, "Confronting the Holocaust: A Mandate for the 21st Century." Nearly 350 people from 17 countries and more than 30 states participated.

During the center's five-year anniversary celebration, Monsignor Murphy stated that the establishment of the center was one of the most significant religious events in the history of the university and the Twin Cities community. Today, the Jay Phillips center for Jewish-Christian Learning looks forward to even larger and more diverse audiences in interfaith dialogue.

ORGANIZATIONS HAVE OFTEN RELIED ON OUTSIDE HELP TO CREATE and market their products and services, from design through delivery. And for years, organizations from a wide range of industries worldwide have turned to Andersen Consulting to help them achieve and sustain dramatic improvement in marketplace performance. ✳ Andersen Consulting has grown to be the largest management and technology consulting firm in the world.

REPRESENTING AREAS OF RECENT GROWTH AND INNOVATION WITHIN THE MINNEAPOLIS OFFICE ARE PARTNERS MIKE DICKOFF, ENTERPRISE GROUP; DALE RENNER, CUSTOMER RELATIONSHIP MANAGEMENT; MIKE BADOWER, FINANCIAL SERVICES; NORM RICKEMAN, OFFICE MANAGING PARTNER; AND MARK PAUTSCH, CLIENT/SERVER CENTER OF EXCELLENCE SOLUTION CENTER.

With approximately 44,000 employees and an international network of offices in 47 countries, Andersen Consulting helps clients manage the complex process of changing to become more successful. More than 1,000 of the firm's people are based in the Twin Cities.

ACHIEVING BEST BUSINESS PERFORMANCE

Andersen Consulting offers a powerful approach to serving clients—business integration. Business integration is the alignment of an organization's people, processes, and technology in support of its overall strategy to achieve best business performance. "While we've traditionally been known for our ability to integrate systems and redesign processes, today our strength lies in helping organizations transform their businesses and maximize the potential of change," says Norm Rickeman, managing partner of the firm's Minneapolis office.

Andersen Consulting delivers business integration services through five worldwide industry groups: financial services, products, health care, government, and utilities. In addition to gaining industry expertise, Andersen professionals develop skills in a specific area of concentration such as strategy, process, change management, technology, or practice management.

Local clients, such as First Bank System, Deluxe Corporation, Northern States Power Company, Dayton Hudson, 3M, and the State of Minnesota, have drawn upon Andersen Consulting's resources. Andersen Consulting is proud to serve the organizations of the vibrant Twin Cities marketplace and often extends its reach further into the community. For example, the firm automated the lifesaving process of matching donors to recipients for the National Marrow Donor Program. Andersen Consulting has also worked with the University of Minnesota Foundation to build and manage the system that tracks university alumni and donors.

Business integration centers are one example of how the firm's industry practices help clients explore the possibilities of business integration. Serving as showcases for industry-specific solutions, these centers or "futuristic work settings" demonstrate how companies can reinvent themselves through a combination of advanced technology and management techniques. Andersen Consulting uses its business integration centers around the world for applied research, education/training, and client workshops for exploring challenges and potential solutions to increase competitive advantage. The business integration centers focus on industry segments and include Logistics 20.20™ in Atlanta, the Financial Ideas Exchange in New York, and SMART STORE® in Chicago, London, Tokyo, and Sydney.

INNOVATIVE SOLUTIONS

Just as it helps clients change to be more successful, Andersen Consulting applies the same principles to its own business, changing and improving its operations to generate greater innovations and success for its clients.

In response to client demands for on-time delivery of leading-edge solutions and lower costs, Andersen Consulting has taken a lead in developing alternative solution delivery models. Many of Andersen Consulting's solutions to clients' large, complex projects are developed in specialized locations called Solution Centers. With repeat use of systems building expertise, infrastructure, knowledge capital, and software design and code, clients benefit from faster delivery, reduced risk, and lower overall cost. The Minneapolis-based Solution Centers, which are among the 20 Andersen Consulting has worldwide, provide state-of-the-art skills in client/server and other leading-edge technologies, as well as enterprisewide business software.

An area of explosive growth for the firm is represented by Minneapolis-based "Enterprises," which are

DAVID ELLIS PHOTOGRAPHY

Andersen Consulting-owned companies. Rather than providing traditional consulting services, Enterprises offer common, network-centric business processes to multiple organizations, often in the same industry. There are currently six such companies, which focus on inventing new infrastructures that benefit industry transformation. For example, PRA Solutions Enterprise provides passenger revenue accounting processes and services to the airline industry, and Utiligent provides a network-based customer information system to utility companies.

A COMMITMENT TO EXCELLENCE

Organizations that flourish understand that success in managing change ties directly to their ability to bring out the best in people. Andersen Consulting is committed to hiring and retaining the best and the brightest employees. Ongoing professional development helps employees build and enhance skills necessary to serve clients and advance their career development. As a consultant progresses in the organization, he or she will benefit from more than 1,000 hours of training, both at the local office and the worldwide education facility in St. Charles, Illinois. The firm invests 7 percent of its net revenues—nearly $300 million—in training each year.

MAKING CONNECTIONS WORLDWIDE

Because nearly 20 percent of the firm's clients want projects implemented on a global basis, Andersen Consulting continues to strive for unrestricted movement of people and knowledge to deliver consistent levels of quality and service around the world. To ensure that the global organization remains connected and able to draw on the collective experiences and knowledge of its people, Andersen Consulting introduced the Knowledge Xchange® knowledge management system to its worldwide practice in 1992. The system, which serves as a backbone for sharing in-

DAVID ELLIS PHOTOGRAPHY

formation throughout 47 countries instantaneously, includes a series of interactive databases that track client engagements, consultants' experiences, and general market information.

Through the Knowledge Xchange and Andersen Consulting's ability to assemble a team of world-class experts, local clients receive the collective expertise of a global organization. "Our goal is to ensure that our clients have access to consistent, high standards of service and our best knowledge, regardless of where our people or our clients are located," says Rickeman. "Geographic borders and time zones do not affect our commitment to deliver innovative business solutions."

ANDERSEN CONSULTING CREATED SMART STORE® IN 1989 AS A RESEARCH AND DEVELOPMENT CENTER TO LISTEN TO CONSUMERS, TRACK TRENDS, AND EXAMINE SOLUTIONS DESIGNED TO HELP FOOD RETAILERS, DISTRIBUTORS, WHOLESALERS, AND MANUFACTURERS PREPARE FOR THE FUTURE (ABOVE).

CUSTOMER SERVICE ASSOCIATES AT NORTHERN STATES POWER COMPANY (NSP) USE A STATE-OF-THE-ART CUSTOMER SERVICE SYSTEM DEVELOPED AND IMPLEMENTED BY A JOINT NSP/ANDERSEN CONSULTING TEAM TO PROACTIVELY AND EFFECTIVELY HANDLE THE 2 MILLION CUSTOMER INQUIRIES RECEIVED EACH YEAR (LEFT).

OTEL ROOMS MAY BE A NICE LUXURY DURING A SHORT VACATION stay, but travelers planning an extended stay in an unfamiliar town need more than just a bed and a bathroom. Midwest Guest Suites, a third-party interim housing provider with headquarters in St. Paul, offers a high-quality, home-away-from-home option to people in need of temporary housing as a result of job relocation, home building, temporary assignment, or training.

CLOCKWISE FROM TOP RIGHT: MIDWEST GUEST SUITES OFFERS A HIGH-QUALITY, HOME-AWAY-FROM-HOME OPTION TO PEOPLE IN NEED OF TEMPORARY HOUSING AS A RESULT OF JOB RELOCATION, HOME BUILDING, TEMPORARY ASSIGNMENT, OR TRAINING.

SUITE ATTENDANTS NOT ONLY CLEAN ROOMS, BUT HELP GUESTS BUY GROCERIES, TAKE CARE OF DRY CLEANING, MAKE APPOINTMENTS AND RESERVATIONS, AND COMMUNICATE PERSONALLY TO THEIR GUESTS WITH DAILY NOTES.

GUESTS HAVE ACCESS TO WORKOUT FACILITIES AND A FULL-SIZE POOL.

At Midwest Guest Suites, guests stay in nicely furnished, full-size apartments with fully equipped kitchens. Telephone and cable services, including HBO, ESPN, CNN, and other popular channels, are hooked up prior to a guest's arrival, and VCRs are available for watching rental movies or training videos. Guests also have access to workout facilities, heated parking, and laundry rooms. They will need only personal items and groceries, and if they're too busy to go shopping, Midwest Guest Services will do that as well. Suite attendants stop in each day to refresh the suite and make sure guests have everything they need for a pleasant stay. There is even a fishing boat available for guests who want to enjoy some of Minnesota's famous lakes. In a note to a suite attendant a guest writes, "Thanks so much for your hard work. My apartment has been wonderful. I notice all the things you do and deeply appreciate them."

What is the cost for such convenience? About 15 to 50 percent less than the cost of an average hotel

room. Mark Thompson, owner and president of Midwest Guest Suites, explains: "We compare to a Hilton or a Radisson in terms of the services and level of comfort we provide. But when you stay here, you can walk into your own kitchen and prepare a gourmet dinner or a late-night snack. You can even make yourself a fresh pot of coffee or tea in the morning. All the conveniences of home are

right at your fingertips—and your costs are significantly lower than if you were to stay at a hotel."

The benefits of interim housing go beyond increased comfort. Studies have shown that employees who are relocating or are on temporary assignment are less productive as a result of the stress and uncertainties of living in a new city. Lane B. Hoage from G.A. Wright Inc. had this to

say: "The staff at Midwest Guest Suites responded on a holiday weekend after all other long-term furnished suites and rentals were booked. I moved into a well-furnished and -equipped suite on a day's notice. It was secure, well maintained, and totally lacking the cold insincerity of just another hotel room. It was as close to home as you can get while traveling." Midwest Guest Suites can eliminate much of that stress by providing home-style living accommodations for as long as a guest chooses to stay—from as little as two days to over a year.

Filling a Market Need

Although there is clearly a market for interim housing, the industry itself is relatively young. Texas businessman Warren Haskin is recognized by many as the originator of this new concept. In 1973 Haskin saw the value in providing an alternative to the small, impersonal hotel rooms in which most business travelers stayed, and staffed his new company with "hosts and hostesses" from his existing service company, Help People, Inc.

Thompson worked for Haskin and saw how well people responded to this personal, homey living environment. In 1991 Thompson saw an opportunity and purchased the Twin Cities location of Guest Suites of America. Armed with nearly 15 years of experience in the hospitality and

interim housing industry, Thompson decided to take the chance. He renamed the organization Midwest Guest Suites and his company hired suite attendants who would not only clean rooms but would help guests buy groceries, take care of dry cleaning, make appointments and reservations, and communicate personally with daily notes to their guests.

In 1992 the company expanded to Eagan; in 1993, to Eden Prairie; and in 1995, to Rochester. Midwest Guest Suites clients include such companies as 3M, Northwest Airlines, IBM, GMAC, Best Buy, The Mayo Clinic, and Barnes & Noble. Thompson maintains an ever expanding collection of notes and letters from his guests expressing their delight and enthusiasm for his staff and their services. "Well over 50 percent of our business is repeat business," says Thompson. "We send out literature to human resources departments letting them know we're here and available. But we've found that people who stay with us come back. And even more important, they tell others in their companies about us, and sometimes tell other companies or their friends and relatives. To me, that says we must be doing something right."

Thompson hopes to continue expansion efforts, developing guest suites in the Midwest and Southwest regions of the United States, along the I-35 corridor and beyond.

Although Midwest Guest Suites is small compared to the major hotel chains, through its membership in the National Interim Housing Network, with more than 20,000 suites nationwide, similar accommodations can be arranged in locations all over the country. Thompson recognizes that the market for interim housing continues to grow—and that his business will need to grow if he hopes to keep pace. "I'm always on the lookout for people who want to help us expand, as well as for opportunities to grow in ways that will benefit our guests, employees, and clients," Thompson says. "But even as we continue to grow, we will keep focused on the personal, customer-service attitude that made us a success, and will help us maintain that success in the years to come."

AT MIDWEST GUEST SUITES, GUESTS STAY IN NICELY FURNISHED, FULL-SIZE APARTMENTS WITH FULLY EQUIPPED KITCHENS. MIDWEST GUEST SUITES OFFERS ALL THE CONVENIENCES OF HOME—AND COSTS THAT ARE SIGNIFICANTLY LOWER THAN AN EXTENDED STAY AT A HOTEL.

WHAT DO DISPOSABLE DIAPERS, BEER, PLASTICS, GASOLINE, AND pharmaceuticals have in common? Like a variety of other manufactured goods, these products require pinpoint accuracy during the manufacturing process. To obtain such accuracy, manufacturers turn to Fisher-Rosemount Systems, Inc., which has helped improve product quality, save energy, reduce waste, and meet environmental, safety, and health requirements for many years.

"In essence, Fisher-Rosemount Systems provides advanced solutions that help customers control 'wet' processes," explains President John Berra. "By that, we mean any material that flows through a pipe—whether it's steam, baby formula, gasoline, or chemicals used to make carpet fiber. Fisher-Rosemount Systems' products are used to monitor and adjust the flow, temperature, pressure, and other properties of materials being processed in a plant. Our digital instrumentation actually tells the plant's manufacturing equipment—such as a control valve—what to do and when.

"Fisher-Rosemount products are so widely used," Berra adds, "that if our measurement devices, valves, regulators, and process management systems suddenly vanished, many of the world's process plants would have to shut down."

Fisher-Rosemount Systems is a family of companies owned by

Emerson Electric. The Fisher-Rosemount family includes Fisher-Rosemount Systems, Fisher-Rosemount Educational Services, Fisher-Rosemount Industry Solutions, Fisher-Rosemount Petroleum,

Fisher Controls, Rosemount Measurement, Rosemount Analytical, Brooks Instrument, MicroMotion, and Xomox.

The Fisher-Rosemount Systems facility located in Burnsville, Minnesota, is one of four manufacturing and technology centers for the systems division, with headquarters in Austin, Texas. Additional facilities located in Canada, England, and Singapore contribute to the staff of 2,000 Fisher-Rosemount Systems employees internationally.

A TRADITION OF EXCELLENCE

Fisher-Rosemount Systems was created in 1992, when Emerson Electric purchased Fisher Controls. Rosemount, Inc., already part of Emerson Electric, and Fisher Controls each had a division for the sale of process control equipment. The two divisions merged to become Fisher-Rosemount Systems. The strong tradition of manufacturing excellence and technological

TRADITIONALLY A PIONEER IN PROCESS CONTROL TECHNOLOGY, FISHER-ROSEMOUNT SYSTEMS CONTINUES TO LEAD THE INDUSTRY WITH INNOVATIVE TECHNOLOGIES.

FISHER-ROSEMOUNT PLANTWEB™ FIELD-BASED ARCHITECTURE ENABLES CUSTOMERS TO DO TRADITIONAL PROCESS CONTROL AT A LOWER COST, AND ALSO INTEGRATE ASSET MANAGEMENT—A NEW AND UNIQUE CAPABILITY THAT CAN IMPROVE PLANT PERFORMANCE WHILE LOWERING OVERALL MAINTENANCE COSTS.

innovations are a part of the Fisher-Rosemount PlantWeb™ field-based architecture. This new architecture enables customers to do traditional process control at a lower cost, and also integrate asset management—a new and unique capability that can improve plant performance while lowering overall maintenance costs. And, because PlantWeb architecture is modular and scalable, customers can define and start up small, high-return, low-risk automation projects while ensuring those investments integrate over time.

Berra sees the company on the brink of creating revolutionary change in the industry, saying, "I personally believe we're headed toward an even greater revolution than the distributed control system revolution. Through PlantWeb architecture, our customers are able to build open process management solutions by networking intelligent field devices, scalable platforms, and integrated modular software. It's the best way to control the process, manage equipment assets, and connect people with the information they need to manage the business."

innovation for each company has carried forward in the creation of innovative technology to better serve the process control industry.

Traditionally a pioneer in process control technology, Fisher-Rosemount Systems continues to lead the industry with innovative technologies as demonstrated by its commitment to the Fieldbus Foundation's development of FOUNDATION™ technology, the introduction of a revolutionary small process control system called Delta V, and a new generation of PERFORMANCE software applications for Asset Management Solutions (AMS). All of these recent

DEVELOPING INNOVATIVE RESOURCES FOR MINISTRY THAT BRIDGE THE gap between contemporary and traditional—and that meet the needs of customers worldwide—is the ongoing challenge facing Augsburg Fortress, Publishers, the third largest of the Protestant church-owned publishing houses in the United States and the publishing house of the Evangelical Lutheran Church in America (ELCA). ✳ Located in downtown

Minneapolis, Augsburg Fortress was formed in 1988 by the merger of two Lutheran publishing houses: The American Lutheran Church's (ALC) Augsburg Publishing House, based in Minneapolis, and the Lutheran Church in America (LCA) Fortress Press, based in Philadelphia. Those publishers can trace their origins to the mid-1800s.

REACHING OUT THROUGH PUBLICATIONS

With its 400-plus employees, Augsburg Fortress provides educational materials, worship music, books, church supplies, and other resources—including computer products—for congregational use. Augsburg Fortress has two book lines, Fortress Press and Augsburg Books, and publishes several magazines, including *The Lutheran, Lutheran Woman Today,* and *Parish Teacher.* The publishing house also develops ecclesiastical art designs, clergy apparel, vestments, and paraments for the church. These resources are available through catalogs and promotional mailings, through church resource specialists who call on congregations,

and through 16 Augsburg Fortress retail locations in the United States, Canada, and Puerto Rico. Augsburg Fortress products and resources are also carried by more than 4,000 bookstores and other retail outlets.

According to Augsburg Fortress President and Chief Executive Officer Marvin Roloff, "At Augsburg Fortress, we are called to create innovative resources and services that help all people find meaning and wholeness and community in the good news of Jesus Christ. Our products and our stores are points of outreach for us."

KEEPING PACE WITH BUSINESS

However, as many businesses have found, it takes more than just good products to maintain—and grow—a successful company. In a move designed to provide better service for customers while at the same time cutting operating costs, Augsburg Fortress recently streamlined its distribution operation by eliminating its 10 distribution sites around the country and opening a new, state-of-the-art centralized distribution center

in Grove City, Ohio, a suburb of Columbus.

"The primary factor in our decision to centralize distribution was the customer," says Roloff. "Eighty percent of our customers can be serviced with a three-day delivery out of Columbus, compared with only 47 percent from Minneapolis, where we formerly had one of our largest warehouses." Centralization also allowed the company to reduce warehouse space significantly, cutting costs for inventory.

Another update is a new computer system to support key functions, including order taking and managing order fulfillment at the distribution center. The system's warehouse module allows bin assignments based on how often a product is picked, rather than numeric order assignment; thus frequently ordered items can be clustered near the conveyor line. The system will track order history, give daily stock reports, and alert warehouse employees when to replenish the bins. Other improvements in the computer system will aid in key accounting activities, scheduling and production, and estimating.

Yet another major change was the closing of the publisher's in-house production plant and the use of outside vendors for Augsburg Fortress' printing needs. "The future direction of the publishing house will focus on dealing with the changing world of the customer," Roloff says. "I look forward to the years ahead as starting a new era of publishing using the new technologies available to help us meet the increasingly diverse needs of the ELCA and beyond."

AN AUGSBURG FORTRESS DISTRIBUTION CENTER EMPLOYEE PREPARES A PACKAGE FOR SHIPMENT (RIGHT).

THE MANY PRODUCTS DEVELOPED AND PRODUCED BY AUGSBURG FORTRESS INCLUDE EDUCATIONAL MATERIALS, WORSHIP MUSIC, BOOKS, CHURCH SUPPLIES, AND CLERGY APPAREL (FAR RIGHT).

PHOTOGRAPHERS

Peter Beck was born and raised in Minneapolis. A graduate of the University of Minnesota, he specializes in stock photographs of families, generations, work, and agricultural landscapes. His previous clients include IBM, Ford Motor Company, Microsoft, and Cargill. Beck's images have appeared in such magazines as *Time*, *Newsweek*, and *National Geographic*.

Cheryl Walsh Bellville, a native of the Twin Cities area, is a freelance photographer who integrates her love of travel and the outdoors into her commercial, landscape, and people photography. A graduate of the University of Minnesota, Bellville is the recipient of the Gold Merit Award from the Minnesota Advertising Federation, as well as of the highest honor for photo illustration in children's publishing from the Wisconsin Library Association. Currently, she is collaborating with Native American writers on two books about the Anishinabe and Lakota tribes.

Annie Griffiths Belt has been a contract photographer for *National Geographic* since 1978. With a degree in photojournalism from the University of Minnesota, Belt is also a freelance photography editor. In addition to numerous issues of *National Geographic*, her photographs have appeared in *Life*, *Smithsonian*, and *Fortune* magazines, as well as in *A Day in the Life of Ireland*, *The Power to Heal*, and *Women in the Material World*. Belt lives in Silver Spring, Maryland, with her husband and two children.

Conrad Bloomquist, who resides in New Hope, Minnesota, is owner and manager of Scenic Photo!, a stock photography agency that specializes in scenic, landscape, and nature images of the United States. His photographs have appeared in numerous magazines, including *Snow Country* and *Woman's World*, as well as in *Encyclopaedia Britannica*, *Compton's Encyclopedia*, and several Reader's Digest publications.

Ed Bock, a native of St. Louis, moved to Minneapolis in 1976. Specializing in stock, corporate, annual report, computer imaging, people, and sports photography, he has done work for Piper Jaffray Companies, Pillsbury, Cargill, 3M, and American Express Financial Advisors. Bock graduated from the University of Miami with a degree in mass communications.

Alec Cartee-Soth, a graduate of Sarah Lawrence College, currently works with the museum photography staff at the Minneapolis Institute of Arts. Cartee-Soth's work has been displayed in one-person shows at Icebox Quality Framing & Gallery and the Minneapolis Photographer's Gallery.

George Caswell is owner and operator of Minneapolis-based Caswell Photography, a studio offering complete photographic services and specializing in traditional formats and digital imaging. A graduate of St. Thomas College, Caswell has worked with such clients as 3M, Land O' Lakes, BellSouth, Anheuser-Busch, and Tonka Toys.

Howard M. Christopherson is a self-taught visual artist from Minneapolis who has won awards in drawing, painting, sculpture, video, and photography. He has documented many exotic places, including the Galápagos Islands, South America, and Mexico. Christopherson is the founder of Icebox Quality Framing & Gallery, a quality picture frame shop and a contemporary fine art gallery in Minneapolis.

David F. Clobes has lived in Mankato, Minnesota, all his life. A self-taught photographer, he is co-owner of CEL Video Productions, Inc. and specializes in Native American culture, wildlife, and scenic photography.

Scott Cunningham has been taking pictures of sporting events since he was in high school, when he photographed football and basketball for Virginia Tech. In 1977, when he moved to Atlanta to attend the Art Institute of Atlanta, he covered Hawks, Braves, and Flames games, and in 1980 was named team photographer for the Falcons. Throughout the 1980s, Cunningham freelanced for such national magazines as *Sports Illustrated*, *Sport*, and *The Sporting News*, and in the ensuing years became team photographer for the Washington Redskins and the Carolina Panthers.

Michal Daniel, originally from Prague, is a Minneapolis-based photographer who specializes in live entertainment and candid documentary photography. His client list includes the Tyrone Guthrie Theater and the Joseph Papp Public Theater, and he was the recipient of the Broadcast Designers Association Design Award in 1991. Daniel's

images have appeared in such publications as the *New York Times*, *Time*, and *Newsweek*, and have been displayed at the Bibliothéque Nationale in Paris.

Walter Deptula, a Chicago native, has photographed on a freelance basis since 1988. His work has been published in several Towery publications, including *Chicago: Second to None*, *Cincinnati: Crowning Glory*, *Des Moines Visions*, *Wichita: Visions from the Heartland*, and *St. Louis: Home on the River*. Deptula is a frequent contributor to the "Chicago Scenes and Events" calendar published by Jeff Voelz of American City Calendars.

Michael K. Dvorak, originally from Dillon, Montana, moved to the Twin Cities in 1992. With a bachelor of fine arts degree from Minneapolis College of Art and Design, Dvorak specializes in assignment and documentary photography. In his short time as a professional photographer, he has traveled from the frozen Arctic to the sands of Saudi Arabia. Dvorak's images have appeared in *Minnesota Monthly* and *Twin Cities Reader* magazines and in *Women of the Road*, published by Shannon Designs in Minneapolis.

Darrell Eager, a resident of Minneapolis, owns and operates EAGER Photo.

Charles and Maridee Farrow are based in Vadnais Heights, Minnesota, and specialize in travel, nature, scenic, and outdoor photography. Their collection of stock photography includes images of Minnesota, Yellowstone National Park, New England, Alaska, and Norway. A graduate of Metropolitan State University, Charles operates Farrow Travel Photography. Maridee also earned a degree from Metropolitan State University and is currently employed as a systems administrator. The two photographers have worked with such clients as 3M, the U.S. Army National Guard, the Norwegian Tourist Bureau, and the State of Minnesota.

Chris Faust is an award-winning photographer from St. Paul whose cultural landscape photography focuses on the conditions that occur in various developmental landscapes. His images have been included in numerous group and individual exhibitions, including shows at the Minneapolis Institute of Art, Minneapolis Foundation, and Minnesota Historical Society.

Robert M. Friedman was born in Chicago and now lives in Minneapolis. Working out of his home, he shoots stock photography of the Minneapolis skyline, nature, and agriculture, and specializes in location portraiture, as well as photographs for nonprofit business publications and newsletters. Previous clients include Cargill, Land O' Lakes, and University of Minnesota Center for Urban and Regional Affairs.

Frozen Images, Inc. was established in 1984 as a general stock agency by eight contributing photographers. Currently, the agency represents 75 photographers, many of whom are natives of the Twin Cities. While the agency continues its emphasis on regional scenics and activities, it has developed a strong collection of international scenics, nature, and wildlife. Its library currently holds 200,000 transparencies in 35-mm, medium, and large format.

Melissa Gerr is a native of St. Paul whose work has been published in several Minnesota magazines and newspapers, as well as in association with PBS station KTCA-TV. Her solo exhibits have included *We're Not All Swedish . . . Finding Ethnic Diversity in Minnesota* and *Pow Wow*. Gerr's river conservation work has led her to her next subject of interest: farmers in the Minnesota River Valley.

Warwick Green, originally from Sydney, Australia, has lived in Minneapolis since 1987. With a bachelor of arts degree from Sydney College of the Arts, Green specializes in illustrative and people photography.

Stormi Greener is an award-winning photojournalist originally from Boise, Idaho. For nearly two decades, he has traveled the world, capturing the heart of such social issues as the plight of the Vietnamese boat people and the refugees of Cambodia. A two-time Pulitzer Prize finalist, Greener is a frequent lecturer at National Press Photographers Association educational seminars, as well as a teacher at the well-known University of Missouri workshops. Currently, he works as a staff photographer for the *Minneapolis Star Tribune*.

Terry Gydesen is a freelance photographer from Minneapolis who specializes in documentary and editorial photography. His images have appeared in numerous publications, including the *New York Times* and *Newsweek*. He has worked with such clients as the Children's Defense Fund and was a staff photographer for Jesse Jackson's 1988 presidential campaign, as well as a tour photographer for the Artist Formerly Known as Prince on the singer's 1993 European tour. Currently, Gydesen is documenting the American political landscape, focusing on the growing polarization of the electorate.

Hillstrom Stock Photo, established in 1967, is a full-service stock photography agency. The Chicago-based firm's largest files consist of images of architecture, agriculture backgrounds, classic autos, gardens, and high-risk adventure/sports.

Chuck Keeler is a self-taught photographer from Minnetonka, Minnesota, specializing in people and corporate photography. His previous clients include Dayton-Hudson, Norwest Bank, General Mills, Pillsbury, Northwest Airlines, and Honeywell.

Layne Kennedy, originally from Anchorage, Alaska, has lived in Minneapolis for 20 years. His editorial photographs have appeared in numerous magazines, including *Sports Illustrated*, *Forbes*, *People*, *Life*, and *Newsweek*. Currently, Kennedy is working on a book about the American bison and taking photographs for National Geographic's driving guide of the Great Lakes region.

Michael Kienitz is a partner in DLM Imaging, an electronic imaging company that deals with the vending and testing of electronic imaging products. His traditional photography has appeared in *Life*, *Time*, and *Newsweek*, as well as other national publications. An electronic imaging instructor at the University of Wisconsin, Kienitz has presented seminars for the National Press Photographers Association, the Society for Newspaper Design, and other state and local press organizations.

Andy King, a native of Boulder, Colorado, worked on newspapers in Colorado and Texas prior to moving to the Twin Cities in 1992. Specializing in editorial photography, King enjoys working with such clients as American Express Financial Services, Carleton College, and the St. Paul Saints. His

images have appeared in *Corporate Report* and have been used by Associated Press.

Gerald Kollodge graduated from the University of Minnesota and Brainerd Community College. Currently, he works as a staff stylist and studio manager at Chuck Smith Photography in Minneapolis.

Joel Larson is a Minneapolis-based photographer who works for Pierce Photography. A graduate of the University of Minnesota and Brooks Institute, Larson specializes in people photography for clients across the country.

and excellence that all started with his father's barber pole, which is now in the permanent collection of the Smithsonian Institution.

Sandy May is a freelance photographer who splits her time between Jamaica and Minneapolis. She has worked with such clients as Dayton's, Target Stores, and IBM, and her photography has appeared in *Newsweek*, *Fortune*, and numerous regional magazines and newspapers. Currently, May is launching Sugar Dumpling, a publishing company specializing in greeting cards and calendars that feature May's images of people around the world.

Gary Mortensen is chief photographer at the Minneapolis Institute of Art, as well as a photographer for the Minnesota Opera. Originally from Chicago, Mortensen now lives in Maplewood, Minnesota, where he specializes in landscape and city scenes of Minnesota, the United States, and abroad.

Tom Nelson, originally from Bismarck, North Dakota, moved to Minnesota as a college student in 1966. A freelance photographer, Nelson specializes in product, industrial, and illustrative photography. His client list includes Onan Corporation, Cargill, 3M, Red Line Health Care, AmericInn International, NK Lawn & Garden, and Pouliot Designs.

Ann Marsden is a self-proclaimed inspirational and challenging artist who is dedicated to the spirit of the image. In her career as a professional photographer, she has worked with America's leading actors, musicians, studios, and theaters, in addition to several national publications and major television networks. Marsden's work has been on exhibit across the country—from the Walker Art Center in Minneapolis to the galleries of SoHo.

William Marvy Company, which offers an array of quality products including tools and sundries used by barbers and beauticians worldwide, was founded by William Marvy in 1936. Today, Robert Marvy, William's son, carries on the tradition of innovation

David McMahon, who has made his home in Minneapolis since 1986, says that he uses his photographic talent to view familiar sights in new and interesting ways. Specializing in advertising illustration, food, and still life photography, McMahon has worked with such clients as the Colorado Department of Agriculture, Pillsbury, General Mills, and Grand Casino.

James Milton graduated from the Commercial Photography program at Hennepin Technical College and currently lives in Minneapolis. Specializing in scenic and nature photography, as well as portraits, Milton works for Ritz Camera and freelances out of his own studio, Flames Photography.

Tony Nelson specializes in promotional and editorial photography for the music industry. Based in Minneapolis, Nelson enjoys candid and documentary photography of people at music festivals and other public events. His images have been published in *Rolling Stone*, *Musician*, and *Request* magazines. Currently, Nelson is photography editor at *Cake*, a local alternative music magazine.

Marc Norberg is a freelance photographer based in Minneapolis. He owns and operates Marc Norberg Studio, Inc.

Judy Olausen, a graduate of the University of Minnesota, was a photographer for the *Minneapolis Star Tribune* until 1989, when she started freelancing. Specializing in corporate and advertising photography, Olausen was named one of the top 10 photographers in the world by the Viktor Hasselblad Aktiebolag camera company in 1983. She has received numerous awards and grants, including a 1979 Cowles Foundation Arts Fellowship to create portraits of American artists, critics, and collectors, which were exhibited at the Walker Arts Center in Minneapolis.

Chuck Pefley, freelance photographer and Washington State native, relishes living in Seattle because of the excellent and abundant coffee, as well as the privilege of doing what many people only dream about—spending days alone with camera in hand recording the beauty of the scenic Northwest. Pefley's stock photographs are used by publishers and corporate clients around the world and appeared in the book *Spectacular America*.

Fredric Petters, a native of St. Cloud, Minnesota, spent eight years working in New York City and one year working in Frankfurt, Germany. A self-taught photographer, Petters specializes in studio and location photography, as well as computer imaging, for magazines, books, graphic design studios, and advertising agencies.

Bill Phelps was born and raised in the Twin Cities area. His portraits and fashion photographs have appeared in such magazines as *Interview*, *Marie Claire* (French), and *Vogue* (Italian).

Keri Pickett is an award-winning photographer who was born in Charleston, South Carolina. With a bachelor of arts degree from Moorhead State University, Pickett has worked with such clients as First Bank, the Tyrone Guthrie Theater, and *Minneapolis Magazine*.

Brian Pobuda is a staff photographer for the *Daily Pilot/Huntington Beach Independent* and lives in Costa Mesa, California. He earned a combined degree in photojournalism, American studies, and film studies from the University of Minnesota. While a student, Pobuda was a staff photographer for the *Minnesota Daily* and served as photography editor for the Arts and Entertainment section for one year.

Jonathan Postal, born in New York City, lived and worked in London, Sydney, Milan, and New Orleans before settling in Memphis, Tennessee. The creative director of *Eye* magazine, his work has been featured in *Rolling Stone*, *Vanity Fair*, and numerous other magazines. Among his many life experiences, Postal's favorite is the time he was trapped in a 20-foot cage with a 15-foot alligator for 30 minutes.

Steve Schneider, a native of the Twin Cities area, specializes in on-location photographs of people, places, and things, and his images have appeared in *Outside* and *Inc.* magazines. Schneider's philosophy on photography is that "a good photograph is a collaboration between the subject and the photographer. And in the dance that is photography, it is the eyes that lead and the heart that follows."

Joel Schnell, originally from Wisconsin, specializes in people and product photography. He has contributed many natural landscape photographs to stock photography files of the Midwest and the western United States. His clients include Best Buy Co., Target Stores, American Express Financial Advisors, and Norwegian Cruise Lines. Schnell currently lives in Hopkins, Minnesota.

Anthony Brett Schreck is a native of Owatonna, Minnesota. He is owner and operator of A.B.S. Photography and specializes in editorial, portrait, and location photography. Schreck has worked with such clients as Edelman Worldwide, Geografix, and United Way Minneapolis, and his images have appeared in *Minnesota Monthly*, *Twin Cities Business Monthly*, and *Twin Cities Reader*.

Joel Sheagren, a graduate of Hawkeye Institute of Technology, is a freelance photographer from Minneapolis. He specializes in people and product photography for such clients as Federal Cartridge, Pioneer, Polaris, and National Car Rental, and his images have appeared in *How*, *Applied Arts*, and *Studio* magazines. When Sheagren is not taking pictures, he enjoys dogsledding and building canoes.

Sal Skog, a native of St. Paul, specializes in editorial and corporate environmental portraiture. With a bachelor of arts in photojournalism from the University of Minnesota, Skog has worked with such clients as St. Paul Companies, Northwest Airlines, and 3M. Her images have appeared in *Minnesota Monthly*, *Family Circle*, *Woman's Day*, and *Twin Cities Business Monthly*. An avid traveler, Skog has documented the local people of such places as Switzerland, Guatemala, and Bali.

Chuck Smith, originally from Sheboygan, Wisconsin, is an award-winning photographer specializing in small product tabletop advertising and fine art photography. A graduate of New the England School of Photography in Boston, Smith is founder and president of the World Timecapsule Fund, a nonprofit education organization. Work created by the World Timecapsule Fund is now featured in the permanent collection of the Minnesota Historical Society, and parts of this project were included in SpaceArc, a time capsule sent into space in 1994.

Richard Hamilton Smith, the child of an air force officer, lived in several places before settling in Minnesota in 1970. He specializes in location photography, having traveled to such destinations as Alaska, New Zealand, Europe, and Tunisia. His nature, sports, and agriculture photography has appeared in such publications as *Ah Wisconsin* and *Wild Minnesota*, as well as *National Geographic*, *Audubon*, and *Outside* magazines.

Paul Stafford is a Minneapolis-based photojournalist. A former newspaper photographer for the *Norwalk Reflector* and the *Hasting Star Gazette*, Stafford has won awards from the Ohio News Photographers Association, Minnesota News Photographers Association, and Minnesota Association of Government Communications.

Jerry Stebbins, born in Minneapolis, is a graduate of St. Cloud State University and has 20 years of experience as a professional photographer. He has done freelance work for Time Life and for *National Geographic* magazine, as well as published three coffee-table photography books. Currently, Stebbins is working on a variety of commercial advertising assignments and building a completely digital commercial photography studio.

Tim Steinberg, owner and operator of Think Visuals, specializes in stock, location, and event photography for the travel industry. A native of Albuquerque, New Mexico, Steinberg has worked with such clients as *National Geographic*, *Sports Illustrated*, and *Time* magazines, as well as the television show *Rescue 911*. His images have won first place in the Olympus photography contest, and he was named Volunteer of the Year by the Minnesota Film Board.

Tom Strand, a lifelong Minneapolitan, works for Fox Studio. His clients include Little & Co., Sietsema Engel & Partners, Carmichael Lynch, Martin Williams, Colle & McVoy, Yamamoto Moss, *Minnesota Monthly*, Dayton Hudson Corp., and Riddell Advertising.

Dani Werner is interested in exploring what is common to the human spirit, regardless of individual differences and social diversity. She has exhibited a series of portraits in Indonesia and is currently working on a project titled "L'Espirit de Bretagne: Photographs of Brittany, France," which will be exhibited in Brittany and later in Minnesota. In the fall of 1996, she began a local project about urban youth involved in community gardens.

Don F. Wong is a freelance photographer specializing in architecture and interior photography. His favorite subjects include geometric abstractions, lonely rural towns, and buildings painted white. Wong is the recipient of numerous awards, including the 1981 A.I.A. Honor Award in Photography and the 1988 A.I.A. Merit Award in Photography. His photographs have been published in *Architecture*, *Architectural Record*, *Time*, and *Architecture Minnesota*, and his clients include American Express, Montgomery Ward, and Pentagram Design.

Daniel Wovcha, a native of Minneapolis, specializes in photographs of industrial landscapes, rural landscapes, and houses. Wovcha is the author and photo illustrator of *Minnesota's St. Croix Valley and Anoka Sandplain: A Guide to Native Habitats*, published by the University of Minnesota Press.

Other photographers and organizations that have contributed to *Minneapolis-St. Paul: Linked to the Future* include Jeffery C. Drewitz, George Heinrich, Langston Hughes, Andy Hyatt, James May, Minnesota Historical Society, and Kenneth Wright.

INDEX OF PROFILES

DARRELL EAGER

Linked to the Future